1595

AND NIGHT FELL

I sank on to the mat, spread out the three grey blankets, folded my black jersey to make an uncomfortable pillow, then prepared myself to sleep at 5.30 in the afternoon....And, in a little while, night fell.

And Night Fell

Memoirs of a political prisoner
in South Africa

Molefe Pheto

ALLISON & BUSBY
LONDON · NEW YORK

First published 1983 by
Allison and Busby Limited,
6a Noel Street, London W1V 3RB, England
and distributed in the USA by
Schocken Books Inc.,
200 Madison Avenue, New York, NY 10016

British Library Cataloguing in Publication Data
Pheto, Molefe
    And night fell.
    1. Pheto, Molefe   2. Political prisoners —
South Africa — Biography
    I. Title
    365'.45'0924   HV9850.5

ISBN 0-85031-524-7

Set in 11/12 Plantin by Top Type Phototypesetting Co. Ltd., London W1.
Printed in Great Britain by Billings & Son Limited, Worcester.

Contents

For Deborah, comrade and wife, who has suffered much, and still does, at my efforts for liberation; and for my children, Gaboipeoe, Maseitshiro, Pule and Phello.

Acknowledgements

To Moichopari and Galetshwane Segwai for encouraging me to submit the manuscript for publication. To Mary Benson and Eugene Skeef for their enthusiasm after reading the manuscript; and to Mbulelo Mzamane for advice.

Note

The word "Coloured" appears often in this memoir. I personally accept that Coloured people are Black. The usage of the word here is for clarity in terms of the different racial categories in South Africa today.

Introduction

My friend:
The Nile will never flow into the Volga
Nor will the Congo or the Jordan into the Euphrates.
Each river has its own springs,
Its own course and its own life.
Our land, my friend, is no longer barren land.
Each land gives birth in due time,
And each fighter will see the dawn.

Mahmoud Darwish
(Palestinian poet)

I find the lines from the writer Frantz Fanon, "The explosion will not happen today. It is too soon or too late," apt in describing the situation of Black South Africans today. The explosion may happen today, tomorrow, any day. It may not happen for a long time to come. But that does not matter. The world will not come to an end with the South African Black man and woman still as mentally, physically and economically raped as they are today. Denied their humanity, love for life and family and, above all, statehood. It does not matter how the White man there equips himself with arms, kills any man, woman or child who resists or challenges his racist régime and laws, or how brutal the White man becomes in suppressing rebellion. It does not matter. The more "laagers" he builds around himself, the less room he leaves for his own escape. And he has little time, for each day that dawns the escape route becomes narrower and narrower, like a rope tightening around his neck. The sad part of it is that he, the White man, knows it. The other sad fact is that he believes in miracles and the strange god of the Afrikaner who has promised him that his flock is the chosen one.

I have suffered since I was born in South Africa. Every Black man there has. My own particular circumstances are a mirror of the sufferings of others before me and — I hope not for long — after me. It is no longer a matter of how the end will come. It is a question of when.

Too many Blacks have died for their beliefs, some of them mere teenagers who had just cut their teeth. Life is rich and has much to offer, particularly to those who have not enjoyed it before. I want to live. In freedom. All Black people want to live, throw off their chains in South Africa NOW.

7

The contents of this narrative are true. The incidents happened to me in real life and, I know, to other Blacks like me too. My experiences were by no means the worst. I have heard of unbelievable cases from my compatriots. I also learn that other Black people go through the same nightmares in other parts of the world.

But I want to live as large as life. To see myself and others in similar situations free in every respect. Free from fear, poverty, from lack of education and opportunity. To be a man in my country and in the world at large. As long as I lack these basics, I shall never cease to be restless, wherever I may be. Nor will the man who denies me these freedoms ever live in peace. I hold firmly to the belief that each fighter will see the dawn. His dawn.

I started writing about my prison experiences at the beginning of 1976. As a result of my past experiences, particularly the last visitations from the men of the Jan Vorster Square Security Branch Police, South Africa, I kept the manuscript drafts in Johannesburg and not in my house in Soweto, as they could come again any night. I did not want to lose my notes again, as I had when they confiscated my documents, among which were my early attempts at writing a novel based on a police shooting I had witnessed during May Day celebrations in 1951 in Alexandra Township, a Black area. I vividly remember one particular Black woman whose leg was smashed by police bullets. Many times I was to meet her limping her way to work on a single crutch years after the event.

Then on 16 June 1976, during the struggling early stages of the book, Soweto erupted. As the student uprising enveloped all the major cities and ghettos of South Africa, almost everything came to a standstill in Soweto. I made contributions to what I had already written intermittently, at night, making furtive trips to the city office where the work was hidden. Wide-eyed, frightened of the police, yet risking the journey from Soweto where life normally began at night for Black people who had been humiliated all day long, where impromptu nocturnal parties mushroomed in many of those compact small houses. Outside, the roads would be full of taxis and motorcars transporting revellers to clandestine pleasantries, or gangsters and ordinary folk going about their miserable lives. But the life of Soweto had changed since the students had taken command of political thought. The good-for-nothing city of Soweto came to its senses and became a good-for-everything realistic little Black city with a sense of a strange mysterious pride. No car could be seen driving aimlessly at night, except the police cars which were easy to identify because of their aggressive, reckless speed. Upon their appearance, every Black person's safety depended on nimble feet. During this period, the memoirs had to wait, watching the birth-pangs of the new society gripping Soweto.

Many of us who had been in jail for alleged subversion watched the flames devouring the White man's images — beerhalls, superintendents' offices and administration blocks and halls — with the "we-told-you-so" eyes. It was bound to come soon, this conflagration, but the White man in South Africa was too drunk with power to listen. So the subsequent eruption of this conflagration was a necessary delay, albeit a painful one.

In the meantime, I had received an invitation to visit the United States. The plane for the journey was departing from Jan Smuts Airport on 23 June. Earlier during the day, I decided to fetch the manuscript from the city. I did not know that Soweto would erupt again. The students had marched into the city to Jan Vorster Square to demand the release of their leaders who had been detained a week or so previously. At 11.30 a.m., Soweto was already in flames. I was standing near a burning bottle store waiting for a taxi. There were no taxis, no buses, no vehicles to be seen at or near the terminal. Behind me, the Bantu Administration-owned bottle store was licking flames into the June winter air. The police had just arrived, armed with all sorts of weapons, in their riot cars and hippos or saracens, to guard the store from being "looted" for the second time in its life. The first time "repossession" took place at this bottle store was during the first fires of Soweto of 1976.

I had the paper carrier bag with the manuscript in my hands. I dared not make a move or run. I would be considered a suspect with the carrier bag, alone, so near to the burning bottle store. Policemen in South Africa go berserk when Black anger manifests so overtly. They could easily have ordered me to stop and searched the container in my hands. The manuscript would have led them to associate me with the fire.

A red beetle car stopped suddenly. A voice shouted at me, "Molefe, what are you doing there?" I ran uneasily to the car as Margaret More, a friend who was driving to my house to bid me farewell, opened the door for me.

9

"Move on," I said, as I kissed her, telling her that she was a godsend. It was that close! Margaret also confessed that if she had known that the area around the terminal was a "no-go" area, she would have taken an alternative route to my house. Indeed, the African gods have worked wonders for me!

Later, I took the plane and awaited the arrival of the manuscript in New York.

1. They came at 3.30 a.m.

My wife Deborah shook me from a deep sleep. Normally, when she wakes me up in the morning, or at any time, she does it gently with a pat on the shoulder. But on this day she did it violently, risking all my wrath. She was not fussing about it. She had to. The knocks at the back and front doors and windows were raining loud and furiously, incessantly violent. When I awoke, torchlights were making angry shafts in the little rooms, the passageway, flashing through the curtains as if to tear them apart with their beams. Those strong torches flashing in the middle of the night or morning can be frightening in the ghettos of South Africa, already riddled by other maladies of this racist state. My ordeal was worse, more so because I had just woken up in the dark interior.

Even before Deborah told me, I knew that it was the police. The ghetto knows that. There was no big surprise about it. It is a way of life. But more. I knew it was the Security Police! Instinct. After some time leading this type of life, instinct becomes a constant companion that nudges one to realities and wakefulness. No one had to tell me.

I knew that their visit was not a mistake. They had come to detain me. But secretly, I wished it were a mistake, that it was not me they had come for. But even to have such a thought was painful. Why should I wish that it were someone else, when no one wanted to be picked up by the Security Police? Of course, it was a question of whose turn it was. It was my turn then. It was as simple as that.

For some time now, I had been active in the Black arts community in Soweto and the country generally. I was a founder member of MDALI (Music, Drama, Arts and Literature Institute). I became its first chairperson and spokesman. I decried apartheid in the arts, demanded that we Blacks determine our cause, recommended a dissociation from White artists and impresarios as long as the colour bar lasted, and I spoke out on the exploitation of the Black artist by the White gallery owners. I had already directed and programmed three annual Black Arts Festivals for MDALI in Soweto, which had aroused the ghettos to Black assertion with work that was Black-orientated. The days when our work aped White productions and people were gone. Gone were White-written plays and poems. The same happened in other media such as music. In the short space of three years the

11

emphasis had become Black pride and nationhood through the arts, drawing on our cultural background: a decided return to our cultural origins.

The Security Police, through their widely established network of informers and pimps, attended these programmes. The knocks at the doors and windows and walls did not surprise me, come to think of it. And only the night before I had closed the last MDALI festival of Black arts.

This was it, then. Goodbye to my sleeping children and my wife. I wondered at the traumatic experience my children were going to wake up to on hearing that I had been taken away at night by the police for God knows how long, where to, and what for. To me, that night of March 1975 was a long one, a night that would not bring the dawn until my release and return to my family and own surroundings.

"Who are you?" I asked, peeping through the kitchen window, where they had congregated.

A strong light blinded my eyes as soon as I shifted the curtain to have a look. I also flashed my own torch at them, which was brave of me.

"Police. Security Police. Jan Vorster Square," a raucous voice from outside replied.

I could see there were three of them outside, all Black, their shapes menacing shadows through the window. I played the light of my torch up and down their faces, in an attempt to see if I could recognize any one of them. The three of them tried to avoid coming into the direct rays of the beam. Meanwhile, I did not react as they did. I allowed their torches to play on my face.

"How do I know that you are police, that you are from the Security?" hating myself for according them the title of "security".

There was silence. I could see one of them frantically searching his jacket pocket. Finally, he produced a card and showed it to me, putting it against the window-pane, allowing my torch to shine on it so that I could read his name and see his photograph. Ben Letlaka.

I had heard of him, and had seen him before. But now I was able to fit his name to the face on the identification card. Ben Letlaka had for some time trailed the Mihloti Black Theatre group. He had shadowed our rehearsals at the Alexandra Health Clinic, in Alexandra Township, just north of Johannesburg. He had also

12

been seen hovering around at most of our performances.

I did not know the other two with him. They were, besides, very evasive, avoiding the window-pane so that they did not come into direct line with the light from my torch. I thought they were ashamed of the work they were doing. Eventually, when I was at last with them, I was not surprised at their earlier reaction. These Blacks were young. At this time in the Black man's political struggle for his land and rights in South Africa, particularly at this moment in Soweto, it was the young Blacks who were voicing their protest for emancipation. These two, by virtue of their age, should have been proud to be counted among the many voices crying out for freedom. They had no business to be involved in what they were then doing. I looked at them, even in my miserable circumstance at that moment, with scorn. They were scum. Scum of the Black world in South Africa.

"Wait. I'm going to dress up. I'll come back to open the door."

I was desperately playing for time, little as there was to play with. Time to pass messages to my wife about what to do and who to contact. This was it. There was no doubt about it. Back in the bedroom, while putting on some clothes, I quickly took a piece of paper and wrote: "This is it. Contact press, lawyer. Hide books!"

Deborah was quick. Every Black person in the ghettos learns to have sharp reactions as we are constantly in an emergency world. Man, woman or child. It is the experience of our lives. The endless stress. Over the years we have built quick responses, quick shorthand sign languages and quick movements. We have since realized that one lost moment could have disastrous results.

On this occasion, Deborah was quicker than her usual slow self, surprising me with her speed. I saw that she more than realized the gravity of my plight. Of our plight, our children included. Only looks and nods and actions. No word spoken. That made me relax. I realized that I did not have to do everything. Everything was happening at lightning speed.

In the meantime, the knocks at the door from the police outside had become louder, accompanied by more shouts. I thought the house was about to fall apart as a result of the three people outside making so much noise at that ungodly hour of the morning. I knew that they had anticipated what I was trying to do inside. They must have been experienced at that sort of thing.

"Open the door. Open this door! Hey, man, open. Quickly!"

Eventually I opened it. They rushed in like a gust of sudden

13

wind. I must have taken an eternity, as far as they were concerned. On the other hand, to me, it was the shortest time in my life in which I transmitted vital messages for my survival.

"What do you want?" I said finally when they were in the house.

"You!" Letlaka screamed.

"What for?"

"We don't know! Just come!"

"Who wants me then?"

"Kernel Visser wants you," Letlaka retorted, pronouncing "Colonel" in the Afrikaans language, referring to this man as if I knew who he was.

"Who is he?" I asked Letlaka.

"He is Kernel Visser. The Kernel!" emphasizing the title more than the person.

I realized that this Colonel Visser must be someone in the top echelons of power at Jan Vorster Square political branch police. The other two lackeys continued the hide-their-faces antics from my searching eyes. They saw that I was desperately trying to focus on them. I wondered why they behaved like that when it was I who was their hopeless victim.

"Your colonel. What does he want with me?"

Ben Letlaka said that he did not know. He was just told to bring me along.

Hell. This Ben knows nothing, I told myself; it was very unnerving. At least I wanted to have some notion of what I was wanted for.

"What is my name?" I continued, waiting to hear for certain it was me they really wanted. Hoping to God they had made a mistake.

"You are Molefe Pheto." He pointed at me. "I know you."

"OK. Let me get some money and tell my wife," I said. I went towards the bedroom, where Deborah was coming out to see what was happening. Ben Letlaka followed me. I saw red, losing what little temper I still had.

"Ben! My wife is undressed. Get out! Wait in the kitchen. All of you," even though the other two hadn't made a single move. "Sit down!"

I was shouting orders at them, as if they were children. It was because of my utter abhorrence of them. The two quiet ones sat down first and Ben followed suit. I surprised myself, and I was

14

taken aback by their response to my commands. They seemed to glue themselves to the kitchen table and the chairs, looking more frightened than myself. Like chickens caught in a storm.

For one brief moment the tables were turned. I was triumphant. I remember wishing that I were as huge as my late father. I would have pulped their heads into powder, despite the guns that I knew they carried on them. This feeling made me wish that nature had reversed my small stature and given it to one of my sisters, all of whom were built like baby elephants. But here I was, the only male in the family, small as a mouse. I came out of the bedroom and told them that I was ready.

During the commotion, my eldest son, Gaboipeoe, had woken up. He came into the kitchen just as they were about to take me away. I told him what was happening. Gaboipeoe seemed surprised that I was leaving without resistance, without putting up a fight. He was 16 then, at high school, and one of the present generation from Soweto who brook no nonsense, particularly from the Security Police; these children seem to have been born hating these police! I was glad that he had woken up, but I will never forget in all my life the look of scorn on his face. It was an indictment, not only of me but of my entire generation.

I knew. I had heard already that the young of Soweto never just surrender or go down without a fight. That, short of escaping, they always put up a fierce resistance to the end, and do not let the police apprehend them easily. It was common knowledge that when one of these youths had to be collected, more reinforcements were always provided.

I was made to sit between the two mysterious robots in the back seat as the cream-toned Kommando motor car raced off with me. I took a receding look at my wife and Gaboipeoe as the car sped off. They remained, stunned, in the street, alone. There was not a single moving object in sight. Even the hungry ghetto dogs that were always foraging for food seemed to have taken fright. The houses seemed asleep as were their occupants. It looked as if I was going far away. Very far. The time was then about 4 a.m.

I also know that I will never forget that image of my wife and son, their helplessness as they stood there looking at the police car racing away with me. That vision has haunted me to this day.

Ben Letlaka drove to Meadowlands Police Station, four or five blocks from my house. On arriving, he pompously showed his Security Police card to the Black policeman on desk duty. He then took the telephone and dialled. I was made to sit on a bench between the two robots, who had up to then not said a word to each other, to me or to Ben. After leaving my house, everything was mute. I had become a mute too. The car had become one, except for its humming as it ate into the road.

I remember wondering if their voices were secret too: inaudible except perhaps to themselves, by some strange mechanism they had developed so that those captured could not hear what they said to each other or what they intended to do with them.

They looked tired, sleepy, and their mouths stank of brandy. They must have spent part of the night at a shebeen before making the raid on my house. In comparison with Ben, they were short and small. Ben towered above their midget bodies. I still wished I was bigger than Ben though.

At the police station, I overhead Ben saying "Kernel" several times over the phone, "jaaing" all the time, repeating the word *"seker"* (sure) several times, nodding as if the "Kernel" at the other end of the phone could see how respectful Ben was. Respectful to White Baasskap. Finally, Ben said "7.30" in Afrikaans. He had received further instructions, which I guessed were that he drive me to Jan Vorster Square and be there with me not later than half-past seven. It turned out that my guess was correct.

I had arrived home at 1 a.m., a habit my wife had learned to live with. Four weeks prior to this night of 4 March 1975, I had been arranging and planning the third annual festival of the Black Arts for MDALI, which had been formed three years ago by artists from the Black ghettos of Johannesburg, Soweto and Alexandra Township, south-west and north of the city respectively, and a few others from neighbouring Black areas. This organization had become a sore thumb in the eyes of the police because it exposed the exploitation of Black artists by White impresarios in South Africa. It spoke of self-determining the artistic activities and destinies of Black artists and insisted on forcefully breaking the chains of exploitation as well as liberating the mental and creative processes of these artists. It was MDALI which, for the first time in South Africa, used the words "Black Arts" aggressively and positively to inspire action towards liberation, in line with the then current philosophy of Black Consciousness. This positiveness, regarded as militant and anti-White, resulted in sharp

16

confrontations between paternalistic White artists, gallery owners and impresarios on the one hand, and members of MDALI on the other. This contradiction for a long time catapulted MDALI to the forefront of Black Consciousness in the arts and made the organization a prime target of the Security Police. The typical South African response towards MDALI, among some Black artists and other people, mostly Whites, was to regard the organization as a subversive political front wearing the cloak of art. But nothing was further from the truth to those who had participated in the formation of MDALI. MDALI was a long overdue necessity. Its anger and annoyance were not coated with sugar — the time to stop differentiating between art, culture and politics had come.

By the same token, personalities in MDALI, participants and others, acquired files at the Security Police headquarters in Jan Vorster Square, Johannesburg. Their statements in the press, their names and theatre presentations, were carefully cut out and preserved in police files for investigation, and the people marked for detention and interrogation. It turned out I was to be such a person.

If MDALI was racist because it did not cater for Whites and stood for Black positiveness, then, speaking for myself, I accept that I am a racist, and healthier for it to boot. I offer no apologies for that type of racism to my fellow Black critics and their White friends, to the régime or to anyone who supports such an accusation against MDALI, especially to the Black critics, some of them poets who flirt with the Whites of Lower Houghton, the rich White suburb of Johannesburg, reading "Black" poetry there.

I was tired. The festival had closed after five days of hard work. I had been programming the various groups, chairing symposiums, introducing speakers, opening the plastic arts exhibition of the festival, directing the day-to-day events and eventually appearing with the Mihloti Black Theatre group. I also read my poems together with other ghetto poets. The festival was over, at least for another year. I was glad. Glad and tired, and I slept like a wet sack at the door after the rains.

They always come in the middle of the night, or in the early morning when sleep is deepest, restful and pleasant. They bang on the windows and doors and walls making a frightening noise, screaming "police, police", their torches flashing through the windows.

17

For some time now, political activists, Black writers and artists and all those who spoke out against the oppressive South African race laws had been disappearing into oblivion or for long periods of time through the hands of the Security Police. In the case of a well-known person, the newspapers would now and then announce the detention of such a person. In the case of a lesser-known person, no one would know. Many people had disappeared and nothing was heard of them again except perhaps by the immediate relatives, who in most cases "preferred" to keep things quiet, in the hope that they were easing the hardships of the disappeared detainee. After some such detention, everything would return to "normal", and life would go on. "Who's next?" would be on everyone's lips. We would live on in the ghetto, following our usual habits, waiting in silence, horror-stricken, hoping all the same to hear more news of the detainee, if we were lucky, because no one knew what happened as soon as one of us was taken away and locked behind those massive prison doors. Detention in South Africa is incommunicado. There is no habeus corpus. No lawyer, no member of one's family, no doctor and no priest is allowed to see detainees. Detainees live and survive on suspension, tension and hope. The cut-off is as complete as a black night. Many break down not out of cowardice, but out of concern for their loved ones left to fend for themselves.

For the past four years or so, these detentions had increased. But the ghetto has always resisted and mounted protest after protest against what was happening to its people, protecting itself with waves of daring outspokenness. The ghetto, fearless, despite all the odds against it. More recently, the news of deaths of those detained has leaked out through the press, the circumstances of all these deaths being the more ominous as they happened at night or at unknown times during police interrogation.

Many times detainees have been secretely transferred to remote jails in the country, far from family and friends. In many instances, to distances of more than 6,000 miles away, known only to their jailers.

2. The Christmas party

We arrived at Jan Vorster Square and drove into a maze of a garage in the basement of the building that comprises this massive police headquarters. I sensed immediately that, once there, there was no hope. Miracles, yes, perhaps. The garage was ill-lit and contained a battery of police cars, some of which I had on several occasions seen in the townships. There was an ominous regimentation that immediately descended on everyone.

I was led to a lift which took the four of us to the ninth floor. There the lift stopped and the door opened, showing us a gorilla-like White man in a glass cubicle. He took a scanning look at us as we piled out. To our right, past the cubicle encasing that hideousness, a steel door miraculously slid and slotted itself into a wall. As soon as we went in, the steel door shot out of its wall-slot back into place. There were no door handles, no buttons, nothing. Just a plain pale pink slab of steel and we were sealed in.

I found myself in a corridor containing what seemed like hundreds of offices, facing each other down the stretch of the passageway. It was still early and the place was devoid of human beings. At that time, apart from the monstrous animal we had just passed, whose job presumably was to control electronically the steel door after assessing arrivals, a few Black, Coloured and Indian Security Policemen were already there, idling, apparently waiting for the Whites under whom they operated. Without these Whites, they were without initiative. Then there were us — Ben Letlaka, myself and the two robots.

The three men led me into a room which I imagined to be Colonel Visser's interrogation chamber. I could feel that in normal office hours, this place must hold people like flies, each one pretending business at this or that. I could feel their numbers even in their absence. And because there were so few then, it felt eerie.

It was not long before the arrival of the important man himself. I did not know him, but as soon as he came in his flourish told me that it must be the "Kernel" in person. He oozed confidence and self-assertion, looking fresh and well groomed. He gave my presence there no importance at all, as if to rub in the fact that I should get it straight, from the beginning, that he had been victorious in having me hauled in.

Soon after his triumphant entry, a whole flotilla of policemen sailed into his room. They rushed into the room where I had been ushered as if they were escaping from someone with a whip who was lashing their backs and behinds.

There were lieutenants, colonels, captains, warrant officers, sergeants, non-commissioned men and new recruits. There were

19

Blacks, Coloured, Whites and Indians. Some of them were very young and some very old, a whole contingent of them, as though an important instruction were to be given. I could see their heads, particularly the short ones trying to get a better glimpse of this important detainee, as I thought. Others got so close to me I almost thought they were semi-blind. A lot of them shook their heads, making clicking sounds at the same time, as if to say that I had had it. Whether this show had been decided as a campaign to make me nervous, and therefore easier to deal with later, I could never tell; or whether the whole spectacle had been stage-managed, I still could not say. What I did feel was that word had gone round that I had been brought in, as if other detainees before me, involved with me, had loaded the whole whatever-it-was on me.

All the police in this room were babbling away, in Afrikaans, at the same time. I ceased trying to follow their excitement which was obviously aroused by me. Many of these peeping Toms were later to be directly involved in my interrogation. Many I never saw again at close quarters except sometimes in passing, as the process unfolded. At one time there were over a dozen policemen screaming for a better viewing point. They made me feel that I was so "important" that they each had to take an individual look at this finally unearthed subversive.

I felt very frightened. Whatever it was, it must be very serious. Colonel Visser, looking fresh and clean, a blond with blue eyes, seemed absolutely satisfied with his work, as if he had himself effected the arrest after a bloody battle in which he had overpowered me.

Ben Letlaka and his two deaf and dumb mutes shared the glory, doing their best to shield their stinking breaths from their White superiors and trying terribly hard to look as fresh and alert as Visser. Other non-White police seemed to share in this success. I got the impression that they all worked as one. One for all and all for one (for you, South Africa), as one of the lines from the South African Afrikaner anthem, "Die Stem" (the branch or agreement), runs.

Their behaviour was like that of ghetto children I had seen at Christmas parties. The only difference was that the spectacle unfolding before my eyes was being enacted by adults. The other difference was that these were the Security Police! — and I was the cause of their "Christmas party." I even had the impression that they were reacting in this manner as if I had been on the run from them for some time and so it was reason enough for a celebration.

The theory that South African policemen, Black and White, were stupid was never better illustrated than it was on this day. In their private confines, they may perhaps exhibit some modicum of intelligence. But I had seen them in public and at law courts, so ludicrously exposed that I found it hard to believe that it was true. I had seen them fumbling and lying and fabricating, half the time not even remembering their own concocted lies to effect a conviction. Many other times I had seen them in the streets not even knowing why they were arresting people. All they could tell one, at best, was, "You will answer in front," meaning in court.

While all this was happening, together with ever so many goings in and out of Visser's room, I was straining my mind for at least one reason for my detention, besides MDALI activities — the most obvious. I could not think of anything else then. But of course, it could be one of many things, or absolutely none, remembering that this was South Africa. No real reason was needed to haul any Black person into prison. But given the existing conditions, it could be one of a multiplicity of things....A conversation, perhaps, with friends, on the political events in the country. I could remember several such conversations I had had with all sorts of people. Ordinarily, there should be nothing the matter with that, even in South Africa. But with so many ill-paid informers all over the place, anything gets blown up out of all proportion. A conversation like that could be interpreted as plotting the violent overthrow of the state. But none of my imprisoners was letting the cat out of the bag and, in agony, I could not find any reason or probability. At the same time, I was doing the best for myself. Reassuring myself that I should relax and not get ruffled by these antics, I told myself to think out my answers carefully as soon as the interrogation started, and I was certain it would begin soon.

I stole glances at every one of them, to make sure I would recognize them if we should meet in the revolution I wished would happen tomorrow. I felt that perhaps I could then avail myself of the chance to repay them in kind. I felt a particularly burning hatred for the Blacks there, more than any other racial group, for having allowed themselves to be used to humiliate their own kind. Next in line were the Coloureds, their next in rank in the South African human hierarchy and, of course, their "cousins", the

21

Coloured population being a result of the early Boers (White Afrikaners) having bedded the indigenous women, some or most of them against their will. Last, the Indians or Asian stock, the super opportunists. I was infuriated and my head was reeling, aching with anger, choking my impotent throat. The Whites I detested for their hateful superiority and contempt of the Blacks, which they had displayed for three hundred years and more for no reason other than that of colour. All this time, I was made to stand like a prize bull in a market, a black one at that.

"Sit," Colonel Visser barked at me, picking a moment when the din had temporarily quietened. He said the word in Afrikaans, which uses the same spelling as in English but pronounced differently, like "set".

This also happened to be the signal for various others to leave, which they promptly did. I suppose business was about to begin and they all knew the sign.

Colonel Visser and I must have been silent adversaries for some time. Only I did not know it. But he must have had me under observation. This was his moment. He had won the first battle. He had me in custody, in his hands and at his mercy. Many of them had left, except those I considered to have some rank. So the room still had some air of the Christmas party. Visser was himself fussing and burrowing into some papers, files and several documents on his desk, one of which was a thick file with my name on its brown cover.

Shit! I'm in hell, I thought, when I saw the thickness of the file.

He opened his mouth, lit his pipe and started. "Phineas Gaboronoe Phetoe," reading from the mountainous file before him.

"Molefe Pheto! I offer that name as it is my right name." I ventured to put the record straight from the beginning.

"Yourr alibis and aliases! We know about them too."

I did not know what he meant by "them" as I had offered him only one name.

All my life, I had been registered through the various South African department offices as Phineas Gaboronoe Phetoe. Besides Gaborone (correctly spelt), Molefe is my ancestral name. I have been trying and fighting all the time to correct the misspellings and to eradicate the inhumanity of being nameless to no avail. But after he alleged that my correct names were aliases, I decided not to crack my head with what I considered an imbecile. Besides,

Visser had already become aggressive.

"Don't lekturre us. You arre herre forr interrrogation. Don't underrmining ourr intelligence, and you mus be rready to ko-operrate."

The Afrikaners, almost all of them, speak English with strong accents on the letter "c", which sounds like "k", and have long rolled "r" sounds. Their "t" also sounds flat. Their English grammar is utterly amusing — come what may, they never seem to master it. These factors made them long-standing jokes in the ghettos of Alexandra Township, Soweto and other places. No day passes without some Black man telling a funny story about an experience involving the Afrikaner and this aspect. In most cases the Afrikaner is aware of this inability and is very sensitive about it. It is worse with the rural Afrikaners, all of whom take exception to educated Black people.

Personally, I am not bothered whether the Afrikaner speaks English well or not. I see it as their planned resistance, as they have not forgotten their historical enmity with the English. But at another level, if anything demonstrates that the Black man has better learning ability, then this is a case in point. With all the facilities and opportunities their government provides for them, the Afrikaners are still incapable. It could also be a reason for their denying us opportunities, for fear of being outdone. Visser was no different, and neither were the rest of the police I was later to come into contact with.

I steadied myself for the worst. Visser kept on looking into the file which seemed to contain everything about me. My life history. He tilted it away from me in such a manner that, much as I tried, I could not glimpse a thing.

Then he rattled out all my past travels abroad. "You have been overrseas," referring to the time when I was a music student at the Guildhall School of Music and Drama, in London. "To London, came back to South Africa, then left again back to England, Frrance, London, Ghana," and here he stressed Ghana.

"You are correct."

He glowered, as happy as a monkey. "You see! Therre is nothing we don't know about you. Now yourr job is to tell us everrything. Not forr us to tell you. Now. What ken you ko-operrate us with?"

I told him that I thought he was to ask me the questions.

"Oo! I ken see you rrefuse to ko-operrate."

He took a deep breath and looked at me through the smoke he had just emitted from his pipe. I believed he was also sizing me up. The others remained fierce-looking, standing like steel statues beside me. All the non-Whites had left. Visser looked at his remaining White colleagues, as if he had to get their acquiescence to continue. Apparently, all the White policemen who had remained behind in the room knew something about what I was supposed to have been involved with.

"Do you know Krris Weimer?"

I tried hard to remember. Nothing happened. I tried harder just in case, to save myself. Still nothing clicked. But I knew that I had never heard the name before. I wasn't sure whether this Kris or Chris Weimer was White or Coloured, since the names of Coloured people and Afrikaners in South Africa are similar both in spelling and pronunciation. It certainly was not an indigenous name. If anything, I had anticipated being asked about people with Black names. This was getting too much.

"No!" I shook my head.

"No?" He imitated me, making it look funny, calculated to solicit laughter from his audience. "I see!" Visser said slowly, his pipe back in his mouth, held back in place by a strong bite.

They all looked at each other. Five White men, three of whom were extremely hefty like the hideousness I had encountered when I came out of the lift with my escorts. Visser and another were not as big, on the elderly side, particularly the other who was sinewy and worn-out.

"Errik Molobi? Do you know that one?" pronouncing the second name so badly I could not recognize it.

I had heard the name before. In Black communities, several clans share the same name. In fact, a cousin of mine by marriage was a Molobi. But his "European" name was not Eric.

"No. I do not know Eric Molobi. I have never heard the name before," I told him, or rather, them. To all intents and purposes, they were all taking part in the interrogation by proxy. They were following everything that was going on and I expected any one of them to throw in his bit at any time, even a punch, if I annoyed them enough.

The five White men again exchanged glances. I had the feeling that they thought I was resisting. But they showed no emotion nor indication of what they thought. I noticed confidence in them as though to say, "You all start that way, but sooner or later you begin to talk."

"Do you know Johnny Rramrrock?"

"No."

"Kenny Klarrke?"

"No."

The questions and names were coming much faster. The fact that Visser was not even repeating them took me off guard for a while. I started thinking that perhaps they believed me and were not really bothered. Well, at last, we were getting somewhere, progress.

"Pat McGluwa?"

"No. I don't."

"A certain Zabane, Aprril?"

"No."

One of them, whom I christened "Mother Hen" because he behaved like a hen over her chicks, with his huge size and busy hands, talkative, walking in and out, raging, menacing me, thrusting his fat fleshy face into mine, annoying me because it had sweat bubbles like wet pimples, said, "He's shitting us, and we'll shit him too."

Then he turned to me and said in perfect SeSotho, one of my native languages, "Hey, we are not here to play. We are working here," his voice loud, as it I had challenged them or was not aware that they were at work.

While I was wondering where he had learnt the language so well, his boast — because that is what it was — alerted me that whatever happened, I should not use any of the vernaculars; the possibility was that a lot of them there could speak one of them. Sometimes I would answer that I did not know what they were asking me, so as to clear my mind when they pursued the question. I had realized that if I didn't give a positive answer, the question came back a number of times.

I did that in the case of Sefton Vutela.

"And Sefton Vutela? Do you know him?"

"No!" I lied.

"You don't know Vutela?" Visser was getting angry. He seemed sure that I must know Vutela. He was right. I knew Vutela very well.

I was aware that Visser was absolutely certain that I knew Vutela, by the way he insisted, showing, I suppose in an off-guarded moment, surprise that I said I didn't. In the meantime, I tried to remember very quickly any awkward moment that might make it difficult for me if I finally agreed that I knew Vutela.

Vutela was a political personality of high courage when I first met him. He had been harassed by the Security Police for a long time in Johannesburg. At the time he was living in Botswana in exile. He had fled South Africa after he had been banned, in the early sixties. He took off while awaiting trial for continuing to engage in the activities of a banned organization, so the charge read. When he was let out on bail, he headed for the border.

I first met Vutela at the Witwatersrand University Library, where we were both employed as "library shelvers", when in actual fact the work we were doing was that of library assistants. We fought many battles together. First, against the library authorities for what we considered unjust treatment of us, and against the university administration's bureaucracy. In all these problems, Vutela stood principled and would never desert, whatever the odds. Indeed, I knew Vutela.

"Oh, yes. I know Vutela... if you mean the one in Botswana!" I had already clearly decided what to say without compromising myself politically, or in any other way. That his exile situation had nothing to do with me. That there was nothing wrong in knowing a man who lived in exile. That politically, I was not involved with him.

However, in South Africa, in interrogation, things do not work out that way. If you know someone in exile, you automatically are involved with him. I told Visser and company that Vutela and I met and became friends when we worked together as library assistants at the Witwatersrand University Library. That I was aware of his political involvement in the country then, and of his status in Botswana. In Botswana, I told them, we had met on the basis of the past and on no other.

"You want us to believe that!" Visser said, enunciating all the words, implying that I was taking them for fools. Of course they did not believe me and it would have been naïve of me to think that they did.

It was the next question that brought out sweat all over me. Over my hands, body and forehead. And it was the first question Mother Hen had asked, apart from the threats that he had made to me.

"Who took Clarence Hamilton away?" He looked me straight in the eye. Mother Hen must have decided that shock treatment was

26

better. Whether I was going to be sincere in my denial or not, it was a chance he considered worth taking. His eyes stuck into me to record my reaction. He had asked the question slowly, clearly, but not too slowly. Just the right pace to produce the effect he desired. I went to pieces inside, but remained stoic. I dared not show that I was shaken.

I knew Clarence Hamilton very well. He had recently joined the Mihloti Black Theatre group, whose performances I directed. Prior to that, he was a drama student at the African Music and Drama Association in Johannesburg, a Black arts learning centre, where I was musical and cultural programme director.

At about the same time that I first met him, Clarence Hamilton had been one of a group of youths who had organized a boycott of lessons at the Coloured school he attended near Johannesburg. He was alleged to have distributed pamphlets encouraging his fellow students not to attend classes as sign of protest against the celebration of Republic Day in South Africa, implying that Coloured people had nothing to be jubilant about as they had no stake in the country, the same as the Black people. The Security Police in Johannesburg reacted sharply to this; coming from Coloured youths, the protest showed the very solidarity that the régime would need to nip in the bud. There were disturbances at his school, culminating in the detention of Clarence Hamilton. He was later charged, tried, found guilty, but was allowed out on bail to await sentence. Clarence did not honour his bail. He ended up in Botswana, the neighbouring independent state, an exile.

"Who took Clarence Hamilton away?" Mother Hen repeated the question.

"I don't know." I had made a quick decision.

So far, my system of delaying tactics was working. But I was sure it was not successful. Somewhere, there was bound to be a slip.

At that moment, one of the older policemen in the room interrupted the proceedings, speaking in Afrikaans: "Where are his things?"

I did not know what things he was talking about. Another replied that they had nothing from me. He was told that I had been collected by Bantu Constable Ben. Yet another added that they had better go and search the house, "*voor die goed verdwyn*" (before the things disappear). The policeman who first asked where my things were continued, still in Afrikaans, "You know

27

how they are," meaning of course we Black people. That given the slightest chance, nothing they could use against me would still be in the house. Books, pamphlets and material like that. We were supposed to be notorious for our stealthy manners; we could not be trusted. He was right. The people of the ghetto would have covered for me as soon as they knew I had been unjustly detained, for that was what it was. No one had the right to detain any Black man against laws the Black man had no hand in making. The ghetto would do anything to frustrate the police. I too would do the same for a fellow Black. It was then that I understood what the "things" were: whatever the search might have produced. So, at that time, there was nothing they could show or refer to in incriminating me.

While the discussion was going on about the "things", I had some respite from Mother Hen's piercing questions. But not for long. He was back as soon as he had had a break. "You say you don't know who took your friend away?"

"No. I don't...." I did not finish the answer I was going to give.

Thud! Mother Hen hit me hard directly on the forehead, dead centre between my eyes, with the three middle fingers of his right fist folded as in karate, the middle knuckle making the first painful contact before the other knuckles. The pain, the force, and the surprise element — like his questions — brought a flood of immediate tears to my eyes.

"We have methods to conscientizing people into remembering. We are working here. We don't sleep," repeating his stock-in-trade remark about them not "sleeping there". Mother Hen was fond of and boastful about what he considered to be the Black Consciousness terminology. He would rattle off the words in as pompous a manner as he could find: "Solidarity, pig, motherfucker, the man, conscientize and afro!"

I could not find any reason for this exhibitionism. If Mother Hen was trying to impress me, I could not see what he would gain by it. Incidentally, he seemed to be the most educated of the lot there. His English was better than that of most Afrikaners I have had the chance to listen to.

Just when I thought the music had begun again, they all suddenly went into another room, summoning a Black policeman, one of the many loitering there, to guard me. But they were soon back.

"*Kom!*" (Come!)

28

These men seemed to conduct themselves in a disorderly manner which at times relieved me from tight corners, while at other times had me with my back against the wall.

Anyway, the order had been given. *"Kom!"*

The Christmas party ended as suddenly as it had begun. Some of the police had come to Visser's room out of curiosity. Some had remained in the room because they seemed to help each other all the time, like actors cuing each other. Some were to remain with me for a long time, day after day, for weeks and months.

Their sudden withdrawal from Visser's room to another must have been to hold a small conference that decided to go and search my house. As they said earlier, I had been brought in by Bantu Constable Ben, who had not searched the house, or was not allowed to do so without White supervision, or was considered not educated enough to know what to look for, or was not even trusted.

"Kom!"

Their demeanour made it clear to me that they knew in a little while I would talk. They showed no immediate hurry to squeeze the information from me. They had all the time in the world, and they told me so; out of experience, they expected me and all detainees to offer resistance, as a matter of course, before the methods to break us were resorted to. They were not in a hurry at all.

"Kom!"

3. *The search-party*

They work very unmethodically, these men. It was this inconsistency that gave me a lot of time to gather my thoughts, to try and anticipate their next move and to answer vaguely when the questions were awkward and needed well-thought-out answers, such as the question on Clarence Hamilton. Even though I may not have known much about him or, I believe, the others about whom they had asked, there could be many pitfalls where I could find myself irrevocably compromised. Since the question about this Hamilton, I surmised that all the other names with non-Black origins must belong to the same group. I had never associated with Coloureds or Indians in either my political or my Black arts work in South Africa, except a lone one here and there. Whites were out

29

of the question. Of that I was certain.

These thoughts gave me no respite as one of the policemen took the wheel of the Kommando motor car for the drive to my house for the search. There were five of them in the car with me. Two Whites, one Coloured, one Indian and one Black.

The Coloured policeman's name was Sons. His was the first name I learnt there that day besides Ben Letlaka's. He was self-opinionated, full of his own importance and officious. He imposed himself on the other policemen, Blacks, Indians and Coloureds. In response, he received sheepish respect, even awe, from the others over whom he lorded. He had the rank of captain, and all the time it would be "No, Captain Sons", or "Yes, Captain Sons". Sons didn't impress me. I particularly hated his Uncle Tom tactics, his pleasantness and perpetual helpfulness to his White superiors. Sons was such a willing horse, a typical "house nigger".

I have yet to see as ill-shaped a person as Sons. His legs were longer than any part of his body, very out of proportion and lopsided. There was this buttockless back of his, straight as a builder's scaffolding plank. Above that, his waist, chest, neck and head were tightly compressed as though he found it hard to breathe.

The White one who drove the car I named "Magosha", a new word which saw its birth in the ever-growing and developing language of the ghettos, meaning prostitute. He got this name retrospectively though. One day, he and the Black one were escorting me from one detention jail to another. We were in the lift, when he excitedly showed this Black one his newly acquired South African passport.

"I'm going to Swaziland," he said animatedly.

"What for?" the Black one asked.

"For Magosha," he replied, showing the Black one a two-finger vulgar sign for sex.

Swaziland is one of the independent neighbouring states bordering South Africa; unlike South Africa, it has no colour restrictions between Whites and Blacks. Many White South Africans, the large majority of them the most ardent supporters of their country's racist ideology, have turned this tiny kingdom into their across-the-colour sex playground because of the prostitution that followed in the wake of independence, as has happened in many independent Black states I have been to — barring as of now Mozambique, whose new Frelimo government wiped out this

30

malady that the former colonial power of Portugal encouraged and abetted. After all, it did not matter to Portugal as only Blacks were prostituted. But Whites go to these independent Black states because they want to have their cake and eat it. They live in two different political worlds excitingly, always to their own advantage. Yet more frightening to the Boers is the fact that apartheid, separateness, is dying. The enraged apartheid bull is bleeding, bellowing its last gasps of racism; outside other internal restlessness from indigenous resistance, apartheid is dying of its own accord and its contradictions are looming large. We Blacks are standing at the ready for its final ignominious burial ceremony.

Then there was the White policeman I called "Purple Suit". He loved wearing that suit. The first time I saw him at Jan Vorster, in fact the very day I was brought in, when he joined the search-party to my house, he was wearing it. To me, a purple suit looked so unique and unusual that I just called him Purple Suit. He always smelt of cheap wine. The first time I smelt the puke, I thought perhaps it was one of those days when he had gone on a binge the night before. He looked like one who did not fit into the Security Police outfit at all, even as just a plain policeman. He occupied a small office where he was always available and on call as though he had no special duty, a lost cog in a wheel. Many a time he looked unwashed and dirty and he did not seem the least worried or aware. That, I decided, was his natural habitat.

Regarding the position that the Indian member of this search-party had chosen *vis-à-vis* the political struggles of the Black man for his rights, I could imagine an armoury of names for this scum. I despised him the same way I despised the two young Blacks who had come with Letlaka to wake me up in the early hours to detain me. When I remember the many people of Indian origin who have carved their names with honour on to the liberation movement, my revulsion for him makes me feel like throwing up on him, into him. He must have heard of the great Indian leader Mahatma Gandhi who defied the attempt to force Indians to carry passes like the Blacks do in South Africa today, and who won for his people the abolition of this most dehumanizing piece of legislation. That was why this scum sitting in the car with me, doing this job, did not carry a pass. He must have heard of the Imam, the Cape religious leader who had been murdered by members of the Security Police while being detained by them. He must have known about Ahmed Timol, another Indian youth recently killed by the Security Police at that same Jan Vorster Square. Timol, whom they alleged had jumped through a tenth-floor window apparently during interrogation. He, this man, might have taken part in the murder of young Timol.

I searched for the most searing, dehumanizing name I could think of for him. He was stocky, with a pot-belly, very short legs and a double chin, suggesting a man satisfied with himself and life generally. He was uncomfortable in his walk, because that stomach was too big for his height. It looked as if he was carrying a perpetual pot there. There is a pot that most communities of the world use at night. It is usually hidden and kept away from the public eye, often under the bed, like an unpleasant secret. I decided to call him that. "Night Pot". In prison, no one wants to empty this night pot, which in South African jails for Blacks is an old tin, hideously filthy, which smells for miles on end. Its stench permeates through many cells, and when you consider that every cell has one, then the multiplication of the stenches must be a mountain of shit. Each time it was my turn to carry the pot out, during the time I was in remand, I felt like digging myself under the cement floor of the cell. Then I would remember Night Pot. During my whole period of detention, I do not remember these pots being disinfected.

These then were the main characters in the car as Magosha belted it along the Soweto highway to my house, as if the books and other important information in my house would suddenly develop legs and run for it. As if the books would know that the men of Jan Vorster Square would come for them too.

Through the window of the car, I saw the Black township of Diepkloof suddenly come and remain behind us, so fast that the toy houses seemed to be spinning on their own. As if the car was sailing through the air. I tried to count the little houses. One, two, four, seven, twelve...jumping the numbers to keep up...Orlando East, another Black ghetto, loomed ahead of us on the rise of the road, and was gone. On my right was the Coloured township of Noordgesig where Clarence Hamilton, perhaps the man for whom I was in this situation, had lived. Then the new bridge emerged and Meadowlands, where my house was, was only an eyewink distance away. I started getting worried about what they were likely to dig up there.

The tyres screeched on the dust road as we reached No. 230, Zone 1, Meadowlands. The time was about midday. On arrival, they all leapt out spectacularly, surrounding the car before I had stepped out. When I did, they encircled me all the way to the door, shielding me as though they did not want the neighbours to see me. I could see the neighbours from the corner of my eye, stealthily parting small chinks in the curtains. Unknowingly, anyone might have thought that my neighbours did not want to identify themselves with me or my deeds. But nothing was further from the truth. That, as we all know in our situation in my country, was only a device to give an impression to outwit the enemy — a survival instinct that the ghetto observed, while the police felt that I was isolated to an extent where no show of solidarity was visible. In the meantime, I also played my protective role by not openly looking at any house in particular. I knew that my captors were watching for any sign of collusion. This ghetto has a loud silent language. There is so much between a chink in the window and a wink in the eye, that anyone who has grown up in the ghetto, is of the ghetto, is the ghetto itself and has graduated in the ghetto ways, will recognize.

I fetched the key from where my family normally left it when we leave in the mornings, either to go to work or to school. Once inside the house, all of them took their time. They took off their jackets and placed them on the couch. At first, they did not go straight to work. They looked at the walls, at the paintings by Soweto's Black artists, at the sculptures in the room, at the array of the huge Mambukushu drums from Northern Botswana, at indigenous musical instruments and other pieces from many Black communities.

I was petrified at Malangatana's revolutionary paintings from Mozambique, fiercely staring at my enemies and captors, with the power, strength and beauty that few works of art possess. But I should not have worried. The Security Police could not read anything from the works — in fact were totally incapable of doing so.

The tone of the work in the house was Black Consciousness. I have no doubt that even if they could not interpret or understand the paintings and other exhibits, they could not miss the aggression of Black positiveness in the house. They seemed surprised that I had all those pieces openly displayed. After all, I had been to England and was therefore "civilized".

In many ways, I felt proud. I asked myself whether that made them feel that they had the right man, or someone genuinely attached to his culture. I fancied the first probability to be what they felt.

Then their eyes landed on the shelves and the books. Apart from relics of my music studies in London, all the books were by Black writers from America, the Caribbean, East, West and Central Africa. A few were by Black South Africans, almost all of them then living in exile. There were poetry books, novels, essays, art journals and magazines. The five looked at each other in disbelief. I could not have made it easier, they must have been thinking. But I knew that I used to make a periodic check as often as it was possible to make sure that nothing on the shelves was banned in the country. Anybody living in a country as sick as South Africa, with restrictions on what ought or ought not to be read, anyone, marked as many of us are, would be stark mad not to take precautions.

"Why didn't you hide these books, man?" Sons said, as if he did not want me to go to jail for possessing banned literature. "You will be gone for a long time, I can see that!" he concluded. "I can already see some banned books there," he went on, turning and talking more to Purple Suit than to anybody else.

Purple Suit sniffed some mucus up his nostrils, making a raucous noise in the process, then swallowed the filth, touching his nostrils and rubbing them hard the while as if deep in thought, breathing out fumes of stinking stale wine into my face. During all this, my stomach turned as if I was going to throw up.

The Black one's face was all ebony, shining, the whites of his eyes indicating that he was shocked at the sight of so many books in a Black man's house. I surmised that it must be his first experience of searching for communist or revolutionary or underground documents and that he was therefore uncertain of himself. Besides, he would not know how to differentiate between the various materials and what to pick out. This would expose him to his superiors and would lead to his automatic exclusion from further search-parties. As an apparently new recruit, no doubt he was ever so keen to do well.

Night Pot and Magosha were in the meantime shaking their heads endlessly, forcing supportive smiles of concurrence. Purple Suit, whose rank I could not fathom, took command. Because he was one of the two Whites there, it was only true to the South African way of life that he be in command. Otherwise, any of the other Whites in the company would have done so, whether or not

34

they were ill-equipped and inexperienced, so long as they were White.

"Take everrything on those shelves off, empty those rreed baskets. Everrything, and pile them herre," pointing to the floor on a spot he had selected during the quiet moments, I suppose. His mind must have been working furiously. "Don't botherr to look. Just take them!"

The Black one, Magosha and Night Pot suddenly sprang into life and went into action, the guns they were carrying impairing their effectiveness. Magosha had his gun elaborately slung under his right armpit, its thin white canvas strap-laces criss-crossing his narrow back and shoulders. The Black one moved his from the right-hand trouser pocket and shoved it ostentatiously to his back pocket, the one on his right buttock, for easy drawing if it became necessary. Sons and Night Pot did some shifting of their heavy metal too. I did not see where Purple Suit kept his.

Night Pot continued a hissing whistle between his front teeth during most of this time, which act increased my intense hatred and contempt of the man. If ever an Indian had his balls squeezed and his manhood drained, then here was a specific example. The noise from his whistling jarred on my ears even more, as I felt he was making me believe he loved his work. These antics of Night Pot also brought Sons into the firing line of my disgust. To me, Sons did not pass for a true Coloured person in South Africa. He was a shade or two darker than me. I kept thinking that Sons was one of those Blacks who posed as Coloured in order to get a better deal than Blacks. There are many such freaks in the country, freaks who want to live on both sides of what is best for them. When the Blacks win the political battle that is certainly poised to erupt soon, these freaks will be there, better-than-thou, even more militant than the Blacks who will have borne the brunt of the struggle. While the Blacks are still at the whip-end of the stick, these same freaks are having their cake and eating it. The same goes for those Coloureds who play White; and for the Whites who sleep with Black women at night, yet scorn them during the day. Many White policemen are known to have raped Black women during patrol duty at night in those police cars. I know of one such incident myself. I had turned the corner just as the White policeman in the back seat of the car was throwing this poor Black girl into the Johannesburg midnight. As I passed them, the police motioned my car to a stop and told me that I should remember that I had seen nothing!

Sons was Black in complexion like me. I only hope that when Blacks have thrown off the shackles of serfdom, Sons will be sought out and reminded of his role before he escapes and disappears into the safety of our numbers. Later, I heard that Sons hated the pure Coloureds who were in detention, most of whom were brought in by him to jail. I was told that during the interrogation of these Coloureds, Sons was more brutal to them, that he hit them hardest, perhaps to prove his loyalty to his masters. He had to be merciless because such Coloureds shamed him, standing alongside and fighting with Black brothers to free Azania (the name now used for our country), a position from which they could easily have extricated themselves. There are many "so-called" Coloureds, men of the calibre of poets like Don Mattera and James Matthews, who have outdone many Blacks in the freedom struggle for our country. The Hamiltons, young as they were. Sons must have felt bitterly the biological misfortune and accident of having a Black skin.

The shelves were emptied. The reed baskets were turned upside-down with hostility, spilling my valuable magazines, journals and books on the carpet. From the other rooms of the house, suitcases, travel bags and other containers were brought into the room they had chosen to work from as the centre of their search operation. They would pry intensely into these various containers, emptying everything on to the carpet. They took every piece of paper, paying particular attention to anything that looked like overseas correspondence.

They found my correspondence with the Moscow Conservatoire of Music, where I had intended to go whilst abroad. These particular letters became prized finds, getting the distinction of immediate isolation from the other documents. The same treatment befell correspondence I had with the Julliard School of Music in the United States.

Beds were turned and knocked about. Mattresses too, the lot. Wardrobes were forcefully and hurriedly swung open, as if the clothes inside would suddenly reveal concealed freedom fighters, or offer resistance. My record player was lifted up and searched underneath for secret compartments, as were the cabinet drawers and the coal stove in the kitchen. The carpet was tested by stamping and feeling with their shoes for mounds that might have been documents. I had the feeling that someone perhaps had told them that weapons and grenades were hidden in my house for the purpose of starting a revolution.

After my later experience of brutality at the hands of these men, I could understand how simple it would be for anyone going through their mill to readily trade his own mother, not to mention a mere friend or acquaintance, for a little respite. Any name that would lend itself became useful for survival.

Bank books, travel documents. Rent receipts and a piece of sculpture with the chain and fist symbol. All these were taken. It was as if I were moving house. I thought they would go for the wallpaper too.

The five men searched from room to room, including the toilet, slowly. I was called to every room they were in at a particular time, made to sit down while they went on. They were mostly quiet except for the consultations between Sons and Purple Suit whenever there was a margin of doubt, but of course there was the incessant nervous whistling of Night Pot. They even found some of my books that I had considered lost, some poems that I normally put in between pages of whatever book I was reading at the time, and some articles and letters I was in the habit of writing that I thought I had hidden from them should they come for me some day, and which in fact I myself could not find when I needed them!

All my collection of books, letters and papers that had taken me the better part of twelve years of steady and careful compilation and filing. Everything dismantled in something like three hours. I was strangely startled by the fact that I recognized every piece of paper, book, journal and letter I had collected over the whole period, each one reminding me of the time, place and circumstance. They burrowed through my house like ants working an anthill.

The pile in the sitting-room had become a heap. A little hill of Black-written books, my most beloved possessions. My whole wealth. My loves. My spiritual saviours. My knowledge of Black America, the Caribbean; my marriage with culture, including the written and the drum language, the "artefacts" that peeped at me each time I swam through the pages of those books. There they were, a painful, miserable, undignified pile on the floor. I felt certain then that the books and I would never meet again. The Black one and Night Pot were ordered to bring six brown government-supply envelopes to pour all the heap into. When

37

they ran short, Sons pulled a pillow out of its slip from my bed and loaded some of the books and other material into the pillow cover.

All the same, I had nothing to worry about, except the letter from the Russian Cultural Attaché in London about my inquiries on music education in the Soviet Union and the Moscow Conservatoire, innocent as that was. Over the years, I had checked and made sure that all the books on the shelves and elsewhere in the house were not on the banned list, difficult as it was to be absolutely certain about that in South Africa, because there was not a week in which a book or journal or some such publication did not come under the hammer of the Publications Board. The fact that there might be an odd book that had escaped my own comb would be an unfortunate accident. I had already resolved that if any were found I would merely own up, telling them that I was not aware of it, and face the consequences. What else could I say?

I saw Wole Soyinka thrown head-first into the pillow slip; the Imamu Barakas that had escaped banning by the Publications Board; Chinua Achebe staring at Purple Suit with his strong eyes suffered the fate of Soyinka; Serote, Mtshali, Senghor, Césaire, Okigbo, the two Diops, Mphahlele, E. R. Braithwaite, Ngugi; my own poems and the first manuscript of my novel joining that august company of Black writers going to jail in a pillow case and six big brown South African government-supply envelopes. In carrying the containers to the boot of the car they used antics calculated to frighten me more, buckling under the "weight" of the contents.

Purple Suit and Sons passed many remarks during their searching exercise. "Hmmm...this!" Sons would finger an item. "What's this?" He would shake his head solemnly. "Moscow!"

"And here is a map. A m-a-p, the borders of Rhodesia and South Africa! Man, whatever you say, they won't believe you at Jan Vorster!" Sons said this after finding a map indicating the areas I had travelled during research projects I had done on indigenous musical instruments.

"And there are bushes. Bushes around here," pointing at the areas he was referring to, "and a road to the Limpopo River". Sons took a mean look at me. I thought he had decided to hate me.

I shivered at my own stupidity and inwardly agreed that I was gone.

Fright played tricks with me. My stomach went out of control and I realized that I had also lost control of my bladder, that some urine might flow at any time. I thought of asking for permission to visit the toilet, but decided against it as giving the game away. My overworked mind told me to behave normally and show surprise that they were making a fuss over everyday issues.

There was no doubt in my mind that if I had had incriminating documents like coded messages and plans for revolution in the house, these would have been found, so thorough was their search. But unless they planted them in the house themselves, I was certain that there was nothing to bother about. In any case, if they had planted some stuff on me, I would not have been able to decipher the code. But I already knew from Mother Hen that they had "methods to conscientize people into remembering", in which case anything planted on me would have had to be "remembered" by me as mine.

I imagined screaming headlines from the government-supporting Afrikaans newspapers about an underground subversive organization unearthed at 230 Meadowlands, in Zone 1, by the surveillance of the overworked, ever-vigilant Security Police, whose efforts were unappreciated by certain sections of the White population. This sometimes happened when the minister of so-called justice, Jimmy Kruger, was challenged by anti-government newspapers to give reasons for some of the detentions. Kruger would reply that the danger of communism was already in the country. In most cases, no one actually saw the subversion this madman promised he would reveal to the country, except copious notes of speeches allegedly made by the detainees, most of which were contentious as the police who took them down often could not by any stretch of the imagination understand what was being said, preferring versions they had concocted in order to bring detained people to trial on some form of charges.

I was delighted with myself that, during all the years of compiling my library of Black literature, I had had the wisdom to send the Nyereres, Nkrumahs, Sékou Tourés, Mao Tse-Tungs, Kaundas, Fanons and others to friends all over the country, sometimes to places as far as 400 or more miles away. I had this unrealistic dream that some day it would be possible to read, as well as to have, these books openly in the house.

After what seemed like eternity, Magosha took the wheel again. He kicked the daylights out of that hissing Kommando car back to Jan Vorster.

On the way back, I recalled every antic of the five men during

39

the search. Magosha and Night Pot meekly taking their finds to Sons and Purple Suit, though mostly seeking, very discreetly, directions from Purple Suit. And Sons now and again darting from here to there, wishing he had a thousand eyes, hands and mouths. He would envelop the whole room with his flailing, awkward, unequally long arms. Magosha concentrated on photographs he found, particularly if there were White women in the picture. He was probably wondering when and how I could have come into contact with them, and where, as sex across the colour line is still a criminal offence in South Africa. Today, this century, when nations are already landing on the moon! Magosha would look at me, at the photos, show me one of the pictures, smiling tantalizingly, his eyes all mischief. He must have thought that I was a "colleague". So, I had White women too.

I had the nagging thought that if Magosha could get a chance to be with me alone for some time, his first question would be to ask what White women were like in bed. And I had long formulated an answer for him: "Not worth the risk." My speculation was wasted. The chance never availed itself. It would have been interesting to observe his reaction.

Night Pot was ranked above the Black one, whose name I learnt was Makhomisane, Alpheus. When Night Pot got an order he did not like during the search, he would immediately bark at his scape-goat, the Black one, "Makhomisane! Didn't you hear? Pick up those things on the floor and give them here!"

The car arrived at Jan Vorster Square with the five policemen still eating the corn-on-the-cob they had bought from a street vendor at the corner of Vincent and Odendaal Streets, Meadowlands, so hungry had they become during the search.

The Christmas party resumed. Every policeman in sight came to life. Old ones, young ones, middle-aged ones, cripples, the lot. They crowded into Colonel Visser's room to inspect the pile from my house.

"*Jesses*! What's all this?"

Whistles of surprise filled the room as they piled in. It seemed as though word had gone around again, for the second time that day. I wondered if this display would ever end. Would it always be like that until my release?

Visser asked me, "Do you rread all these books?"

I told him that I had read most of them, that some were new, or that I hadn't had the time to read them yet.

"And you wrrite all these materrials?" referring to the poems and articles and letters.

"Yes."

"Mun," pronouncing "man" as it sounded in Afrikaans, "this Kaffirr kan wrrite!"

Some of them gave me the dirtiest looks despite the fact that they did not know what the Kaffir had written. Sometimes it must have been envy — they must have thought that I was one of the educated Blacks they did not like.

The only thing going through my mind at the time was the map that Sons had concentrated on in the house. I searched the depths of my conscience for what to say to excuse it. But I found no feasible reasons to advance. I felt that any other reason would get me into a worse mess. The best was to hold on to my decision that it was a research map and never depart from that line. I decided to have no nightmares before the actual ones, if these were to come. Thus the little anecdotes they now and again let slip off their tongues, sinister in all probabilities, had no visible effect. But those were little brave acts on my part. I was as frightened as a hunted animal that had at last been cornered. The anecdotes certainly found their intended mark.

As it was already late in the afternoon, Makhomisane and Night Pot were ordered to take me down to the cells. I thought to myself that action would start on the following day. On the way to the cells, a crippled Coloured policeman joined the two escorting me. He was also on the short, stocky side, very poor-looking as though he worked for charity. His face spelt extreme sadism. I guessed correctly.

I noticed that he had a limp in his walk when I became brave enough to have a good look at him, "taking him from shoe to head". Limp, step, limp, step next to me, as we quietly went on, somewhere towards the belly of Jan Vorster Police Station, where the cells were. Jan Vorster Square, a beastly looking building, as beastly as John Vorster himself, after whom it was named. The building is mostly of blue glass and opaque windows. In the meantime, there was this limp, step, limp, step next to me.

Quickly, Limp Step jumped next to Makhomisane. With a hideous smile on his face, he asked ominously, "Has he been dry-cleaned yet?"

Makhomisane shook his head from side to side.

Limp Step said softly, "Let's do him now," as he feigned an awkward jab at my ribs.

The lift arrived. We walked in and he limp-stepped himself in too.

The cell allotted me gave me an eerie feeling. I tried to read any meaning into it all. Bare, with two filthy old grey stinking blankets. The smell of old cloth from the blankets was dominant, and the cell itself added its staleness and airlessness. The blankets had been over-used and overslept in and had not been washed for long periods. They were so thin I could see through them without having to put them against the light of the solitary centre bulb in the room. The cell itself was dirty, the dust as thick as thin linoleum, leaving prints of my canvas shoes as I explored it. A piece of thin grey mat lay in the middle of the cell. The doorless built-in toilet gaped at me endlessly, the stench choking my nostrils and throat. I did not have to try to bring my upper lip up to serve as a buffer for the nose. The reek from the toilet eventually took over and I felt covered by it. On entering the cell, I had quickly glanced at the number above the door-frame: 320. Was this a home from home? I asked myself. The twist in my house number and the one on this cell, to me, foretold that I had "come home".

When night came, I reflected on the incidents of the day. I concluded momentarily that they had, in their anxiety, forgotten about Clarence Hamilton. That it had been a close shave. But had they...?

4. Character Personae

The Security Police at Jan Vorster Square are numerous, so much so that after a while I gave up trying to count them, and I could not remember their identities. However, a certain group had begun to emerge, assuming a permanence that told me I would be with them till the end. Whatever the end.

In the meantime, I had developed my system of nicknaming them for my own comfort and easy identification. To be absolutely certain, I double-checked by watching to see if their characteristics suited the name I had chosen. Difficult as this was, I never had to change a name. They refused to disclose their real names to me but all the same, I got to know some of them by overhearing their conversation when they referred to each other by name.

During my boyhood days in the slums of Alexandra Township, my friends and I had great fun checking on people whose facial features resembled certain animals. The most popular of these were goat, monkey, horse, owl, hyena and dog. In most instances, the names were more fitting in our vernaculars than in English, because often they were suggestive of some mystical qualities or were onomatopoeic. I found this childhood pastime standing me in good stead in my predicament.

Sergeant Patose, a Black staff member whose name I found out later, was one such case. He reminded me of a tearful hyena. He had that firm, long nose of a hyena, starting from somewhere between his eyes and beyond. He had a narrow head, slightly flat like the top of a Volkswagen beetle car. His head was always clean-shaven because he was beginning to go bald. He had a noiseless semi-knock-kneed walk, a kind of sideways glide. His mouth was large and wide, accompanied by a permanent smile showing strong teeth which resembled a hyena's. He always addressed the White policemen as *Marena* (kings). A small belly was developing which almost negated the hyena image.

Hyena confirmed my feeling that all the policemen in South Africa that I met, Black and White, are unintelligent. He had been in the police force for more than fifteen years, he once told me, impressing upon me that his experience enabled him to see beyond my attempts to fool them. But to my mind it had been fifteen years of continuous indoctrination. Even after those years he still could not speak Afrikaans intelligibly, though he tried pathetically hard. Hyena was excellent in one aspect of his work. He could carry out instructions given him by his White superiors as faithfully as a dog.

"Watch him," the Whites would tell Hyena each time they left the room in which they had been interrogating me.

"Yes, *Morena*," he would answer.

As soon as the Whites were out of sight, he would interpret the order to me and immediately put it into effect.

"They say I should watch you. Now, stand still...there, just where you are. Don't move. I was not there when you and your Communist friends were planning all those 'nonsonses'," pronouncing "nonsense" in the African manner. Hyena talked to me mostly in SeSotho, one of the main languages spoken.

During his *Marena*'s absence, Hyena would avail himself of the opportunity to interrogate me. His questions made no sense. I wondered why I wasted my time, my strength and my breath responding to inane questions. Perhaps I was afraid he would beat me up, something I knew the police were capable of doing. So I responded. I also realized that what I said went in through one ear and simultaneously left through the other. On their return his superiors would ask him what had transpired in their absence.

"Wat seg hy nou?" (What's he say now?)

Hyena would shift apologetically on his buttocks, scratch his ageing head and reply, *"Hai, Morena, ek weet nie."* (No, King, I don't know.)

I discovered he was from Lesotho the day I listened to him talking to another policeman called Malie, who had recently been to Lesotho to inspect the progress on the house he was building there. Malie intended to retire soon to go and settle there.

"Have you built your house yet?" Hyena asked Malie.

"I have the materials ready, but I can't find good builders. The people at home," meaning Lesotho, "are lazy. All they do is watch women all day long. How is your house coming along?"

"I'm just from home. Yes. Last week. It is about to be finished. And I see, it's about time to retire and take my family back there." Then he turned to me. "Pheto and his friends have made me old."

There was a short pause. He looked at me again. "Pheto! Can you see what you have done to me?" he said, touching his greying head.

Just before they finished their conversation, Malie inadvertently gave me Hyena's name.

"Hela, monna, Patose, I'll see you later. I'm avoiding these fellows so that they don't send me out." He was referring to the White policemen.

Patose was a mercenary. If things became difficult for his ilk in South Africa, he could easily leave. He would have earned his money and built his huts, and would retire back to his country of Lesotho.

At least Malie and Patose were not South African-born Blacks. I also found out that most of them there were from rural areas. The story was more or less the same in the case of Magoro, who came from the Transkei. He also turned out to be an opportunist of the first order and mercenary no less, of the same kind as Malie and Patose. Now that the Transkei was "independent", Magoro hoped to emigrate there and seek a position in the police department,

44

presumably a high-ranking one based on his "experience". In the meantime Magoro was doing fine for himself.

From some of their conversations on which I always made it my duty to eavesdrop without showing that I was interested in what they were saying, I could not help but draw the conclusion that most of them intended running away to some quiet asylum as soon as the opportunity presented itself. Perhaps in their own way, through their long careers in this work, they were able to perceive the rising anger among Blacks in South Africa, which sent warning signals particularly to them.

As time went on, I found myself detesting Magoro more than smelling shit I might occasionally step on on the pavement, and the immediate attempt that would ensue to prise the mess off the shoe. He was short and had a pot-belly too. His face sometimes appeared coffee-smooth, sometimes pitch-black, sometimes a mixture of the two plus some pimples. I could never understand the kind of skin ailment he suffered from. His head was as round as a ball, and evoked a strong desire in me to kick it as hard as I could. He had a shrunken left ear, a little stump of a thing. Either he had been born that way, or had met with an accident which had half amputated whatever ear there had been before. I secretly wished he had been born with it, as I knew his boyhood friends would have made him the butt of their pranks.

Magoro seemed to develop a kind of complex against me, or perhaps that was his way with all of us who were political detainees. He was in the habit of hurling political arguments at me, knowing full well that he would "win" each time. On the occasions he permitted me to speak, I would seize the chance, laying it on as hard as I could, deriding every Black policeman and other lackeys of the régime. He would stand up, come very close to me, his half-ear almost touching my face. "Shut up. Look at what happened to Nkrumah and the others. Amin. As soon as they come into power, they take other people's wives, start a campaign of terror and murder." He said he was better off in South Africa.

I would shut up because there was nothing else I could do. I felt sorry for myself for not being able to let him know that I had great admiration for Kwame Nkrumah. The only satisfaction I had was that nothing could erase the impact of Nkrumah on me and thousands of other Black people all over the world.

On several occasions Magoro asked me what qualifications I had.

45

"Academic or technical?" I would ask.

"Shut up!"

All Black policemen had that in common. As soon as the Whites were out of the interrogation chamber, having become tired or going to tea or to the gymnasium, the Blacks would vent their frustrations on me.

"Pheto. You propagandize Black Power. Consciousness. But you are an educated man without logic. Logic!" This was one of the many harassments from Magoro.

Here we go again, I would say to myself, looking up at the ceiling in deep thought. In the meantime, Magoro looked like a lecturer before a class of admiring students. Perhaps he thought he was impressing me, gesticulating and punching the air to stress the points he was making.

"This because of that! That because of this! A man must have logicality!" 'Magoro would spin round on his heels and face me with his *coup de grâce*. "Give me logic and tell me where you travelled abroad, and we will be at par! You see!"

While the other Black Security Policemen would at least leave me alone at such moments, Magoro seized every opportunity to get at me. I already knew his routine. He should have been able to realize that I despised him for picking on the bones left by his masters. I would swallow my thoughts and pride as soon as he cleared his throat.

"O my God! This shit-house is at it again!"

One day I decided to surprise him as soon as we were alone. "What's your name?" I asked him out of the blue.

He sat up, cheek in palm, his elbow on the lifeless police-supplied table. His red eyes looked at me with a vacant stare. A long silence ensued. Our eyes locked and neither of us gave an inch. He cleared his throat, shifted, blushed, then belched.

"Magoro! Captain!"

Captain Magoro never uttered another word that day. He remained deep in thought until he was relieved by Makhomisane.

The mind boggles trying to remember all the police at Jan Vorster. They came from all sectors, although most of them were from the White sector. There were old ones, probably grandfathers who should have retired; new ones, most of whom were Black, coming mainly from the rural areas of South Africa, a good number of them young. I was certain that their parents did not know the kind of police work they were engaged in; that their

46

sons worked shamelessly for the régime in direct political support as well as frustrating the liberation efforts that their own great-grandfathers had been prepared to give their lives for, many of whom had died in the land wars against the White intruders.

Back to numbers again, I hadn't seen the first three, Ben Letlaka and his two colleagues, since the Christmas party. They probably belonged to the pick-up squad, one of the many. Not all of us had been picked up by the same squad. Many other policemen whom I saw I never got to know. Just faces passing by, like bees or flies in summer cascading over a dead dog, like shadows coming in and out.

On very rare occasions, I would see someone being brought in. I do not know how I differentiated between detainee and policeman, but I could feel the difference. I could sense it from the manner in which those who were brought in walked. Their frightened eyes darting and searching into every corner of those ominous interiors and long corridors, trying to locate fat White police interrogators in their offices. The offices were on both sides of the corridor, and remained closed at all times. I hoped that those brought in saw me too, if only to reassure themselves that they were not alone. There were detainees brought in every day that I was at Jan Vorster Square.

At first I was not certain whether he was Makhomisane or Makhombisane. I settled for Makhomisane as I had no time to check on specifics. I had to learn to survive as quickly as I could. Knowing his name was no problem. He was the football that was kicked in all directions, on which occasions his colleagues barked his name as they issued instructions to him.

Makhomisane had recently been recruited from Vendaland, one of South Africa's homelands, which has since been granted "independence", like the Transkei. He was a terrified man, uncertain of himself in this "high echelon of power". He behaved like someone who had been warned that unless he improved he would be fired. It would appear he wanted to survive by pleasing everyone, Black, Coloured, Indian and, of course, White. Patose poked fun at him for his clumsiness, even to me. Visser and another policeman called Struwig were discussing Makhomisane one day, wondering how he had come to be recruited, and they gave me the impression that they merely tolerated him. Struwig could not stand Makhomisane.

47

Makhomisane knew little or no Afrikaans. He would be on the trot before he had grasped what it was he had been ordered to fetch, only to return to ascertain what his real errand was; or he would come back with something he hadn't been sent for. It always amused and annoyed me at the same time. Why wouldn't the fool listen or ask?

But behind the steering-wheel of one of the big motor cars he was allowed to drive, Makhomisane became a different person altogether. He would slide sideways behind the steering-wheel, play it with one hand, cigarette dangling from his big hanging lips — real big time in his immaculate clothes. He did dress well, come to think of it.

Although all the other non-Whites did messengers' tasks at Jan Vorster Square, such as cleaning cars, sending tyres to the garages for patching, checking petrol levels, being sent to buy cigarettes and the like for their White seniors or to pay house electricity bills for their White counterparts, fetching the White policemen's wives from hairdressers and driving children to school, Makhomisane was the super messenger.

He was also funny and given to sudden outbursts. When he was left alone to guard me, the silence would be like a block of wood. Then, without warning at all, with a shaky voice reinforced by his endless cigarettes, he would blurt out, "So? You have travelled to England!" And just as suddenly, he would add: "Ya," breathing out, surprised that such a thing could happen, that a Black man should travel to England. After that Makhomisane and I would be back to our solid block of silence. I had no doubt that other than marvelling at my travels abroad, he was fully convinced that I was involved with "subversive" organizations in communist countries, information he had gathered during my interrogation from inferences made by the Whites who questioned me.

Much later, in the cells, I learnt that the other detainees had named him "One and six".

"What does it mean?" I asked in the darkness of my cell.

"One shilling and sixpence."

"Hey, Frank, why do you call him One and six then?" I half whispered, half shouted.

"The boys," meaning the other detainees, "think he's so scared he's like a whore who charges only one and six!"

That's when I realized that my habit of using nicknames was common practice among detainees to identify their interrogators, to use in communicating with each other, and that the methods whereby they arrived at a name were the same as mine.

The first policeman to assault me was a hunk of a man called "Tiny" van Niekerk. It was strange that they called him Tiny because he was a 300-pound bully with an equally heavy voice. He was as stupid as the other Afrikaner policemen. Invariably, all the policemen it had been my misfortune to meet at Jan Vorster Square and elsewhere in South Africa had been those who had failed to make the grade at school because they just did not have the brains. Magosha once asked me how I had managed to obtain such high musical qualifications, in England of all places, and what my future intentions were. I told him I wanted to study for a Masters degree and finally for a PhD.

"Oo! Something like a dokterr?" he said.

"Yes. Something like a doctor," and I thought I had closed the subject. But the numbskull went on:

"I kould neverr make it orr do anything at skool. I did not have the cleverrness. That's why I joined the police forrce!"

I believed that he really was dumb. Here he was, my captor, telling me that he was so stupid that the only thing he could do was to join the police force. The revelation reinforced the belief we had in the ghettos that the police force will accept any White reject, as long as that reject is willing to "chase, catch and shoot Kaffirs".

Tiny van Niekerk was no different. Brute force and ox-like strength must have contributed to the rank he had, a warrant officer. He was almost a second Mother Hen, except that he was hasty. There was nothing he wanted to miss out on. He disliked controversy or answers that did not meet his demands during interrogation. Many times I realized how little these men who were supposed to be in charge of the security of the country actually knew about the very security laws under which they had detained me and the others.

It was after the Easter weekend, after I had complained and reported to a visiting magistrate that I had been assaulted during interrogation by one van Niekerk, that he had me hauled from the cell first thing on the Tuesday following this long weekend. After making heavy weather and failing to explain why I had been arrested, he decided to read me part of the "Terrorism Act Clause". "That you arre herre forr interrrogation, and that you will be held herre until the state is satisfied that you arre not withholding any inforrmation koncerrning terrrorrism in South Afrrika and orr its borrderrs...and that you arre herrer to be interrrogated and not to have yourr arrse licked!..."

I did not think for one minute that their law said that. But that version, backed by van Niekerk's brutal fists, was possible. But as luck sometimes favours the weak and undefended, the small like me, van Niekerk tired very quickly. I could not imagine how my 140-pound frame could survive a beating from a 300-pound brute. Sometimes, the Black gods were merciful...In the circumstances, I had great fear of this man, his looks, his booming voice, his being and his fucked-up mind.

I had finally met the man who was my direct jailer, under whose immediate orders I had been detained. This was Ben Letlaka's "Kernel", who had to be telephoned at 5.30 at his house. I was that important to him. He had woken up, the Colonel, prepared to drive to Jan Vorster to meet me, weigh me and finally decide which way things would go regarding my activities, whatever these were. At that moment, I was still in a daze, having been harassed out of bed, ill-clad, confused and unwashed. He, clean and fresh, after a good breakfast with his family. I, with my family in disarray. My wife was probably at that moment running helter-skelter, trying to inform family and friends that I had been detained that morning by the notorious Security Police. Gaboipeoe, my son, if fully recovered and at school, was probably finding it difficult to inform his teachers and friends that I had been taken away. Then my other three children, Maseitshiro, Pule and Phello, waking up to be told that the police had snatched me away during their sleep. My youngest daughter, Phello, would not know anything. She was only nine months old.

I compared the problems my wife was burdened with that morning and wondered where Visser's wife was. We were looking at each other from two different positions. He was sitting behind his clean desk. I was standing in front of it. I had already been standing for a while before Visser arrived.

As soon as he entered the room, the non-White policemen jumped to attention and remained as stiff as cabinets. Those who were then standing froze, until Visser gave the command for them to relax. It was amazing for me to watch how seemingly normal people suddenly became robots at the command of someone. The Whites also accorded Visser the respect due to him because of his

50

rank, although they were less rigid than the non-Whites.

I took one look at Visser and decided that there would be no love lost between us. I resolved that I was in that predicament to the finish.

Colonel Visser was certainly the best dressed of all that motley crowd that tried pathetically hard to look clean. His clothes were well cut and fitted him well. For an Afrikaner, his clothes had style and class. His hair was neatly brushed back, though it was an uncontrollable as Black resistance. Despite his rank, Visser was like the rest of them, a numbskull. He asked the same questions with sickening monotony. In an attempt to confuse me, he would vary the phrasing of a question. I concluded that he was trying to convince me about how brilliant he thought he was.

"Do you know Vincent Selanto?" he would ask.

"No. I don't."

"You don't know Vincent Selanto?"

"No. I don't."

"Vincent Selanto. You say you don't know him?"

"No. I don't."

"You don't know Vincent Selanto then?"

"No. I don't."

"You surre you don't know Vincent Selanto?" by which time I would have a strong desire to hurl abuse at him.

"No. I don't know Vincent Selanto."

"Is that so?"

"Yes, it is so!"

He would realize that I was taking the mickey out of him by imitating him, though I did not give the faintest indication that I was playing the fool because by then I was bored stiff. I gave the impression that he wanted me to answer his questions in parrot fashion, and that that was what I was doing. He would get annoyed and hiss like a snake. One day, when I refused to write what he wanted me to write as my "statement", he came over to me and hissed through his teeth:

"Therre arre too many disused mines in Johannesburrg forr people like you!"

And so, I thought to myself, that is where most of us disappear to. I imagined being thrown down one of the mines in the middle of the night with no one in sight. I imagined that at the bottom of the mine I would drown in the filthy mine water full of garbage and that there would be large snakes down there which would immediately feast on me, as steady death crept over me. I realized then how much I desired to live. I imagined a little light penetrating through the hole through which they would have thrown me in, and how I would still attempt to survive.

I wished I knew who this Vincent Selanto was, if it would save me from being thrown into one of the disused mines. It was the ultimate in sadism for him to even suggest the mine when I was at that moment in a tortured state. When Visser spoke in Afrikaans he sounded like a cackling hen after laying an egg. He nattered as quickly as a machine-gun with the capacity to fire 500 rounds a minute. His "r" rolled as if it came from a light engine with a whining sound.

I gained the impression that Colonel Visser liked his work. He tried to keep his desk very clean. He would blow the dust and pipe ashes away, put this and that in its designated place, and begin to interrogate with "Is that so?" It annoyed me that after all those days he had nothing to ask me except "Is that so?" Shit. I swallowed my feelings in my breast. Colonel Visser spoke English badly. He conceded as much on one occasion, when Deborah had been allowed to see me and bring me clean clothes as well.

"You speak Afrikaans?" he asked her.

She shook her head to indicate that she did not.

"We speak only Afrikaans herre. We kan't speak English. Now, talk to yourr husband into the mikrrophone...." I grinned at his faulty English even before he had finished, hoping that Deborah had been listening to English as spoken by an Afrikaner, Visser, one of the "lecturers at the University of Jan Vorster Square interrogation rooms". But at that time I had been reduced physically and mentally by what I had gone through so that I could not indulge in the pleasure of poking fun at these tormentors, as we normally did in the ghettos.

Colonel Visser was always tired. He would start yawning as soon as he was comfortable on his desk, his eyes drooping as if he was under the influence of some drug. I was soon to find out why. They held interrogation sessions right through the night, working in shifts and in teams. Most of the offices at Jan Vorster Square on the tenth floor had detainees standing up all the time, hidden from everyone except their torturers, for days on end.

I had by then endured two months of being subjected to all sorts of interrogation processes. I was made to write a "statement" under the watchful eye of Lieutenant Visser, no relation of the colonel. The name Visser in South Africa, among people of Afrikaner stock, is as common as Smith in England. But the two men were as different from each other as day is to night.

I picked up Lieutenant Visser's name when he also became a permanent member of the team that interrogated me. I was all ears and eyes most of the time; little escaped my attention which I considered important for my survival. During the writing of the statement, I had to include the word "lieutenant". I could not spell it. I asked Lieutenant Visser to spell it for me. After all, he was one.

"Eh...eh...e...hm..," then he tried, "L...i...." He gave up. "Oh... just write 'Lit.'."

I wrote: "Lit.".

Lieutenant Jan Visser, Mother Hen or Heystek, and Colonel Visser were like triplets. They worked together, shared opinions and at times bombarded me with questions simultaneously, sometimes in competition with one another or so it seemed, as when Heystek asked me about Clarence Hamilton, only for another to get me off the hook inadvertently. When this happened, I found it a blessing in disguise. I would pretend to pay attention to one of them, while escaping what I considered the most difficult question.

The general lack of knowledge and basic common sense among the police was a boon to us detainees, though this caused us severe beatings for being more knowledgeable. Lieutenant Visser was the worst of them all. His big head used to remind me of my high school days, when I sat not far from a boy called Maduna. No matter how hard our teachers tried, Maduna could register nothing in his big head. Lieutenant Visser was worse than Maduna.

Lieutenant Visser was the epitome of physical fitness. He was a *karateka*, well built, bull-necked with a small waist. He walked upright and was straight as an ironing board. His hair was closely cut, well-brushed and shining with ointment. He had a deep voice, and very thin lips — just an opening like a fish mouth. He had penetrating eyes, slits like sharp razor cuts. All detainees who had been beaten up by Lieutenant Visser during interrogation regarded his brutality as living death. On the occasion he assaulted me for an hour, he never looked tired for one moment.

During interrogation, he lacked originality. He leaned heavily

53

on his two friends, Heystek and Colonel Visser, picking up tips from them, like someone depending on morsels falling from the table. His colleagues were aware of his shortcomings and always came to his rescue by redirecting the line of questioning to save him embarrassment. However, his friends also depended on Lieutenant Visser to do the butchering. He left me wondering what it was the police found creative in assaulting frightened, defenceless detainees under unbearable circumstances.

"Hela, monna, Pheto. Re tla ho bolaea mona!" (Hey, man, Pheto, we will kill you here!)

That was more or less my first contact with "Mother Hen". Heystek was not easy to read. He was a very busy man, walking in and out of his overdecorated office, into other offices where interrogations were being conducted. I would pick up bits of information from the numerous conversations they had. One of the police would walk into the interrogation room in which I was being questioned and ask loudly: "What's that one's story?" At another level, they may have been stage-managing all this to give me the impression that someone being interrogated and apparently connected with me was breaking down and telling them whatever they thought I was keeping away from them, so as to get me to panic and talk. During Heystek's visit to the other offices, such as Colonel Visser's, where I was mostly kept, he would throw out a few questions, assess me and, just as quickly, move on, carrying a pile of files with him. In many instances I was assaulted in Heystek's office. It was in his office also that Tiny van Niekerk read me the "Terrorism Act". His office contained a Van Gogh print that watched many detainees being assaulted. Heystek would watch the assaults sitting behind his massive desk, gloating like an inflated mummy, continuously urging us to talk.

Heystek was typical of most White policemen. Huge too. He had a mountain of a chest, a big stomach, large arms and fat hands. On top of this he had a double chin, with a sneer on his lips which he could twist into a droop. His office had a steel desk; an outsize decorated ashtray made in some valuable stone; with a matching, well-polished pen and stand, both of which were never used. There was also a photograph of himself and, I presume, his wife on the east wall. Opposite that was the Van Gogh print, which made me hate Van Gogh for doing nothing while we were being assaulted. I lumped Van Gogh together with the others in my hatred of South Africa's racial attitudes, because he, Van Gogh, was White too.

Heystek was an all-knowing braggart. For good measure, he spoke SeSotho very well. Many White people in South Africa speak various Black dialects badly. Not Heystek. He was excited over this feat and made me feel this immediately. I had no admiration for the freak achievement. He had acquired the knowledge for nothing, pretending at the time to love the Blacks who taught him the language. I am certain that those who taught Heystek this language had no idea how he was going to use it to further Black oppression in South Africa. If they knew how he was going to use the language, they would have been sorry for their lack of wisdom when they taught it to him. Besides this, there was his boast about his familiarity with Black Consciousness terminology, some Marxist–Leninist literature as well as Black theatre and art.

"You know yourself that theatre is a very dangerous medium in a situation such as 'ours'."

I wondered whether Heystek included me in his "ours". If he did, I could not understand how I had suddenly become one of them. I suppose when the boat is sinking, then we are all South Africans!

"No, Jannie," he would say to Jan Visser within earshot of me. "We have no time for this man. Let him stand there until he talks." Or, he would continue, "We have all the time. We can keep him here until 1977. For as long as we like."

It was then 1975.

I had grown to hate him too with a particular vehemence. He would raise an argument, giving me to believe I could speak as I saw fit, but as soon as he started to fumble in defence of the status quo he would put me down in the same way as Magoro did. Heystek could not hide the fact that the Black Arts movement of MDALI and its Pan-Africanist orientation had made inroads into the Black ghettos, and he reminded me of it. Whenever he exhibited his usual sneer, a twist of his lips, particularly if he had his dark glasses on, I thought that the day for my execution had come.

"Phineas, you are the worst liar I have ever come across in my whole police career!"

I do not know whether he meant what he said. But if he did, then it was probably true. I had lied. Sometimes willingly, and at other

55

times because I did not know what they wanted from me. I knew nothing about the allegations regarding the Coloureds that they were forcing me to make, the confessions that they wanted from me. I lied, too, when their fists started to thump me, their boots hitting forcefully into my ribs, karate chops and back-hand swipes at my protruding frightened eyes. I lied to get them off my back, anything to keep them off me. When they were satisfied that I had told them the truth and they needed verification, we would be back to square one. I simply told them that I had lied so that they would leave me alone or stop assaulting me. Deep down, I was convinced that even if I had known anything, I would not tell. At least that is what I hoped I would do. I now know that there is nothing more difficult than that!

Breathing hard in exasperation, deflating his large stomach of all hope that I would deliver the goods, he would look at his Jannie and say, "I told you, Jannie, *hierdie man moet ons lankal dood gemaak het*," (this man we should have long killed), using English and Afrikaans as though the one language needed the other to make its point. But as the days went by, Heystek began to tire. He would come in with the faithful Jannie behind him, ask one question, then slump over his sumptuous desk. He made one more effort before he ran out of threats. One last effort to get me to my senses.

"Hei, man! The stories that there are murdering, torturings and assaults here are true, but only if you don't co-operate."

Even Heystek made some boobs in English. It would have been surprising if he hadn't and I would have been disappointed. He tried to dress well. I had the impression that they received an allowance to replace clothing that ended up bloodstained after assault periods and torture of detainees. But the non-Whites, men such as Limp Step and others, made me revise my assumption, because they looked terribly miserable and ill-clad.

Many more police mushroomed, played their part, and disappeared as suddenly and mysteriously as they had emerged. Day after day the process was repeated. Days that never seemed to end. I talked to God. "God, will it ever end? Which side are you on, God, whose side?"

Before I knew the names of Heystek and Jannie Visser, I had questioned Patose, as they left me in the interrogation room where he had been called in to guard me.

"Patose, who is he, this 'kind' one?" I played up to Patose,

Mother Hen's and Jannie Visser's side-kick, hoping to get him off-guard.

"Oh! This one who speaks our language. Captain Heystek! This one is king. He won't do you anything." Patose showed me his hyena teeth, pleased that he knew them so well!

"*Kea leboha.*" (Thank you.)

5. What kind of nightmare is this? I

I had already been in detention since 5 March, and I had been interrogated every day. They brought me up from the cells between nine and eleven in the mornings and kept me standing, asking me questions until about three in the afternoon. The questions were the same as those they had been asking me since the 5th, the names of people they wanted to know something about; there were new variations now and again, but the routine they were using had not changed at all. I already knew everything by heart, as I had enough time in the cell to think over and re-run every day's event. I was kept alone.

It was now 12 March and nothing had changed. It was about three in the afternoon and time to be taken down to the cell, to my solitary thoughts and to anticipate the next day...

Colonel Visser had been doing the interrogation from the time I had been brought up that morning.

"Do you know Wiseman Hamilton?"

"No. I have read in the papers that he has been detained. But I have never met him before," I said.

"Do you know Krris Weimerr?"

"No."

"Do you know Frrank Molobi then?"

"Yes. I know him."

"How do you know Frrank Molobi when you say you don't know Errik Molobi?" he exclaimed.

Frank and Eric are cousins. Their fathers are related. My wife is their cousin, so the two men are my cousins-in-law. I had never met Eric before, but my wife had already introduced me to Frank. By this time, I had long ago told Colonel Visser that I knew Frank. He must have asked me about Frank and Eric a million times. My boredom at having to recall this was beyond endurance.

But then, according to their "logicality!", the type with which

Magoro had made his *coup de grâce*, if I knew and had met Frank, I automatically must have come across Eric! The manner in which they all think alike is frightening.

At this time it was clear that my interrogators wanted me to fall for certain suggestions. They wanted me to agree that I knew the names of the people they had been asking me about, to "agree" to an association of sorts, to "agree" that these people had military training programmes they soon wished to undertake, and that I was assisting them, and that I was arranging to send them to some mysterious rendezvous "somewhere in Botswana or anywherre in Afrrika!" When they failed to make any inroads into me, their line of approach changed. They suggested that I had been approached by Clarence Hamilton and that Clarence was their contact man; the link being that he, as a member of my performing group and a former student at the African Music and Drama Association where I was director of programmes, had reason to be close to me. The reason why I fitted into this position was that I had made contact with Communist organizations during my stay abroad.

By this time, I could certainly swear that all or most of the people I was being interrogated about had been detained. In many ways I had anticipated this, as my major pastime was allowing my mind to foresee their next line of thought. I had no doubt that they too did the same. We had to outwit one another. But I had resolved not to acquiesce to anything and not to be party to their infamous and nefarious schemes for sending Blacks to prison on trumped-up political charges. Besides, they had already deprived me of my limited "freedom" by keeping me there without being able to prove that I was the link man they thought I was. They were trying to save face by creating a reason for my detention. However, at this time, the reputation of the Security Police had sunk so low among the Black population that there was nothing on earth they could still do to salvage any credibility from this racial group. The international community was also at last waking up from its purposeful slumber because it had become embarrassing to them to continue being openly identified with the blatant racist brutality of the Kruger–Vorster brotherhood.

My own stubbornness was due to my utter detestation of White South Africa's attitudes. I wanted my rights and my land back, no less and no more. The intricacies and dynamics of their often-sung excuses that we Blacks wanted to drown them in the oceans where they had come from depended on how the Whites would adjust to their defeat by us.

Also, during my interrogation, the name of the banned African National Congress kept coming up. I deduced that the Coloureds with whom I was being implicated were either linked with the African National Congress, or had been "persuaded" to admit to it — persuaded by those steely-blue eyes in the middle of the night on the dreaded tenth murder floor of Jan Vorster Square.

If my guesses were correct, then being linked with the African National Congress, which was known to have offices in various countries abroad for the purposes of pursuing the liberation of South Africa, doomed my chances of survival. I had no doubt that I would never have knowingly entered into any involvement or arrangement with anyone undertaking ANC work, or worked under their banner. I personally do not believe in the politics of multiracialism espoused by the ANC. All the same, I wished the people involved all my Black luck, as their enemy was also mine.

I did not know how the police had come by all the information they were trying to force on me, and I was amazed to hear the details of discussions Clarence and I had had surfacing from them. Could it be that Clarence had told someone, who had passed the information to a confidant, who in turn had whispered titbits to yet another person until the matter had become an open secret, which secret finally had me thrown in jail? Or was it a police ploy, which meant that the police were accurate deductors, and not the numbskulls I had always thought them to be!

Uppermost in my mind was the disturbing fact that I might be someone's stool-pigeon, the pawn that was not supposed to know the name of the game, the one that was not meant to survive, the sacrificial lamb! I told myself that if that was the case, I was on my own, master of my own destiny, and I would have to get out of the mess unaided.

Given the chance to be involved with honest comrades for liberation, I would commit myself to any undertaking, even if my chances of surviving were nil. But I would hate to realize that my sacrifice in the struggle was sealed in some "higher" quarters without my knowledge. That to me would not be comradeship. To me, comrades are those who care for each other and are prepared to die for each other.

"Tell and agrree to us that the Kolourreds wanted to do militarry trraining in Botswana orr anywherre in Afrrika, and you know it!"

Visser plied me with questions that I found most difficult to understand. One thread kept me in hope, which was that, much as they tried, they could not produce a single proof of my collusion with the Coloureds, even with the aid of their biased legal system.

"How can I agree that I know anything about these people you allege are my friends, when I don't even know what they look like?" I would reply, and I meant it.

"Yes, Clarrence Hamilton was theirr man. He was sent to kontact you!" As he said this, Visser would be near tears, burning me with his eyes.

My interrogators had given me to believe that they knew everything. That my duty was to volunteer what eventually would be the final statement, which I would then have to write to their satisfaction. I had already written three such statements, which had been torn up by Heystek as unsuitable and therefore unacceptable. Heystek had thrown them into my face after refusing them.

What was happening was that I was being slowly fed all this information so that there should be little I did not know regarding what the Hamilton group had been caught attempting. I had pieced this together bit by bit, instalment by instalment. All that remained was fitting the names to their owners. I could not work out how they were going to let me pass that test, short of showing me the men themselves, or their photographs. I started choosing in my mind what information I could disclose and what would certainly send me to Robben Island, and to avoid disclosing the latter with all my wits, overworked as they already were.

Many times fate worked against me. There were coincidences that kept creeping into their questions that were difficult to handle. A circumstance, a name or a place — all ganging up against me with nasty conspiracy. At times I would myself take the plunge, believing that I saw a loophole, only to end up in a worse situation than if I had kept my big mouth shut. One such instance decided my future reaction if another chance should offer itself. That was not to jump to conclusions nor underestimate their snail-speed brains, but to say as little as possible, offer nothing, but wait.

I had had a student learning the trumpet and ear-training with me called Raymond Zabale. On a certain day, I had to cut Raymond's lesson short because I wanted to visit the local passport office with the intention of getting my expiring passport endorsed. I was due to visit Botswana shortly. I had left my place of work earlier than usual so as to be able to have time to stand in the usually long queues that we Blacks in South Africa have to contend with. Services for Blacks are so poor that at times, even after long periods in the queues, it is common to return home unattended to. The pass-office is one such place. Crowds and crowds of Blacks waiting to be served, as a result of this piece of paper called the pass, a notoriously hated document that all Black men and women in South Africa have to have on their persons all the time, and to produce on demand by the police, or face immediate imprisonment if it is not there, or was without some detail such as an employer's signature at the end of each month and before the 7th of the ensuing one. The document that dictated a Black man's life in seeking work and delineating where, that decided his application for a house, his tax-paying, passport application, banking and withdrawing his own money at banks and building societies. The document that must be produced for furniture and motor car purchases, for getting married to one's chosen spouse, needed for acquiring children's birth certificates and for proof of death and for permission for burial.

There are many such places where Blacks have to wait in these long queues. The worst queues were the old pensioners' on their trips once every two months to collect their meagre allowances. These poor old Blacks would start emerging from their homes to go to the White superintendent's office the night before. All through the night, they would be seen plodding their slow way there. Small, bent, frail, moving phenomena in the unlit night. At two, three or four in the morning it would be the same story in the different locations. If you happened to travel a lot at night, as I did in my car, from organizing or to organizing, from meetings or to meetings, these human landmark dots in the night would frighten you. Many times we gave the old people lifts. At times they declined because they did not trust young people in Soweto at night. I know these instances only too well. My mother used to leave at 4 a.m. By 5 a.m. these old men and women had formed an endless huddled line on the grounds around the superintendent's offices. At daybreak, they would be part of the Black norm. Yet another queue at the offices of these White men who control Black lives. The Black man's lot is simply to fall in line, follow this line inch by inch, with accompanying insults being the daily burden from those who are supposed to serve us.

Ours is one long life queue.

Aware of this hazard, Raymond had told me that his brother was one of the clerks in the pass-office department. He suggested that I look his brother up and tell him that I was his teacher so that he should attend to me quicker, ahead of the other people. After all, no one in the line would complain as all would rather shut up and get attended to meekly, as it were. Blacks more or less begged for these services. There was no nonsense about some tax-payer claiming some non-existent rights. Blacks simply had to behave themselves!

Just as Raymond and I had expected, the queue was very long, more so because it was nearing a long weekend. Over these long weekends, many South African Blacks were anxious to take a little break from the perpetual oppression and escape, no matter how briefly, to one of the nearby independent countries of Lesotho, Botswana and Swaziland for some respite. Raymond's brother was helpful, and I was through in a short time.

While all this was going through my head, Colonel Visser was on the other side of his desk with me in front of it, facing him; and faithful Captain Magoro was sitting down, listening, waiting to pounce on me should Colonel Visser leave the room.

"Do you know one Zabane?" he asked me, the same as ever, with no change in the pattern.

I knew that I did not know a Zabane. But still I tried to crack my mind, for all it was worth. Eventually I had to submit that I did not know him. To them, this proved that I was resisting. To me, it did seem strange that I did not know all the people I was apparently involved with. In fact, I thought this aspect made me more suspect to them.

"No. I do not know Zabane." Then I made the plunge I was to regret. "But I know a Zabale," I added, emphasizing the "le" at the end of the name.

"You know Zabane then?" Visser insisted.

"Not ZabaNe, but ZabaLe," I also insisted. The small difference could cost me my life if I did not press the point home.

"What is his firrst name?" he shouted at me.

"I don't know his first name. I was just told he was Zabale, so I referred to him by that name," I continued.

"Why don't you know his firrst name?" he belaboured the point.

Colonel Visser must have thought I had made a mistake and that

62

I was trying to wriggle out of it. But on this question of Zabale, he almost became human, instead of one of the merciless animals all of them were during interrogation. There must have been a reason for his change of attitude, despite our differences on the last two letters of the name.

On the other hand, my predicament arose from a conflict of cultures. It is a common custom among most Blacks from my part of Africa to refer to each other by our second names, that is, our family names or surnames. Sometimes, the second name was preferred because it expressed respect or deference, and most certainly, warmth and affection. I was in the habit of addressing all my close friends in this manner.

"This Zabale of yourrs," Visser said, giving up the argument of the "Le" or the "Ne". He probably thought it better to go along with me in case something meaty presented itself. "You say, wherre is yourr Zabale?"

I knew that Zabale was serving a prison sentence at Leeuwkop prison, half-way between Johannesburg and Pretoria, for allegedly "fixing or forging" passes and selling them to rural Blacks, and also to local ones who did not "qualify" to be in certain parts of South Africa such as the cities, like Johannesburg. Blacks who had left the impoverished rural Bantustans (designated areas for Blacks) for the cities to find work needed this pass document more than anything on earth. The "racket", as it was called, did a roaring trade in the ghettos. Some White officials working at the various pass-offices were involved in it too. But they seldom took the rap. Blacks were the scapegoats.

"I understand he is in prison at Leeuwkop," I told Visser.

"Forr what?" he barked hurriedly.

I told Visser what Zabale was supposed to be in prison for. I should have anticipated it. I cursed myself. I was a shit-house. What could I hope to achieve by volunteering that information? I told myself that I deserved what was coming. "Those who kill themselves have no one to weep for them", we say in Africa.

"And what about the passports? Did you not see him about forrging passporrts? Yourr passporrt and yourr frriends" too, forr yourr militarry trraining!' He gloated at this. In the meantime, I went completely cold. I couldn't win.

"No. I did not. My passport has always been in order."

Colonel Visser called for assistance. A White man called Bouwer came in, a senile dry old man of about 60 who turned out to be a frustrated waste of humanity. Bouwer must have thought that every Black man was a stud. Interrogation under him turned into a session of comparing the sex performance of Black and White women, lurid and nauseating, and he would do that right in front of his superiors, such as Colonel Visser.

When Bouwer came in, I again got confused as to who was senior at Jan Vorster Square, not that it mattered. It looked as if he had been waiting in the wings to show his seniority too. He tore into me about Zabane and Zabale, insinuating that I was inventing names that did not exist, and that I must know that he was smarter than me, that in the end he would come up with the facts, and I would come out singing.

Visser asked Bouwer to telephone Leeuwkop prison and find out if they had a Zabale there. He told Bouwer that I claimed that I did not know Zabale's first name because "his culturre says he should call people by theirr second names only!" Visser could afford to be sarcastic at my expense, but I did not like it one bit.

Bouwer sat on the edge of Visser's desk, took the telephone and rang Leeuwkop prison. He let his legs hang over Visser's desk, swinging them to and fro as he waited for Leeuwkop to respond. I heard him arguing with someone at the other end of the line about something to the effect that Blacks had the same surname. The person at the other end suggested that if he was supplied with the first name, then the whole matter would be easy.

While waiting for Leeuwkop to check through numerous Zabales, Bouwer turned his attention to me. "What is this *nonsons* about not knowing yourr frriend's firrst name?"

Bouwer sang Visser's chorus even before he had learnt the song well.

"Well..." I was about to reply when he swung his emaciated legs away from me, responding to Leeuwkop.

"*Ja? Julle het hom?*" (Yes, you have him?)

Bouwer turned to Visser and whispered to him that apparently there was a prisoner named Zaba.... "What is it again?" he asked Visser.

"Le." Visser replied.

"*Ja!* That 'Le' of yourrs." He peered at me, then turning away he told Visser, "But without the firrst name, they have it difficult therre."

Bouwer looked at me. "I'm going to see this Zaba...le. And if he says you werre seeing him about forrged passporrts, what will

64

you say, because he will say so!"

I kept quiet for a long time. Stunned, thinking. I found his suggestion sinister. They could easily have forced Zabale to agree to the fact that I needed forged passports for what they had been trying to insist I was involved in. After all, Zabale was at their mercy. Which Black man would not grab at the chance to buy his freedom in a South African jail, given its inhuman ill-treatment of Blacks, assaults and what have you, by warders and police, if an offer was made that all that Black man needed to do was to tell a lie in court against a political prisoner? And suppose Zabale just became unscrupulous and took his freedom, whatever the consequences to me? I would be sunk through my own big mouth anyway. In court, I would not have a leg to stand on. I knew of so many Blacks who had been convicted on trumped-up charges. The White magistrates and prosecutors were notorious for their bias. They listened only to the side presented by the police, even if there was a great element of doubt in evidence. In any event, by the time the prisoner appeared in court, he would have been so beaten up already that he would offer only token resistance. Those who escaped always found themselves back in jail on some trumped-up charge, by the same police who might have failed to procure a conviction the first time. One of those endless vicious circles of Black life in South Africa.

This is not idle talk. I nearly went to jail for a concocted traffic offence. The White traffic officer who had arrested me made it clear to me that he hated the fact that the car I was driving was new, and mine! After the magistrate had sentenced me to thirty days or a fine of R30 (fifteen pounds), the traffic officer made a point of meeting me outside the court to tell me, "Since when do Kaffirs buy new motor cars!" He arrested me on two other occasions.

Then there was the time I was stopped and asked to produce my driver's licence. I could not understand it because I had committed no traffic offence. I was locked up at the Kliptown Police Station, charged and tried the following morning. I was found guilty, but was allowed until eleven o'clock that same morning to produce the licence without being given time to go home to fetch it. The magistrate had found me guilty at a quarter-past ten! It turned out the Black policeman who had arrested me was a regular customer at a shebeen I used to frequent. He hated the idea that the shebeen owner had a soft spot for me. I was told this by the lady who owned the place because the policeman had returned to show off to her that he had arrested me to "put me in my place", and that he would do it again.

I still have to come across a Black man who, by the age of 30, has never been arrested. My father used to boast to me that he had never been in jail in his life. I knew that it was not true. What he meant was that he had never been to prison for a criminal offence and that he would not wish to see me in prison for that reason. However, at the age of 63 he was arrested for a pass offence. I did not remind him of what he had once told me. I was bitter at the fact that, old as he was, he could be locked up for not having a pass on his person, and be made to spend the night at the Fordsburg Police Station, near Johannesburg. He told me after we had paid his fine that there had been many of them in the cells that night, young and old.

A lot of police rookies achieve promotion for their "vigilance" and "dedication" to duty for clearing the White cities of South Africa of dangerous Blacks who move about without their passes. The Bouwers and the Venters and the van der Merwers passed up the police ranks at the expense of innocent Black lives, and the White farmers found cheap Black labour from the prisons for their maize and potato harvests.

I was quiet, but all the time these thoughts were ravaging me. It would not surprise me if Zabale said that I had seen him about passports. I found out, bitterly, that the interrogation of detainees takes a long time here. The interrogators jump from one thing to another like children trying to fit a puzzle on a jigsaw board. It is more confusing when one is interrogated by six or seven anxious policemen, or more. I found my mind moving confusedly from one interrogator to another.

"Why do you trravel to Botswana so much? What do you want therre?"

This time it was Tiny van Niekerk. There were three of them in the room, Colonel Visser and Captain Magoro being the other two. I told van Niekerk that I was descended from Botswana, and that I visited my relations there, but I knew he suspected other things. Blacks criss-crossing the borders of South Africa were suspect. They could be linking up with exiles in these independent countries for advancement of their political work. It was worse in my case, as I had travelled in Europe before. But I also told him that in my work for MDALI I had to travel to collect enough work for exhibiting at our art festivals.

"Why don't you damn stay therre if you have yourr rrelations therre? I'll tell you," he paused. "South Afrrika is too good forr you. You would starrve to death therre. That's why you won't go."

Van Niekerk went on as though he would never stop, saying a lot that hurt me because I could not reply and wrenching my heart out with all those comparisons we have heard from their babbling politicians about how South Africa was the best country for Black people in the whole world: how well we Blacks were treated, having so much done for us there, how well educated we were, how the wages received by Black people were better than anywhere in Africa, the housing schemes and so forth.

I was hurt and I wanted to tell him that he was talking a lot of rubbish. To tell him that at that very moment he and his colleagues and their laws had me in detention against my will, through laws made by White men only. That I had not seen my family since his friend Visser had decreed that I be detained, and that I wished to see my family as I was worried about their welfare. Could he, van Niekerk, tell the whole world that every morning I was brought up from the cells, kept standing from nine till three in the afternoon, asked questions which I answered to the best of my ability, yet got nowhere near being released to rejoin my family and community? That during the days I had been in detention I smelled from lack of washing facilities, yet I could hear other prisoners not far from my cell splashing water during their bath-time; that I already had bugs sucking my blood, thirteen of which I had only last night killed after searching for them on my body and clothes, killing them by putting the damn things on the cement floor before pressing them to their death with my thumbnail! Yet I was supposed to LOVE this South Africa, LOVE it?

My throat was hot. My eyes were swimming in a stream of burning tears which I could feel about to burst down my cheeks. I knew that I could not take the insults any more. Eventually, I decided to tell van Niekerk and his friends what I felt.

"I would have no problems in Bots..."

Van Niekerk did not allow me to finish. I was lifted off the floor by one of the hardest, quickest punches, the heaviest too, that I had ever taken on my jaw. The force of it threw me a little distance from the trio, under a table. Its sudden impact blinded me for a moment. Blood immediately trickled from the corner of my lip. I had sustained a cut on the inside bottom lip. Because I did not have a handkerchief to wipe my blood with, I decided to swallow it. I felt no pain then. Only surprise and fright.

Colonel Visser did not move an inch, but Magoro had already jumped into action like an uncoiled spring that had been long suppressed. It seemed that what they were then doing was something they had done many times before. I stood up by sheer instinct. Before I could get on my haunches, I saw his towering legs near the region of my face. As I raised my eyes to take in this whole structure of massive humanity in front of me, another punch made a fat-fisted, soft-thudded landing on my cheek bone, returning me to the position I had just risen from.

"Stand up, you bastarrd. Stand up!" His big voice bellowed like his two heavy punches. My head felt so heavy I thought I would not be able to raise it again.

"Face that way. You think you arre a herro. You like being beaten up!"

I turned a little, afraid of this huge man behind me, seeing Magoro manoeuvring for a shot at me too.

"Face that way!" van Niekerk boomed again with impatience. I must have been slow.

As I did, van Niekerk smashed me on the neck and on my right ear again.

"Tell us. What do you want in Botswana? What is MDALI?"

Interspersed with the questions, his blows kept on raining incessantly. When I tried to turn my face towards this man who was assaulting me, he would bellow that I should turn my face away from him so that I should not see his blows coming my way. Sometimes the force of the punches turned me round.

"*Ya. Ek wil alles hoor van daai MDALI.*" (Yes. I want to hear everything about that MDALI.)

"MDALI is..."

Whack! Bam! I fell to the floor again.

"Up, herro!" I tried to rise. Blast! Thud! Swoosh! As he swung his leg and kicked me. I groaned.

"Pick him up. Stand up!"

Another attempt to stand on my legs. But he was back on me before I had come half-way up. Slam!

"What is MDALI?"

"MDALI is..."

Whop! I heard the sound of something like a stick through the air before it found its mark on my neck. It would appear that

68

during questions and punches he had picked up something to hit me with. Perhaps his knuckles had been hurt.

"Com'on, MDALI..."

When will it ever end? Are they never going to tire, this 300-pound man and Magoro, whose job is to prop me up each time I am down, like setting me up? I thought this sort of thing only happened in stories. Magoro kept on pulling my beard up and down whilst at the same time holding my trousers at the waist, pulling them up and down for no reason at all. Is this humiliation going to stop?

It stopped suddenly. As suddenly as it had begun. Van Niekerk was tired. He propped one leg on one of the chairs in the room to get more air into his throat and on his neck, which seemed to be sweating inside his tight collar. Meanwhile, Magoro had a field-day jabbing my ribs with awkward punches. There was such a searing pain already shooting through my ribs that I was sure something serious was wrong.

Colonel Visser sat on his chair with his pipe eternally dangling from his mouth, cackling like an angry hen after laying an egg on a hot day.

Van Niekerk came back to me about MDALI. "Now," he said slowly. "That MDALI of yourrs. Tell us. And we know everrything!"

He was panting, but apparently did not want me to realize that he was dog-tired. He gave me the impression that he was halting for a while for me to talk.

I told them: "MDALI is an organization of artists formed in Soweto in..."

"Listen!" Heystek, who had come in during the commotion, shouted at me. "Don't shit us! Why don't you say Black!"

I had purposely omitted the word Black because I could not afford another beating. But I soon realized that I would get assaulted more, this time, for not using the term "Black". Either way, I had no choice.

I had earned this assault because of my own stubbornness. Van Niekerk had anticipated that I was going to give him a little lecture and take apart the claim about the so-called better lot of Blacks in South Africa under the apartheid régime, when compared with the conditions of Blacks in other states in Africa. In fact, I was going to tell him there was no chance of starting the argument as the comparison should be between us Blacks and the Whites inside

69

South Africa. In human terms alone, the relations and values thereof, the treatment of our lot by Whites in South Africa did not rate at all. That he and the Boers and the rest of the Whites could keep South Africa for all it was worth. Their Johannesburg too. The bloody lot and the gold. But that freedom was something unnegotiable. That I had travelled and stayed in foreign states and had been shown courtesy and respect I had never dreamt I was worth. That I'd sooner be in the "poverty" of Botswana, whose wealth of culture had still to be outdone by the culture of the Boers, and that they, the White men, had been all over other nations' territories where they had pillaged, plundered, stolen and robbed everything from land to culture to art, had raped and behaved like beasts. What, then, was so "marvellous" after all, about Blacks leading a better life in South Africa with their supposed high "per capita bullshit income per annum" than in this "Botswana of mine!" or other African states?

I quickly remembered that van Niekerk had assaulted me because I was just about to tell him that it was not true that the life of Blacks in South Africa was better than in other Black states. It also seemed obvious that Heystek knew the MDALI constitution. On the other hand, I had resolved to use the word "Black" as much as I could, knowing that they did not approve of the positive image of "Black" as used by us. I felt that I should pay them back with the only weapon I had, although *they* had insisted that I use the term "Black". Their insistence was a ploy to frighten me more. In the circumstances, one would be afraid to do so. I started: "MDALI is a Black organization of Black artists formed in Black Soweto...."

"We know Soweto is Black!" Heystek screamed and cut me short. The medicine was working and it had hurt him so much that he could not tolerate it. But my humiliation had reached its limits. All the same, I took the hint.

"As I was saying, formed in Soweto, to mobilize the Black artist against White exploitation...."

"But Blacks also exploit Blacks! Why do you say White exploitation?" van Niekerk bellowed. He seemed to find similar faults in Blacks that we found among Whites.

"*Hy is nog sterk!*" (He is still strong!) Heystek could not contain himself or stomach my cheek.

"He is playing herro," van Niekerk said, positioning himself closer.

70

"Oh, hell," I cried. "He is coming again," blaming myself for letting my humiliation stupidly dictate how I had reacted. I watched him and raised my hands to protect my face and head.

"Go on!" he said menacingly, icily. I felt that they did not like what I had said, and the manner in which I had said it. Anyway, that had been my intention.

"MDALI means to protect...."

"Conscientize!" It was Heystek, red with Afrikaner anger. "Why don't you use your terminology today?"

"No. I'm coming. I'm trying to lead step by step," I told Heystek, choosing him from the group.

"*Laat hy maar raas.*" (Let him continue making noise). Colonel Visser woke up from his stupor.

I went on all the same. "We in MDALI also want to free ourselves mentally, and we want to judge our own standards a..."

"*Magoro, hy praat net kak. Vat hom weg.*" (He is talking shit. Take him away.)

Magoro called Makhomisane and another policeman to take me back to the cell.

"*Het hy sy kos gevreet?*" (Has he devoured his food?) Visser asked Magoro, before the other two took me to the cell.

Makhomisane was sent to get me a carton of food which I took down to the cell but could not eat. I sat on the mat and thought from the time they left me there until it must have been very late at night. I went over my day's experiences, tried to anticipate what was to follow, imagined the questions they might ask, formulated my answers and invented lies that might sound convincing. I thought of ways and means of strengthening myself against further assaults and humiliations, and realized that I did not improve my lot by annoying them further but rather suffered more. I reasoned that I was useless in prison to my family, myself and MDALI. Their abrupt dismissal of me that afternoon made me feel that although I was saved by the lateness of the day, my nightmares had just begun.

I did not eat their food. I felt that I would be contradicting my injured pride.

It was a Wednesday. Apart from my torn lip, I was certain where the most damage had been inflicted. I remembered a friend of mine, Ben Zwane, who one day told me, after one of his many detention spells, that whether one liked it or not one would

71

eventually tell the Security Police something once the beating started. I remembered saying to Benzo, as we affectionately called him, "If there is nothing to say, what are you going to tell them?"

"Anything! You must say something. Anything!"

The day that Benzo related his jail experiences to me, I could not imagine what I would say if the Security Police ever detained me. Now, that moment had come, and I was here in the cell thinking of it. That day seemed so far off then, dancing to jazz music in our house in Diepkloof, Soweto.

"Ya. Tell them anything. And, anyway, put on as many clothes underneath, as well as a jacket if you have one in the cell. Jerseys too. So that when they kick your ribs the impact does not penetrate the skin and bones. They could break your ribs!" Benzo continued to dance.

I wondered at Benzo's non-concern. He had been detained more than four times in his young life since I knew him. And each time, he told me, he had been beaten up by the police before he gave in to what they wanted, though conceding nothing he wanted concealed from them. I told myself that I needed Benzo's fortitude then. I know that Benzo told me the truth. I remembered that one day, from his hospital bed, soon after one of his detention spells, he sent me to the city to certain White people who gave me some money for him. These were some of the people he had been involved with but had managed not to sing about their involvement.

I fell asleep thinking of Benzo, and that he had died during July 1974, after only about a month outside, from one of his numerous detentions. I fell asleep seeing him in the house at Diepkloof, dancing and saying: "Tell them something. Anything."

It must have been about 1 a.m. when I came to. I did not have any sense of time in those cells, but I could tell if it was late at night or very early in the morning. My cell was dark, awkwardly placed for natural light to filter through. If you were lucky, you might be locked in a cell that allowed some amount of light. I had been unfortunate.

A distant pain was searing my side, gripping me like someone had a tight hold of me and was intent on breaking my ribs. I could not breathe. I was in a daze and sweating. Momentarily I could not remember where I was. But as I was slowly realizing that I was still at Jan Vorster Square, it dawned on me that I had woken up in response to the pain which was becoming worse. With difficulty, I slowly eased the weight of my body off the painful spot, which was on my right side under my armpit.

It all came back. The blow on my ribs when van Niekerk had had me turned away from him and his blows. I remembered that at that moment, my arms were raised to protect my already torn lip as well as my face and ear from further damage if punches were aimed at the injured places. But as I had been forced to turn away from him, I had no idea where he had intended to hit me next, or when. That's when my right side felt as though someone had torn it out of my frame. The pain I was then feeling had been the result of that rib-tearing blow.

Was my rib broken? I tried searching for the exact spot, feeling my way slowly so that my searching hand should not descend abruptly and cause me more pain. I did not understand why I still tried to locate the exact spot, or its enormity. I knew the cause. But my curious hand continued to probe around the area until I found the place. When at last I did, I had to withdraw my hand sharply from it as if I had touched a hot plate on a stove. After many attempts, I was satisfied of the exact location. That done, I decided to make the least movement on the affected side. I hoped it would be possible.

I prayed that they would not come for me on the Thursday morning.

6. Refrain

Early in the morning. Every morning. The usual hard metallic knocks with a teak baton on the steel doors. I could hear the knocks all the way down the hollow corridors. From cell to cell, steel door to steel door. Getting nearer or fading away into the distance of the inner precincts of the jail corridors. Then the voice.

"Everrything all rright?"

I could not hear the responding voice of the detainee. Instead, I could hear the next metallic knock. But as the knocks came closer, faint responses began to be audible.

"All rright!" I would hear the answer.

I learned later that it was the prison Major doing his morning rounds to find out if the prisoners were fine.

"Everrything all rright?"

"Yes, Major."

73

Then it would be my turn.

"Pheto, everrything all rright?"

I never understood why this Major referred to me by my name.

Pain stopped my voice. I could not answer. In any event, the checks were so fleeting that if one had anything to complain about, it were better for that person to shoot up from the stinking blankets and wait in readiness near the door to shout at the top of his voice, even before the Major had finished asking, and tell him that his rib was broken, whether the rib was broken or not, as in my case. There was certainly something wrong.

This Major always shouted at the top of his voice. He never waited for an answer, nor did he seem to care. It was mainly routine and a job. Nor did he expect any prisoner to complain, particularly the so-called common prisoners, who were treated like pieces of cloth that needed to be thrown out with the dishwater.

The Major was always accompanied by a Black policeman whose duty was mainly to knock on the steel doors with his baton, then quickly and gingerly step aside to attention. That done, the Black one would lightningly, on tiptoe, with the daintiest nimble footwork in the world, dash to the next cell in the line, so that in a little while over three hundred cells and prisoners had been checked and "everrything and everryone was all rright!"

All that Thursday I was in pain. Mercifully, I had not been collected for further interrogation. The mere thought of them coming for me had already tortured and weakened me.

I lay on my left side, or on my stomach with difficulty. I could slowly roll over and lie on my back after a long struggle. Lying on my back was the most comfortable position.

When the food was brought in, which I normally went to the door to collect, I signalled to the Black policeman who had brought it to leave it just inside the cell, on the floor. The policeman did not ask me if there was anything wrong with me, he simply left the carton of food where I had suggested. He was quite mechanical about it. I thought he knew that I had been assaulted, or perhaps he was used to being abused. But he gave me the impression that he knew what happened to us political prisoners on the tenth floor of Jan Vorster Square. He had seen us lying stiff and still many times before.

I did not get up to collect the food because I could not. Even then, I could not have eaten it as I had lost my appetite. The pain had given me no respite either. By then, I had a swelling around the spot and I was certain that van Niekerk had broken a rib or two. I blamed them all. Van Niekerk, Colonel Visser and Magoro.

Friday the 14th. It was early in the morning. I heard the knocks on the steel doors as usual, from afar. In fact, I had been waiting so that I should hear the very first knock, and be at the door by the time they reached my cell. I could walk a little, albeit with difficulty. I started for the door, racing against their approach, anticipating the time they would reach cell 320. As the Major peeped through the spy-hole, before the hard knock on the steel door by his Black partner had stopped, and before his "everrything all rright?" had been fully shouted, I strained every muscle of my voice.

"No, Major! No. My rib," I screamed like a madman.

He heard me. With an equally loud scream, he asked. "Pheto! What is wrrong this time?" as if I had been in the habit of complaining.

"My rib. The rib. Broken!"

"What happened?" he asked.

"I don't know. But broken. The doctor."

I had to stress my message quickly, otherwise he would have been off. I was afraid to tell the Major that I had been assaulted. I thought that I would reserve that for the doctor, if I might be taken for an examination. I had no hope of that happening, but I was in pain and had to do something for myself, despite the fact that the Security Police, the Vissers and the rest of them would not have liked it.

The Major left without letting me know if he would do anything about my complaint. I heard the knocking baton on the steel doors disappear into the distance. I wondered why I had bothered myself. Nothing happened the whole day long. I had not been collected for interrogation either. That meant that I had two days of respite, except for the constant pain. I had given up waiting for some reaction, and I had been doing my best to endure the pain in silence.

I heard the keys rattling in the steel doors. I wondered whose turn it had been to be taken up, mine, or someone else's. Then my cell door swung open. It was about three in the afternoon. Patose peeped in and said, "Pheto. What is it now? We hear you want to see the doctor. Hurry. We are about to knock off." The Major must have told the Security Police.

I was first taken to the Commissioner of Police whose office was on the ninth floor. He was wearing a uniform, but I realized that he was senior to the Security Police as well. He asked me what the matter was. He looked unsympathetic, unconcerned and very matter of fact. He rubbed his eyes after he had removed a very thick pair of glasses. Patose was there of course, watching me. Just at that moment, van Niekerk filled the door frame with his massive body and peered at me. Shivers went down my entire body. In the meantime, Patose had been shouting at me and I had almost not heard him.

"Tell the king what's wrong with you. Talk, man, or I'll make you shit just now!"

Patose had spoken in a dialect with me. The Commissioner, who, I thought, would check Patose's roughness with me, did not understand what we had been saying to each other. Van Niekerk continued to peer at me, the message in his eyes being: "You dare say a thing and you are as good as dead!" But he said nothing. He just watched and listened. He too could not understand what Patose and I had been saying.

"How can I tell your king that I have been assaulted when you see that the one who assaulted me is here!" using my eyes to indicate van Niekerk to Patose, shouting at him also.

Van Niekerk knew that the technique had worked. All the police must have used it many times before. As far as I was concerned, that was the reason why van Niekerk had appeared at the door. The Commissioner looked stupid to me, and had not been helpful at all. He wondered what it was Patose and I were shouting about.

"Talk, man. Pheto, talk!" Patose looked worried. Apparently, I had made him look ineffective in front of his most senior boss.

"Doctor, sir. Doctor, my rib," I blurted out.

"What is it?" the Commissioner asked.

"I don't know. But I need a doctor."

"Take him to the doctor," he said finally in Afrikaans.

Bouwer, Colonel Visser and Patose ultimately drove me to the doctor a short distance from Jan Vorster Square, off Bree Street, in Johannesburg. They had made me sit in the back seat, with my wrists handcuffed. For the first time in nine days I saw people in the streets of Johannesburg, the sun shining on the glass windows of the shops, and I realized how there was no sun in prison. But nobody paid any attention to the car with the two Whites and two Blacks in it. There were so many cars in Johannesburg going about their business. Why should this particular one have been special? In my situation, I had had vague notions that perhaps Black people were all eyes for those who had mysteriously disappeared from their midst into the clutches of the Security Police. That they would be concerned because tomorrow it might be their turn. But these had been mere fantasies which had been created by my situation. It wasn't that our people were not concerned. The mere thought was in itself far-fetched. Detentions happen very often and are facts of life. If someone had seen me in the car of the police, so what? There was nothing they could have done about it, except to send a message to my wife to say that I had been seen and I was still alive. I realized that I wanted that to happen so much, for myself, for other detainees, and for those awaiting our release from detention.

The visit to the doctor was useless. It turned out that he was one of the state doctors. The first thing that caught my attention in his office was that his desk and table had initials standing for the South African Police imprinted on them. During the examination, Colonel Visser and Bouwer stood on either side of the doctor and me. Patose manned the door behind me. The whole scene was a repeat of van Niekerk menacing the Police Commissioner's door. I was afforded no chance to tell the doctor that I had been assaulted by the police without being overheard by the others.

"Were you assaulted?" the doctor asked me.

"No. I was not assaulted."

"What's wrong then?"

"My rib. It's swollen and it throbs with pain."

"Oh, maybe you slept badly on it! I'll give you some pills to take."

"My ear also," I said, realizing that I had lost the one possibility of bringing my plight to the surface.

"Which one?"

"The right one," pointing to the ear that had suffered under the avalanche of van Niekerk's fists and punches. The ear ached, feeling like it had been stuffed with something and could not hear. It had developed a tender swelling just under the ear-drum. Now and then it would start hissing.

The doctor directed me into another room. Bouwer, Visser and Patose followed me as though they were glued to me. The doctor joined us shortly afterwards. He had a number of instruments which he poked into my ear. The old doctor, of Jewish origin, flushed it after having examined it. When I asked him what the matter was, what he had seen in my ear, he replied that my ear was dirty!

I least expected that from a doctor of Jewish origin. At his age, did he not realize that Hitler had been reborn in South Africa? Or was it that this man of 65 had chosen to be on the safe side, should history repeat itself? I knew he was a Jew, and his age, because the two White policemen had made unsavoury remarks about him in the car on our way to his office. That the "poor sod" should have been on a pension but would not take it because he had financial problems. They had also mentioned that the doctor's son was a very good rugby player.

In that same room where the doctor had looked into my ear, there were two Black nursing sisters whom I knew through my wife, who is also a nurse. I chose the farthest from me and used sign language to indicate that I had been assaulted. Through the reaction in her eyes, I knew that we had communicated. I hoped that she would perhaps pass the message to my wife.

When the "examination" had been completed, we went back to the car and I was driven back to Jan Vorster Square. Patose had surprised me by asking me if I knew the nursing sister I had signalled to. Patose had seen it all, yet I was certain that I had taken all necessary precautions, as I could have created problems for the nursing sister, and worse ones for myself. How the old hyena had seen me baffled me no end, and why he had not told his superiors was all the more confusing. Perhaps he became discouraged because he could not communicate well in Afrikaans.

"No. I have never seen her in all my life!"

Visser had become suspicious of our conversation. He asked Patose what I had been saying.

"*Hai, Morena, hy se niks,*" Patose answered, touching his head, smiling. (No, King, he says nothing.)

During the drive back to Jan Vorster Square, I accepted with resignation that all roads to bring my plight into light were closed. That the system was too tight. That even doctors, whom I had always believed were governed by their ethical code, were equally hopeless.

7. Coincidences

There is a large number of Black, Coloured and Indian informers for the special branch police in South Africa. They swarm round the country from urban townships to rural areas like summer flies. They come in all shades. They could be respectable-looking Blacks, poor Blacks, or Blacks who have failed to make it in their chosen fields. Added to that, there is a bunch of unscrupulous ones, a shabby lot that prey on their community for disgraceful rewards. The most difficult to expose are the "respectable"-looking ones.

Then there were those planted in shebeens, among one's neighbours, in the teaching profession, and recently some students at the so-called Bantu universities had been suspected of collusion with the Security Police. Social, community and meeting places and organizations such as MDALI and the African Music and Drama Association were also hives for these social pariahs and clandestine hyenas.

Suddenly, an unknown from virtually nowhere would become a permanent landmark in a given vicinity. He would be very friendly and well informed on issues relevant to Black needs. This person would manage to worm his way into being accepted by Black activists he had been assigned to watch and he would, in many instances, be successful. His credentials would be impeccable to the point where he would be allowed to join the organization he had been assigned to infiltrate. Sooner or later, he would disappear as suddenly as he had appeared. The police would swoop down on the members of the groups he had infiltrated. After the swoop, he would reappear. Of course, the detentions had occurred during his absence on "business" elsewhere. He would be equally "surprised" and "angry" that Molefe Pheto, Boitumelo Thabang and others had been detained. "Man, these police are finishing us,' he would exclaim and mourn with the ghetto. If the group he was trying to infiltrate had been vigilant and suspected his credibility, he would have to be very guarded, but he still couldn't afford to miss the day-to-day gatherings, even at the risk of his own life! His brief would be to identify faces, know names, monitor events, lay his hands on documents, minutes and constitutions post-haste, if he could. He suffered from constant pressure from his masters to supply these items. He would find himself threatened on both sides, the angry ghetto on the one and his impatient masters on the other.

At times, the informers became so desperate for information that they would follow groups they had not been successful in infiltrating into meeting rooms; when challenged, they would excuse themselves by saying they had entered the wrong room by accident, or that they had been looking for a friend whom they thought might have been in that particular room or meeting. During that brief moment, their eyes would have inquisitively panned from face to face, like a snake, missing nothing.

From the period since June 1976, and a little before that time, many of these informers have received thorough beatings and removal from gatherings by young Blacks. Those beatings were called workshops. Those young, brook-no-nonsense Blacks periodically made our meetings no-go areas for the police informers. Those informers who were already known kept their distance.

One morning I had been driven from the Fort, or Number Four, one of the three jails I had been kept at during my detention period. Makhomisane and Patose had driven into the hidden basement garages at Jan Vorster Square. A Black businessman was keeping a rendezvous in the garage with Heystek. The businessman had driven there in his own big cream-white American car, and they were deep in very friendly conversation with each other. As we passed Heystek and the man, Makhomisane and Patose shielded them from me and told me not to look in their direction. But it was too late. I had had a good look at them and my mind had started working. I had long put two and two together, and I certainly did not end up with five. Having spent some time in detention and solitary confinement, I had become extremely quick and observant, perhaps as a result of fear and for my own survival. However, I obeyed the instruction not to look in the direction of the two conspirators.

On two other different occasions when I had again been brought in, but from the Hillbrow Police Station, two well-known photographers were keeping a similar rendezvous with Heystek. The photo journalists did not behave as if they were being detained, and their camaraderie with Heystek was most suspect. Unfortunately for these two, they both saw me and knew that I was in detention at the time. One of these photographers had been under suspicion for some time from the ghetto political activists. I had known that long before I was detained. If my sighting him on that occasion proved anything, I could not wait to be released.

No one really knew Somkelo Khumalo or where he had come from. He appeared suddenly at the African Music and Drama Centre, as large as life. He became one of my students, learning musical theory and other allied arts. He became very active and was well received by all and sundry. His story was that he had skipped the South African border into Swaziland to evade political harassment by the Security Police some time in the late sixties. But he had since returned secretly and was trying to acquire a pass and other residential documents and permits.

But everyone knew that, short of co-operating with the special branch, no exile ever returned to the country. Whether this co-operation continued or not was neither here nor there. The only exiles who returned were those who continued underground, never surfacing.

I assigned Somkelo's trumpet lessons to a colleague of mine, Cyril Khumalo, with whom I shared a large contingent of trumpet students. Somkelo himself decided to be taught the trumpet by me.

"Mr Pheto, I want to be taught the trumpet by you instead of Mr Khumalo," he pleaded.

"I'm sorry, I'm already full. Unless someone drops out, at the moment I can't find the time. Besides, you have Mr Khumalo who is an excellent player," I told Somkelo.

"No, Mr Pheto. I prefer you because you are strict."

I decided to be firm with him as I did not want to encourage the students to undermine the staff. The situation could make it difficult for me to administrate and would cause unpleasantness to those affected.

"It's my duty to allocate students to teachers and vice versa. At the moment there is no valid reason for a change in your case."

Somkelo then told me that Cyril Khumalo was his relative, and that he did not want to be taught by him on that score. I was aware that they shared a family name, but had not known till then that they were in fact related.

From that time onwards, I kept Somkelo at arm's length. He could not have afforded going into exile for his convictions, then return to successfully enjoy the luxury of openly avoiding surveillance and special branch swoops. As far as I was concerned, he would have been target number one. When he realized I had kept my distance, he came out into the open with me.

81

"Mr Pheto, I think I should tell you the truth. Be open with you. Since becoming a student here at the African Music and Drama Association, the Security Police have been pestering me." Somkelo paused. I watched him. I thought I would have been surprised if they hadn't. But what he told me was contrary to my expectations, even though I had not been taken aback. He continued. "They have asked me to keep an eye on this place," meaning the whole building and indicating its size with his hands. "They have mentioned particularly MDALI, of which you are organizer, and Phoenix Players downstairs."

I realized how relieved he was, at last having off-loaded his burden. He was unsure about my reaction and had awaited my response with impatience. I wondered if I were not being framed, though I could not say how. Phoenix Players was a White-run organization purporting to promote the Black arts. It was located on the first floor, sharing the same building with the African Music and Drama Association, which was on the third floor. I allowed Somkelo free rein and waited.

"But my conscience won't allow me to do this to you. So I refused," he volunteered.

I had waited for a long time to hear what his reaction to the offer had been, but I had not asked him.

"I think they are wasting their time," I replied. "But why don't you eat their money?" I was as caustic as I could be because something told me he was trying to improve his image with me. He knew he had fouled something up really badly.

Somkelo never came back to me with his problems and mission at the African Music and Drama Association. On the other hand, his "confession" had sealed my attitude towards him permanently. As far as I was concerned, there was to be no love lost between us for all time. He eventually joined a choral group for which I had played as one of the trumpeters. Soon after, I left the choral group.

Every Saturday morning I collected Elina Templin, a White music teacher, from her house in Greenside, a suburb of Johannesburg. Elina, a Canadian, was teaching the piano and general musicianship to the children under my music programme in Soweto. I had personally asked her to join the staff, because she was a good musician and as fine a person as one could ever wish to know. She had no problems about teaching Black children, and her own personality was that of one who had no hang-ups about the colour of one's skin. After she had agreed to take the position, I remember the difficulty I had in procuring a permit for her to enter Soweto for the "purpose of teaching piano to Bantu children". She was finally allowed to enter Soweto for: "Piano teaching only, from nine in the morning till three in the afternoon only, and on Saturdays only".

One such morning, as we arrived at the Young Men's Christian Association in Orlando East, where the lessons were conducted, a well-dressed and well-spoken Black man approached us.

"I have been interested in what you are doing for our children here, you and your lady-friend. I would like to meet her and show my appreciation. I am a teacher myself, but I am presently awaiting a post," he went on.

For a long while, he had been a mystery to me. We had seen each other several times at the YMCA, greeting and lightly commenting on the day-to-day issues. We had talked a little about Nigeria and other Black states. He said that he admired the West African cloth shirts I always wore. I had been teaching there on Saturdays and weekdays for over two years by then, but I did not know where he had come from. He had just "grown" there, and become a part of the "landscape".

"Oh! This is Mrs Templin," I said, surprised.

"Mrs Templeton! Glad to know you." He extended his hand to shake Elina's.

I was about to correct him when he left hurriedly, after he thought he had her name. I forgot about the incident and dismissed him as someone who was being too inquisitive.

Elina asked me about him as soon as we were settled in the piano room. "Who is he?"

"I don't know. He's always around here," I told her simply. Elina was unhappy. She had become wary of people watching and staring at her. She was a dedicated person and must have aroused a lot of suspicion. It was rare that White people could work relaxedly, unofficiously, as she did, among Blacks in the ghettos.

I had just finished teaching an afternoon music class. I went to the YMCA cafeteria for tea before driving to the city for an adults' class. There he was, as usual. This time, I was determined he should tell me who he was. But I let him lead as soon as I had joined him at one of the tables. I told him about my past, that I had been a music student and was then teaching. It was his turn to tell me about himself. He told me a similar story to that which Somkelo Khumalo had told me! I was just on the verge of asking him if he knew Somkelo as they had been in the same small country (Swaziland is not large) for the same reasons, almost at the same time, and were both back in our South Africa under similar conditions. A sixth sense warned me that the similarities were too much! I let him off without any reaction or comment.

Visser, the Colonel, was peering at me from behind his desk on the ninth floor. I was, as always, made to stand in front of him, on the other side of his desk, with my back turned from the door. It was again one of the many sessions. From the cell, to the ninth or tenth floor, back to the cell, up again the next day and so forth. One day Patose complained to me about the many journeys he had to make fetching me and returning me to the cells. "Pheto, man. Talk, man. All your friends have long talked. You are the only one we are still dealing with. I am already tired with you. You are not the only one here."

I told Patose that if his kings did not believe what I had told them, there was nothing I could do about it.

"You will talk, I tell you. You will talk!"

Now, Visser was questioning me. "You have mentioned all the teachers underr yourr prrogrrames, White and Black. But why do you hide this one!" he asked, putting emphasis on "this one".

"Which one?" I asked, wondering who on earth he meant.

As far as I was concerned, I had not left out a single person who had been on the staff at the African Music and Drama Association. Visser came nearer the edge of the desk, tensed before he delivered what he considered to be his *coup de grâce*. "Templeton!" and very slowly, he repeated. "Why did you not tell us about T-e-m-p-l-e-t-o-n?"

He had the habit of referring to "us" even if he was alone. I had found this strange and amusing because Africans from my part of the world always use the plural form in the same manner. I was certain that somewhere in history, when the first Whites had arrived in my country, they had been influenced by the people they found there. I doubted if Visser knew anything about royal plurals anyway.

For a while I could not rake this "Templeton" from the bottom of my mind, despite the fact that the name had not been far from Templin. I recalled all the White personnel who had worked at the

African Music and Drama Association again, softly, but audibly, more for my benefit than for his. Jellin, Martiz, Leveson, Broere, Thompson...to no avail. However, I reminded myself that the name had to begin with a "T".

"No!" I gave up. "I do not know a Templeton."

"Yes!" he bellowed at me, like a dying bull after the first knife had entered its throat. "The White woman you drrive to Soweto everry Saturrday!"

Oh, hell! How could I have forgotten Elina! How was it possible! But I suppose that in my frightened condition, apart from the fact that Elina had resigned from the African Music and Drama Association a while ago prior to my detention, she had gone out of my mind. Besides, Colonel Visser had made it quite clear that he was interested in those Whites who were still serving at the cultural centre then. All the same, I should have remembered Elina. Her contribution to the programme at the arts centre had been incomparable. I almost shouted her name.

"Elina Templin. Elina. Elina Templin, not Templeton!"

I had scored one off him, the clot. I was certain that whatever they tried to do, they could not shake me. But Visser had reminded me who and where I was, and what my station was on the rungs of the ladder of race hierarchy in South Africa.

"Mrs Templin! Not Elina!" he barked. I had not been aware that in my anxiety I had aroused the wrath of Colonel Visser, indeed of Afrikanerdom itself! "Does she allow you to call herr Elina!"

"Well, eh...Mrs Templin. She resigned about six months ago. You wanted me to tell you about those teachers who were still on the staff," I said morosely.

While this had been going on, my mind was working overtime in a million and one directions. Something about "Templeton" was forcing itself on me. That I had heard the name somewhere, and that it was important that I should remember the connection. I kept on relapsing into other thoughts instead of concentrating on Visser in front of me. But when the circumstance of the Templeton episode fell into place, it was as clear as a clean African stream cascading down a mountainside. The well-spoken man, the "landmark" at the YMCA, the Saturday morning!

I felt glad that I did not get the opportunity to correct the "landmark" at the YMCA then. I felt I was on top of this Visser moron and the relief was great. My mind eased into some peaceful repose, peace that I would find it difficult to explain and

85

share with someone else.

In the meantime, Colonel Visser had been trying pathetically hard to get out of the mess he had made. He needed to do so with dignity. What he had thought was his *coup de grâce* had ignominiously shattered to pieces like so many bits of broken glass on a floor. I could count the numerous bits laughing at him, and to have realized that I had been the architect of his débâcle elated me.

For a while, Visser must have been thinking about the informant, the unscrupulous informer who had been the cause of his appearing foolish before me. The bastard that had been paid to bring doubly-checked information about White communists in the ghettos, and this one had floundered on a vital piece — the name. Worse still, when this "Templeton" had stopped coming to the YMCA, the swine had not let his masters know that I had long stopped bringing the White woman to Soweto on Saturday mornings. On the other hand, this Black informer, "his mother" I cursed under my breath, had made me suffer unnecessarily. It had been no intention of mine to keep Elina in the dark for there had been no reason to. Elina and her family could have suffered from these bastards of Jan Vorster Square. At least, the landmark should also have told the Vissers what Elina's mission in Soweto was, although they would have seen further than that, as they already had. And what about the landmark's appreciation for what Elina was doing for the Black children of Soweto!

But on that Saturday morning he had asked to be introduced to Elina, he had been appropriate, suave and proper, the first Black "parent" to have expressed appreciation to Elina. Elina must have felt that it was the best compliment she had received from the community, far better than the meagre honorarium she earned for her sacrifices.

"And Zabane? Do you know Zabane? A cerrtain Aprril?"

"No. I have never heard of Zabane. But I have a friend whose name is Zabale." I had stressed the "Le" of the name.

This time Colonel Visser had been cautious, and rattled too. He dared not repeat the mistake as he had made in the Templeton case, and I knew that they would check my correction every bit of the way.

"You surre you don't know Zabane?"

"No. But I'm sure I know Zabale."

"Wherre is he, this Zabale of yourrs?" he continued, having

conceded defeat. I told him where Zabale was.

"Yes!" That was Bouwer who had been detailed by Visser to find out about Zabale at the Leeuwkop prison. "But we know he worrked at the passporrt offices, and he said that you saw him about passporrts, and you werre with that White woman of yourrs."

I replied that their information had been incorrect.

"What if Zabale bearrs us out?" Bouwer was thoroughly enjoying himself.

I knew that it would be easy for them to arrange indemnity and release for Zabale if he would agree to testify against me. In his position there was nothing he could have done. They needed a conviction against me to prove that there was communist subversion in South Africa, so that they could coerce the frightened White constituency behind them. I realized that Zabale might reason that he had been placed in a more awkward situation than that of an ordinary "criminal" trial. That that in itself would have made him acquiesce to anything they required of him.

The unfortunate coincidence was that I had seen Zabale about my passport, and had also inquired whether it would be possible to acquire passports for over a hundred children, who were in the arts scheme, to visit Botswana. But the White woman Visser and Bouwer referred to had nothing to do with me or Elina. In this instance she turned out to have been a local impresario, Bertha Egnos, who exported African musicals such as *Ipi Tombi* to England and America. She had an African personnel officer, Meshack Kungoane, whom I knew, doing most of the work of procuring passports for her troupes. Sometimes Meshack went with her or some other White woman to the passport offices because a Black man's services were quicker at government offices if the Black man was in the company of a White person. One of the clerks who told me of Meshack's ingenious solution to the long queues advised me to find a White friend for the purpose. Most Black people knew of the ploy and used it well. I had used it too. Some years ago, when I had landed my first job in Johannesburg as library assistant at the Witwatersrand University, I had insisted on being taken to the pass-office for registration by one of the Whites on the staff. I was eventually accompanied by the then deputy librarian, a Mr I. Isaacson. We were in and out of the pass-office complex, with its enormous queues trailing behind us, in no time. I had come out holding a cluster of permits and papers and the perpetual pass-book still in my hands as the counter service had been so fast and "polite" I had hardly had the time to return the numerous pieces of paper to my pockets.

But a White woman was still the quickest service route in government departments in South Africa. The senile old White men employed there suddenly came to life at the sight of one. So Meshack had played his part well, and I could not blame him, except for the mix-up poor Zabale had ended up in.

A particularly unenviable and awkard coincidence. God! If ever a man had been caught in webs not of his making, that man was me. There were times, many times too, when I believed that I was under a curse. For instance, when it was my family's turn to be evicted from our stand (plot of land) and the five-roomed house my uneducated father had sweated his life to build for us in Alexandra Township to move to a government scheme in Diepkloof, I had tried hard for us to be resettled in two of the so-called small houses the government offered as there were fifteen of us all told. My mother, my sisters and their children, me and my wife and our own three children. The government officials had refused. I was told that there was a housing shortage, and that there had been worse conditions than mine, where families of as many as twenty had been squeezed into one small four-roomed structure.

True as that statement may have been, the reality of the matter was that we could not live, all fifteen of us, under those cramped conditions. I ran the gauntlet of all the necessary offices I had been referred to, from one superintendent to another, sometimes to someone I had been told was the most senior superintendent, to no avail. Finally, I had to give up, and all of us, less two of my sisters who were then with friends and relatives elsewhere, squeezed into the little hovel provided. I still blame myself for not having fought hard enough so that the whole family could be together.

A cousin of mine who knew of our predicament was due to leave for the United States. She needed someone to remain in her equally small house in Meadowlands, only a stone's throw from Diepkloof, until she returned from her nursing studies. She offered me her house, which I readily accepted. She had told me that I would have to share it with her young nephew called Torch. She had assured me that Torch was a quiet young man who would pose no problems for me.

There could be no argument about it. Staying in my cousin's

house with Torch and my family was far better than fifteen people making do in one tiny Soweto house. So there would only be six of us in her house. Her name was Tiny, because she was slightly built. She arranged that I and my family be transferred into her permit as her subtenants. She did this before she left, and on the eve of her departure we moved into her house. Torch, the quiet young man, could not be found. We waited. Two weeks went by. I became worried about him. Torch could be in jail, in hospital, or dead. He could be anywhere. In South Africa, when a man disappears he most probably is in some trouble with the law. But Tiny had told me that Torch was only interested in his studies. I asked the neighbours. They told me that Torch would soon be back. He was, they said, in the habit of going away to visit relatives in the country. On such occasions, he would be away one week, two weeks, something like that. Two months went by and still no Torch. Instead, one afternoon, the Security Police arrived in my office at the African Music and Drama Association.

"Phineas Phetoe?" the Black policeman inquired, after having been told by the secretary where he could find me.

"Yes?"

"Come!" he said, closing in as if I were going to run.

I thought that they were gangsters, and wondered what on earth I could have done to annoy that element, where or when.

"Who are you?" I fumbled because it all happened so suddenly.

"Don't you stay at 230 Zone One Meadowlands?"

"Yes, I do. But who are you?" I insisted.

His colleague answered and said that they were from the Security Police at Jan Vorster.

"We want you. No," he corrected himself. "They want you there."

That confrontation had left me and my students agape as I was about to begin teaching.

On the way to Jan Vorster, I was thinking about Tiny in America. Could she have written a letter which had contained controversial political information which the Security Police had intercepted, landing me in this mess? Could she have addressed a meeting about a Black man's plight in South Africa, or on the political struggle for liberation, Tiny, there, in the safety of America? "Anyway, I'll see when I arrive at Jan Vorster Square."

At Jan Vorster, a tired-looking White man took over.

"You arre Phineas Phetoe, I believe?"

"Yes, I am."

"You studied in London?" as though it were criminal to have done so.

"Yes, I did. For four and a half years. In music." I decided to finish the issue for him instead of him feeling important about what he thought he knew about me.

He kept on consulting a file which contained a lot of newspaper cuttings about me. It also seemed to contain some forms and other information. Then he asked why I was staying at Meadowlands when the records he had before him stated that I had been officially resettled in Diepkloof. I explained how I had ended up in Tiny's house.

"Wherre is Torrch?"

I was totally stunned. I had almost forgotten about Torch. I had given him up and had already written to Tiny to let her know that I hadn't seen a sign of him. In this situation, I wondered where the young man could be. I immediately thought that this policeman asking me the whereabouts of Torch had him imprisoned somewhere in that political dungeon for Blacks that is Jan Vorster Square, and that he, Torch, had already been interrogated and brutalized. The police normally do that. They would haul someone in, a friend, a neighbour or nearest relative of the person already detained by them, to ascertain for themselves if anything was known about the particular individual in their claws. I suppose that if they assured themselves that nothing was known about that person, then they had a clean slate for killing or permanently holding such a person. But I could not imagine how Torch might be there except that, as a young man, he might have been involved with some underground political activists. If my guess was correct, then I felt proud of him, wherever he might be. At that time in the country, there were many such underground activities and groups.

I told the White policeman that I did not know where Torch was. That I had been expecting him to come home since I took occupancy of my cousin's house at Meadowlands, and that I had never set eyes on him so I did not even know what he looked like. The last word from the policeman was that he would be contacting me soon.

Three weeks later, they were back. I was at work again and I was bundled to Jan Vorster.

"We have it to ourr inforrmation that Torrch has skipped the countrry and ıs in Botswana heading forr Zambia forr militarry trraining!" The White man tried to hypnotize me with his eyes when he told me.

"What ken you tell us about that? When Torrch skipped the countrry, wherre he is going, who is arrranging forr him and is he coming back?"

I told him that I knew nothing at all, that the situation had not changed since the last time I had been brought to his office. In the meantime, the Security Police had been to my neighbours to find out everything about me. It would appear that the neighbours had verified what I had told him before, though it was many months before they told me the Security Police had been making inquiries about me, and about Torch too.

For the second time they had let me go, but not before they had driven to the house with me to search for anything that belonged to Torch. They took exercise books, and other books which had Torch's name on them. They did not ask me to sign for his effects. They merely confiscated the property.

But I was rationalizing like a civilized man, which I am. My tormentors did not think that I knew about simple courtesies like that. These my dehumanizers. These people who were supposed to have led me from the barbarity of the kraal to the new era! These Christian men who were supposed to respect other people's property. But I remembered that their ancestors had not respected my land which they had stolen from my ancestors, and that at that moment their government leaders were busy desecrating the sanctity of my fatherland into so many pieces called "Bantu Homelands", and were reserving the most fertile of my ancestral lands for their own use, meanwhile cramming me into only 13 per cent of the most soil-eroded portions.

Now, here, in this cell, and for the third time in detention and interrogation, I was being connected with another run-away young man, a student also, more or less the same age as Torch. I was again being connected with recruiting for military training, which Torch had apparently gone to.

The whole picture was fitting into place like so many fragments that needed putting together. My smartness would eventually come to an end as their watchful eyes and investigations would prove.

The worst coincidence was the cell number into which I had been unceremonially thrown — 320. My house number in

Meadowlands was 230. What could fate be doing to me? I asked myself. In other words, would their superstitiousness confirm their belief that the Afrikaner god was indicating to them that I was a real bad Black cannibal who would swallow Afrikaner babies? That I had just been moved to a home from home, hence the number of the cell, which was a mere twist of the number of my house? And come to think of it, this particular cell was larger than 230. Of course, the cell was usually packed with over sixty prisoners. It was just that in my case, they had deemed it necessary to hold me in solitary confinement. We all know that the Afrikaner doggedly believes in his god. The Afrikaner says, and shouts it at the top of his voice to the world at large, that his god has singled him out as the chosen of this earth, as an exclusive race blessed with the wisdom that will show the world how wrong it is. The god that would prove to Britain, America and the West as a whole that the Black man belonged to a subhuman species that should be kept in bondage. The species that should not be allowed to vilify its women and children and the entire non-Black human race. And that if these Blacks were to be freed in South Africa, it would be over his, the Afrikaner's, dead body!

Ian Smith, then bogus premier of Rhodesia, once uttered, "not in a thousand years" and "over his dead body" rather than have Black majority rule. But now it is history that the Zimbabwe African National Union (ZANU) pompously proclaimed the state of Zimbabwe less than ten years after Ian Smith made his empty boast. The Afrikaner further down south will see this history repeated because the flames of Pamberi na Chimurenga are sweeping down across the Limpopo River into southern Africa's grasslands like an angry storm.

I wondered why my own ancestors had deserted me in this hour of need. Why my gods appeared weaker than the Afrikaner one, and also wondered on whose side the real god was, the one I was made to learn about at school and church when I still worshipped according to the dogma of the White man.

One of my major preoccupations in prison was planning how effectively I could pass on the little I had learned, seen and observed during interrogation, the goings on of informers there, and who they were. How could I disseminate information that would keep our surveillance at its sharpest? I had heard, for instance, from boastful Heystek, how the police normally had more than one informer attend a meeting or infiltrate an organization, unknown to each other, meaning that these informers were actually policing and outdoing each other. That these informers were the least trusted, hence the double, triple check or whatever the number used. And that, if the Heysteks of this world found some of these informers wanting or unreliable, they unhesitatingly exposed their cover by revealing their names. That the Heysteks were aware that some of them were in it for the money only. Sometimes, the Heysteks used this ploy of revealing their pimps' names in order to sow further distrust amongst the Black community. But at the same time, it was very possible that the Heysteks were using innocent people's names, and particularly those that were the real militants of our struggle.

On my release, I told my close colleagues every detail, name and circumstance of what I had observed whilst in prison.

8. *What kind of nightmare is this? II*

During the first nightmarish assault I was rescued by their own inefficiency. That had given me a breather. It had taken their concentration away from the various names they had been interrogating me about, and from MDALI, before I had made a mess of whatever answers I may have given. I was taken down to the cells before I had disclosed or "agreed" to anything that might have compromised me. My thinking had taken many directions. On the one hand, I was fighting for my survival. On the other, trying very hard not to allow them to get any foothold on useful information. In a little while, I knew that we would be back, in the same room, for the same routine.

"So, you arre still not prreparred to talk."

Then they would ignore me totally, whoever was interrogating me then. In the meantime, I had been aware that they were busy with all sorts of matters relating to other detainees, not necessarily connected with me. They would be going in and out, or coming in and gathering in a corner, audibly discussing some tactic. Something like: "That one gives us no trrouble," or, "That one needs to be killed."

I had no idea who the "that ones" were, but the impression I gathered was that I had been stubborn, which fact made me frightened as I imagined that more drastic steps would have to be implemented to make me as easy to handle as the "that ones". The insinuations had other unnerving effects on me; maybe some of the detainees connected with me had talked, and I worried no end as to what they might have said.

On 23 March, I was told by Colonel Visser that as I had not been willing to "ko-operrate", other methods were going to be used on me. He told me that he had been gentle with me, but that others would not be, and that I should remember that "Therre arre too many disused mine dumps in Johannesburrg forr people like you. Now wrrite!" he said, pushing heaps of paper in front of my face. By this time, Colonel Visser, Captain Heystek and Lieutenant Visser had rejected and torn up three "statements" I had written.

"This is nothing. Nothing! We want the rreal thing. Yourr involvement with the Kolourreds, the kommunists you met in England, what they told you to do with the forrged passporrts that Joe Slovo and Rruth Firrst have given you, the people you have alrready rrecrruited forr military trraining and yourr kontakts underrgrround forr the Afrrikan National Kongrress and the money you brrought frrom Botswana forr Joyce Sikakane!"

Names and more names of people I was supposed to have been involved with. Joe Slovo was a White exile apparently working for the African National Congress. Ruth First, I believed, was Mrs Slovo. I had known the two a long time ago when I was still with the African National Congress in Alexandra Township. Recently, I had only read about them. In London, I did not remember having met them personally. Joyce Sikakane was a former detainee who had fled the country and had been a friend of mine. I had done a little political work for her, but I had not known that the Security Police had wind of it because we worked very tightly and half the time she did not know when I was going to "deliver" the goods. Somewhere, someone might have talked.

"You see, we told you we know everrything. Even what you don't tell us. But we want you to tell us," they would gloat.

Then there would be more of the incessant short intervals and conferences to decide on their next move.

I was very tired. There was nothing left that I could tell these men. I had told them who I had met in Europe, my friends and the circumstances of our meetings, and what MDALI was. They had torn up three attempts at a statement. Whatever I wrote again would be the same. It was then 23 March. A short time in the life of a person under ordinary circumstances. But a long time to me during which much had happened. The "education" I already had

94

was extremely useful in surviving further, and I used that to the fullest advantage under the circumstances.

Colonel Visser came in alone. "Frrom tomorrrow otherr people will deal with you, unless...." I decided to wait for tomorrrow.

Heystek added a final warning to the many I had already had as he and Lieutenant Visser escorted me to the cell. I decided to hold on. "*Tshwara thata*," as we say in SeTswana. I wondered where their Black sidekicks were on that day, when Heystek and Lieutenant Visser had to escort me. Maybe, I thought, the two were not taking me to the cells.

"Ya, Phineas," Heystek was saying this in SeSotho. "Tomorrow you will tell us. We have time. You can rot here too."

Lieutenant Visser said nothing all the way, just now and then flexing his overblown body, his neck, shoulders and arms. He walked next to me, and Heystek was on the other side.

All night through, I rehearsed lies, defences, blocks to ward off their blows, falling positions and breakfalls to protect my testes and penis and other vulnerable parts of the body. All this was happening in my mind, recalling tricks I had learned during my boxing and judo days. Those days were many years ago, but there was much I had not forgotten. I made it a point also not to forget to put on a lot of clothes for padding, remembering the advice I had had from Benzo.

The worst part was spending the night knowing what my fate would be the next day. They could have taken me by surprise, thus sparing me the misery and added suffering I went through. When I recalled the severe beating I had taken from van Niekerk, I wondered if what I had been programmed for would be worse, and if so, by how much.

I died many deaths that night.

The morning broke unperturbed. Cruel, without the slightest care in the world. Prison routines were followed as usual. Petty pass offenders were woken up to be taken to court. Major came for his shouting rounds. I felt like telling him that I was going to be assaulted that day, but I could well conceive the reply he would have given. "Well, it has not happened yet. Get assaulted first!"

"Yes, Major," I might as well have replied, and at nine or thereabouts the keys rattled in the steel door of my cell. Heystek, as big as Jan Vorster Square, Lieutenant Visser, his neck as thick as Cape Town, and yet another scrawny White one that I had

95

never seen before, were at the door, after Patose had unlocked it.

"God! They have come for me!"

"Pheto, you have not decided yet?" Heystek spoke in SeSotho. "*Ha re tsebe ka sheku.*" (We don't know today.)

I was frightened again. I tried to say something, but my voice seemed to have stopped working. I tried to imagine what it was going to be like, how long it would last, or how long I would be able to endure it.

On the way to their offices on the tenth floor, to the same rooms where so many "suicides" had happened, apparently during interrogations, Heystek had taunted me all the time. "*Amandla.* That's what you say. Power!" He also said that Blacks take a long time to die anyway. Heystek was already breathing heavily from climbing the many devious ways up some stairs, down others. From long walks, short ones, left and right turns, before we reached some lifts to the ninth floor, then another about turn to a short flight of stairs to the tenth.

I hoped that he would be the one to assault me, if there was going to be any assaulting, as I imagined he tired quickly. Lieutenant Visser continued to mumble incoherences, in Afrikaans, now and then fixing and loosening his shirt collar. The only clear sentence I had him utter was "He will talk!"

Faithful Patose had been with them all the time. All he had done was to open the cell doors and disappear into their shadows. The new one they were with kept on asking them who I was. They told him that I had undergone military training for subversive purposes whilst overseas, and that I was dangerous. The new one took one look at me. His reaction made me realize that he believed them. They had kept me unwashed so my hair was matted for lack of being combed. It had all been calculated so that I fitted the image they wished to present of me. I had resigned myself to my gods.

Heystek collapsed into his chair as soon as we finally arrived in his office. So, Colonel Visser had meant what he said when he had warned me that other people would take over. I looked at Van Gogh on the west wall and pleaded with him for mercy. None came. Lieutenant Visser stood beside me. The questions began.

"Yourr passporrt. We arre now tirred."

At that moment another White bull blew himself into Heystek's office as if someone had forcefully pushed him. He was totally new to me, and the ugliest I had seen of all that lot, with blobs of huge

96

pimples on his face, some of which were as big as large bird's eyes. He was in shirt-sleeves. He sat down, then looked surprised.

"Is this the thing?" he asked, indicating me with his upturned left palm. His tone told me that he had expected and prepared himself to deal with a strong Black man, and therefore had a big job on his hands. At that time, I must have weighed 135 pounds, including all the clothes Benzo had advised me to use as padding.

"What's his name?" the new one asked them. Heystek told him, and at the same time gave him a résumé of my life.

"Oh, ja! England, heh! What's the best kountrry in the worrld? Have you seen the slums therre, in the East End! I tell you. South Afrrika is the best kountrry in the worrld."

I concurred that South Africa was indeed the "best" country in the world.

Lieutenant Visser resumed. "Who trravelled in yourr passporrt? What happened to the missing pages in the passporrt?"

I realized that they had all the time been going through the books and other writings, property and other documents they had taken from my house. I knew about the passport, and that some of the pages were missing, though at the time I still did not know who had stolen the pages they were referring to, and for what purpose.

It so happened that during my stay abroad, someone had surreptitiously laid their hands on my passport, had neatly and expertly torn some pages out of it. In the meantime, I had not been aware of what had happened until a week prior to my return to South Africa.

It had been nerve-racking to discover it, to say the least. Investigation after investigation led me and a few trusted colleagues up blind alleys. But with the help of highly equipped and trained liberation comrades (not belonging to any of the South African liberation movements), we reduced the clues to three possible areas of supicion. The South African régime's agents in London, because I had been active with one liberation group, hopefully, under cover. We also suspected a break-in for the purpose of securing the pages from the passport, as there was no evidence of any other documents having been disturbed. The break-in might have come from some unknown South African liberation group which knew I had a valid passport, and had need of it.

The final suspicion we cast around a liberation movement whose interests in South African passports were obvious. Our conclusion had been that such a group, or any relevant organization needing that type of assistance, could have approached me, proved their bona fides and made their request, telling me of their particular need for the passport. I knew in my mind that if any group had done so, and I had been satisfied that they would treat everything in the utmost confidence, I would have given them any assistance they needed. Knowing myself as I hope I do, I would have kept my mouth sealed under any sort of pressure unless I became aware during interrogation that I had been betrayed or that the Security Police already had conclusive evidence. I would realize that the game was up and I would have prepared myself for the consequences of imprisonment. As it turned out, I realized that the poor sods knew little or nothing of consequence about my overseas connections by the way they were shamefully grasping at every fancy that chanced their way.

I had wanted to return home as there was much I had to do there. We threw caution to the winds and went straight to South Africa House in Trafalgar Square. A friend of mine, Christopher Strang, a Scot, who was married to the secretary of the African Music and Drama Trust that had sponsored me in London, accompanied me. We reckoned I needed to take someone the Boers at South Africa House could not touch without causing diplomatic heavyweights to come into the fray.

By the time Christopher and I arrived at South Africa House, we hadn't had time to orchestrate our line of attack. We handed in the truncated document and applied for a new one! The Boer behind the counter wanted to know what had happened to the missing pages. Christopher threw a humdinger at him.

"We believe, and are certain, that it must be your agents who are responsible for the missing pages! No one else would be interested in that sort of activity."

Though I was totally unprepared for the line Christopher had taken, I was most impressed that he had taken the apartheid representative's bull by the horns.

The Boer sweated from forehead to his thick neck. He apologized profusely and found it difficult to categorically deny the accusation, which he could have done, as we had also speculated. He told us a cock-and-bull story that the passport would have to be referred to South Africa and so forth, and that it would take some time. It did not. In the end, within about four days or so, I had been granted a new passport, different in design from the old one, and that, to my mind, had been the end of the matter.

I had travelled home not without incident though. The plane from Ghana, where I had stopped over, was due east. Again, I made a mess. The security at the Ghana immigration section had found a letter on me addressed to "Revolutionary Comrades" in Zambia. All the same, the letter was returned to me after it had been read.

In the plane, I had avoided liquor and asked for coffee. After the coffee, I "slept" comfortably for a long time, and missed one touch-down completely. When I woke up, my body was heavy, lethargic, and not co-ordinating well. I looked at my watch and knew that something had gone wrong. The passenger next to me said that they did not want to disturb me during touch-down, but that I had not missed much anyway. I then discreetly went through my pockets and realized that they were not as they had been when I boarded the plane. I checked my camera case. It also had been disturbed. I concluded that my deliberate plan not to fly European or South African planes had misfired. I thought that I would have been safer in a plane owned by an African country rather than one owned by a western country. Also, the reason for having flown African had been to put my money where my mouth was — Africa.

Hunters and hunted sense each other. I had decided to scan the passengers on the plane for the security men on it. It did not take long to spot who I thought they were. When nothing had registered for some time in terms of reaction, I pretended to go to the toilet. Two men stood up even before I had left the seat. One had been sitting next to the first-class cabin en route to the pilot's controls. The other had been sitting right behind me. Thereafter, I had no problem. To me, hunters and hunted had accepted the presence of each other.

"How much is meat therre? Kould you buy meat? What kommunists funds did you use?" Pimples persisted.

"Meat? I . . . ."

"Madali. Who is he? I want to know him!" He didn't stop harassing me until I was totally confused.

Heystek was about to tell him that MDALI was not a person, but a Black artists' organization, when he suddenly bellowed, "I don't karre! I want to know this Madali, who he is!" The whole

99

thing had seemed funny, but it wasn't any longer because the new one was not showing off. He just could not understand that MDALI was not a human being.

"MDALI is . . ." then the blows began. Suddenly. Hailstones of them. From all angles, incessant. Visser. The new one, Visser. Many blows that I could not see. I collided with the blows. In the air. On my feet. On the floor. I had become a ding-dong, as if they were playing ping-pong with a human table-tennis ball. The punches were coming so fast and my closed eyes kept on seeing flashes like lightning, sharp streaks of light, despite the fact that I shut my eyes tightly. I clasped my arms around my head and face, cursing in the meantime that two hands were not enough. If thrown on the floor, I would pull my legs up to my body and fold up like a lamb feeling cold in winter. But nothing helped. Quickly, I would be picked up by one of them. I would find myself totally unprotected and at full stretch. Then my ribs would come under the avalanche of their blows, on my back, neck, head and arms. Their shoes . . . an eternity of silence except for the sound made by their punches, blows, boots as they connected into their target, me. There were groans and grunts from me, and the frosted glass top of the door of Heystek's office and walls shook as I was bounced in and out, this way and that, by Visser and the new one. My confused eyes saw the blows, when I did see them, their kicking legs, Heystek's large desk, Van Gogh on the west wall all as a collage in motion, the different moving angles ganging up on me, depending on the position their blows had thrown me, either on my feet or on the floor. Down, or half-way in the air, or just somewhere indefinite between the ceiling and the floor.

"What kind of nightmare is this?" I whispered to myself during the furore. When I was upright, they punched me to the floor. When I had fallen down, they booted me up.

"O my God!" I cried.

I was dripping with sweat. At that moment, the many clothes I had on were the worst hindrance. I was hot from all the jerseys and shirts and jacket which clung to me and weighed me down. I thought of Benzo. He had advised that I should put on as many clothes as I could. I cried softly that Benzo had ill-directed me.

After what seemed to be an age, they stopped. The new one again asked me what Madali was. Lieutenant Visser followed up about the passport, whilst Heystek, still on his chair, said, "You will tell us. We don't play here. We are working."

100

Sweat was pouring down all over me. But just as I was about to tell them that I was ready to talk, they started again. As suddenly as they had stopped.

"We have methods to conscientize people into remembering. The stories that there are beatings, torturings and murderings are true, if people refuse to co-operate," he concluded. Later in the cell I remembered that I wondered when Heystek, like all Afrikaners, would speak English like the rest of them. It would have surprised me if he had not obliged me during all that time that I had been in prison. He had been a bit suave, but then, when the chips were down, he could not be any different.

"My kaffertijie, you will kall me baas!" ("My" here was pronounced in Afrikaans which in English would be like "May"). The new one had gone berserk. He was a complete beast. Wild. "You will fly like a kite with a motorr karr without wheels!" as he wheeled around with his hands and body simulating the motor car he was talking about. He had looked really funny, more ugly and beastly than he had been. It was a long time afterwards that I thought at last I had managed to analyse what he had been trying to say about the motor car, which in my mind went something like this: "That I would be like a motor car without wheels (wheel-less) flying (through the air) like a kite!" or better still, "That I would be like a wheel-less flying motor car". All the same, I finally gave up analysing what he had said without being satisfied that I had cracked it.

The one time I opened my eyes during the spell when I was being beaten up and caught Lieutenant Visser's eyes, I thought that he too had gone berserk. He had lifted me up by the lapels of my jacket, had banged my head six to seven times against the wall, just under peering Van Gogh. Thereafter he had tried to lift me up by my hair, but two huge tufts of hair had ripped from my head and remained in his hands. For one brief moment it seemed as if he had shit in his hands. I was so grateful that the hair had broken because I do not know what would have happened otherwise. While I had been suspended by my hair, brief as it was, the pain had been excruciating. Lieutenant Visser threw the tufts forcibly on to the floor, wiped his hands on my jacket and told me to clean the mess up. As I reached for my hair on the floor, the pimpled beast kicked me hard in the rib that van Niekerk had smashed twelve days ago. I remembered stiffening suddenly and being unable to breathe.

101

I do not know what happened afterwards, except later, when I had found my breath, being told to sit on a chair. It seemed like a long time of having been nowhere. I could not see a chair where they were indicating, but I dared not use the one the beast had sat on when he had flown into Heystek's office. When I looked at them in surprise, Visser pointed at nothing and said, "Sit". I still did not understand and was slapped again by the beast, flash on my unguarded face, with the back of his left-hand palm. Again Visser lost his temper with my "stupidity". He forcefully pushed me down, holding on to my shoulders, pressing on until my knees bent and when I reached "chair" posture, he told me to remain like that. "Now, sit!"

I could not maintain that position for any length of time. He was on me as fast as lightning. I had disobeyed them by not sitting as instructed. The two then thumped my thighs with their knees until the muscles were numb and my legs unable to support me. The muscles around this part of my body just collapsed.

It must have been an eternity before they decided to go out for their usual conferences without which they did not seem able to interrogate. Makhomisane was summoned from somewhere. He came running to guard me during their absence from the room. He shook like a leaf when he saw the condition I was in, his eyes glinting and shifting in their sockets. He told me that I was to remain standing, but he was not in command of himself, and his voice was shaking. Eventually my hands slipped from Heystek's desk as I tried to support myself. I next found myself sitting on the floor, still sweating, with Makhomisane holding a mug of water to my mouth telling me that they had told him to let me drink the water.

When I was returned to the cell, a journey that normally lasted only three to four minutes took fifteen minutes; I tried hard to walk quickly as Makhomisane and Patose were claiming that they had to rush somewhere, but I pleaded with them that I could not walk any faster. They part pushed me, part walked me and part carried and dragged me. They could not have dragged me all the way back to the cells as we passed many prisoners and other police staff along the corridors. Everything had to be made to look normal. They kept everything terribly secretive, away from possible eye-witnesses.

On the way, Patose said that he had warned me a while ago to talk to save myself from what I was going through, but I had not listened to him. He said that my friends had tried to resist like me, that they had tried to shield my name, but had eventually broken down. He finally said that it were better that I made up my mind and tell them for my own good, to save myself from further assaults.

When Makhomisane and Patose finally locked me up, I flopped on the cement floor for a long time. The will to crawl to the blankets was there, but the body would not obey my wishes. Soon, I realized that the floor, cold as it was, was as welcome as a block of ice on a hot day.

It was an age before I reached the stench that was my "bed" to rest, and to do the routine playback of the day's events in my mind. I realized that I had been crying from the frustration of being assaulted without the chance to fight back.

9. *The rattle of the keys*

Before Makhomisane and Patose had been instructed to take me back to the cells, Heystek told me that they had not finished with me yet. He said that it had been only the beginning, and that I would be fetched from the cell on the 25th for more interrogation.

On that day, I had waited on the mat but under the blankets, all ears for any approaching sounds. I listened and heard every footstep within earshot either approaching or receding. Listened to all the noises and the echoes made in the hollow corridors. To voices which ate into my aching flesh and hurt pride — to voices of policemen and prisoners, the so-called pass offenders and petty thieves and loiterers as they were brought in or taken away.

The most jarring noise was of the rattle of keys on the steel doors, first the outer one, then the inner, and finally the one constructed out of steel bars that were as thick as the branches of young trees.

The noise came from policemen bringing food, or locking in prisoners or checking that there had been no escape. The police had a sadistic habit of banging hard on the doors, first with their teak batons which they always carried with them, then shoving the keys violently into the keyholes with devilish force so that the eardrum was jarred. Sometimes, when they were not opening the cells, they would be just sauntering down the corridors swinging the big bunch of keys, producing an endless restless rattle which

103

was most annoying to us in solitary confinement. Every action by the police was violent at Jan Vorster, in fact at every police station I had been to in South Africa. Force lives and rules. That also included the language used by the police, the most vile, strings and volleys of swearwords full of sexual vulgarity and downright venom. I have never stopped wondering how these men could have been the preservers of law and order.

Before I was detained, I was used to their violence as it spilled over into the streets of the Black ghettos. It might be their massive trucks gouging their way recklessly into crowds of people, irrespective of whether there were women and children about. I had myself, within a period of five weeks, witnessed the death of two children, both little girls, run over by carelessly driven police trucks. Both girls were killed at the same spot, in Jabavu, Soweto, in a busy shopping complex where the pedestrian crossing was well known. I remembered that on the second occasion, we who were there erupted into what White South Africa refers to as a riot, usually Communist-inspired. We stoned the police who had driven the truck, turned it over and were about to set it alight when other police reinforcements arrived. We ran for it. I also continue to wonder why it was that as soon as these men wore the police uniform, they went through some transformation during which they became power-drunk, particularly the Black ones. I was almost certain that the White ones gave them the gun and told them to shoot every Black bugger in sight, and these Black police had obliged.

Recently, when Soweto had erupted during the students' protest against the system of Black education, the Black police went on the rampage. They opened fire on us wantonly, as if they were on an animal hunt. They shot children of their own communities with no remorse. They had assumed the power of God, short of being God himself. Rumour had it at one time that Hector Petersen, the first Soweto pupil to be shot dead, only 13 years old, had fallen from a Black policeman's bullet. I could believe that, as there were so many of them. Perhaps when we begin to write our history, the truth will still emerge.

And the White police? It would be folly of me to even try to spend any energy on them. They are beasts that no living person can ever be reconciled to as human beings. At least, I understand the background from which their atrocities emerge, and the side, born of and fed on ignorance, on which they stand. They are defending a position of racism, hate and fear.

All through the day then, and even later, when interrogation had long been over and I was just rotting there in one of those Johannesburg prisons, the key's rattling noise gouged my soul each time I heard it. Whether it was in the doors of the cell I was occupying or elsewhere, it was the same. The rattle of those keys was the indication that someone was either being taken away or brought in. I would find myself ending up tense, wondering who it may have been, and whether I knew the person or not. I would also wonder when it would be my turn to be let out.

I had resigned myself to the fact that they were not going to come that day, the 25th. The third meal of the day had been eaten and I already knew that after dinner, the chance of the keys rattling in my cell were almost nil, though at times the last meal of the day was as early as two in the afternoon. That would be the day when the night would be exceedingly long.

Hated and annoying though this noise made by the keys was, at least one good purpose the noise served was that of roughly indicating what time of day it was, because most of the cells were in constant darkness and one had no idea of time. I used to hear the keys at about 6 a.m., then at roughly 11 a.m. and thereafter at 2 p.m. These three instances were absolute certainties each day.

Even if they had come, though, that would have been the day they would have had to bring a stretcher to carry me to interrogation. But I now know that a stretcher would have been a luxury! They carry the dead bodies of those they have murdered out of the murder cells with the same dirty stinking blankets issued to prisoners to sleep in.

I was in poor shape. The rib had been shooting regular but intermittent pins and pulses of pain. My thighs were still numb, as though paralysed. My neck ached as if it had a hole just above it. The right ear had a distant buzz that went on continuously. As a musician, I thought I had reached the end of the road. I could foresee nine years of study in South Africa and a further four years in London gone to waste.

10. *The visiting magistrate*

Detention prison routine in Johannesburg is the same, day in and day out. They did not come on the 25th. They might come today, tomorrow or the day after. They could come any day. As long as I had not yet made the statement, there was no telling when the game would end. Wondering, waiting, listening for the echoes in those corridors of power, the keys, the footsteps and the bullying commanding shouts of the police, the frightened, constantly running prisoners, the roll-call preparing the petty prisoners of apartheid for court appearances, the usual continuous beatings and the weeping of those assaulted.

I knew then that I had received the worst beating because I did not yell or beg for mercy. I was told that my attitude was interpreted as resistance and it galled those that were assaulting me, particularly the beast. I whimpered and groaned but I did not yell out. Perhaps I had been too frightened and the sound would not come out of me. Perhaps I had been too deep in thought, concerned about permanent disablement that might occur because of their brutality, or perhaps that I would be ashamed of myself for the rest of my life if I did cry and beg for mercy; I knew that the police would give the earth for me to have responded in such a manner, about which they could gloat for a long time. But I learnt later that I had been stupid. That I should have screamed at the top of my voice and should have called out, "Please, baas, I will talk." However, even if one's chips were down, political dissent based on one's beliefs kept one fighting. I disagreed with what they were doing to me and their methods to get information from me. They had not yet established nor told me what it was they had detained me for. All the same, even if they had told me, I would still have stuck to my beliefs, coupled with my hatred for their system of racism.

Of course, the honeymoon of the key not rattling in my cell could not last long. And there could have been other reasons too. I heard them, as usual, coming from a long way off. My hearing and other responses I did not know I possessed had developed beyond my expectations. So I heard them, though there was something unusual, an unbelievable difference on this particular day, the 26th. There had been no shouting or screaming commands. There was no anger or forced entries. The voices were quieter and they had taken a long time in their procession towards my cell.

I heard subdued, refined talking, civilized and human. Every cell on the third floor that contained a "terrorist" detainee had been visited. I reasoned that I would not be the exception. I strained every muscle to lift up my battered body. I started a long crawl to the door. Then I hoisted myself up and hung on, just below the high window, pressing my left ear to the bars to catch every sound. The voices were nearing, and were still polite. I heard voices I could not recognize. Could it have been a priest? Or Kruger himself, their Minister of Justice! I was hoping for too much. I am the type that never learns.

Eventually, cell 320 was opened. A Black policeman travelling with the entourage had done that, and then cowered back. There were three White men in all, one of whom I recognized as Bouwer. Another was a greying, portly person I had never seen before there. When the steel door finally opened, and I saw all of them, the short portly person had a pen and several sheets of paper. First to advance nearer to talk to me had been Bouwer, who "introduced" himself! Hell, that was good, and things were changing. For Bouwer to actually introduce himself? Bouwer had become politeness personified.

Bouwer asked if I was "Peyto".

"Yes, I am."

"This is the visiting magistrate," he said, indicating the greying person. "Is everrything all rright?"

Since when had everything been all right? Or, would Bouwer have cared in any case, after his colleagues had assaulted me?

I thought inwardly that the exercise had been one of their many tricks.

The magistrate asked me if all was well with me.

"What!" I thought.

The magistrate came closer so Bouwer was forced to make room by moving aside.

"Don't fear anything. Have you any complaints?" the magistrate asked again.

"Com-what?" I could not believe what was happening.

I threw a furtive glance at Bouwer and his other small-built friend behind the magistrate to assess if they could overhear what I intended to disclose.

"Fear nothing," the man pressed on. I think he suspected that I wanted to say something. "Or are you all right? It's Pheto," he said, referring to some papers, "is it not?"

"Yes," I agreed that it was me, and "Yes, I have complaints to make."

"What is it?"

Behind the magistrate I glimpsed Bouwer's eyes stabbing fear at me. His cheeks had suddenly gone red with blood. He exaggeratedly mouthed and whispered some threat, shaking his head vigorously, scowling all the time. The magistrate in the meantime was not aware of the drama that was taking place behind and in front of him. I understood Bouwer's antics, although I could not lip-read what he was trying to convey to me. He was "wetting his pants now" as we say in my mother-tongue. I was concerned only for my safety. I had already take far too much from these brutal Security Police, and I was prepared to do anything for my survival. I calculated that if I missed any opportunity, such as this one of the visiting magistrate, there might never be another.

The other little White man, dressed in a grey check suit, moved away from the magistrate, throwing his arms into the air with resignation and despair. I immediately realized that he too was on Bouwer's side. Meanwhile, the benign magistrate was listening. Everything was happening quickly.

"I was assaulted during the course of making a statement." By that time, it was too late to rescind my action. It was too late for Bouwer and his little colleague to threaten me. It was too late for the magistrate not to have heard me.

I told the magistrate that I was first assaulted by a policeman called van Niekerk, and that the assault took place as recently as the 24th. That I had again been assaulted by Lieutenant Visser and another policeman whose name I did not know then, and that the latter assault had taken place in the presence of Captain Heystek, in Heystek's office.

The magistrate took down the details on a sheet of paper. He wrote the names of the police, the reasons and the circumstances as well as the time, which I had mostly guessed as I had no way of telling exactly at what o'clock the assaults had taken place. He then read what I had told him to make sure that I was satisfied. When the magistrate left the cell door, he told me that nothing would happen to me again.

I had my own doubts, but I felt that I should do everything to save myself from further abuse. And if I should die in there, at least I felt that these records, such as the visit to the doctor and the report to the magistrate, would serve to expose strange circumstances which would be cause for concern.

But I was being very naïve. Who did I think I was to be able to expose that system? And who did I think I would be exposing the system to? After all, these men were carrying out mandates of a White society that had voted into power the politicians on whose behalf they were acting. It had not even been a question of silent connivance of the voting Whites, but their salient support. The inhumanities and debasement suffered by Blacks in South Africa were common knowledge. No one cared but we Blacks knew that every allegation we made was a fact. And at this time of our struggle, I thought that my efforts were a wasted risk. I should have been satisfied with the fact that whatever happened, my grave would have been but another monument to the already overflowing detention deaths. That with time, those of us who survive to carry the freedom struggle to its final victory will eternally remind those who have perpetrated these cruelties. That our mothers have not mourned in vain, and that those who have fallen have not done so in vain.

Before the magistrate left, I called him back and told him, "I'm not trying to put anyone in trouble!"

Shit! I felt disgusted with the coward that I am. I hated myself and wondered what I was doing in the struggle. The magistrate also wrote down the last bit that I had told him.

All that done, I did not feel for a moment that the magistrate had taken sides with me. I remember that Bouwer had stolen a chance before the steel door was locked, as I had called the magistrate for the last rejoinder. "Peyto, what is it now?" and his teeth and eyes jutted out of his red face. I remembered seeing the movie *Frankenstein* when I was 12 years old in Alexandra Township. Bouwer had looked like the monster I had seen on the screen then.

The surprise visit by the magistrate had been on a Thursday, late in the afternoon. It was the Thursday before the Easter weekend. I remembered how one day, early in the same week during my standing sessions in Heystek's office, the police had been fussing over Easter preparations for their families: that Patose had been instructed to drive to Heystek's and Lieutenant Visser's houses, collect the "missusses" and drive them to their communal hairdresser. In the meantime, he was also told to fetch the children, then return to pick up the missusses from the hairdresser's and take them all on shopping sprees for Easter goodies. I remembered also the many phone calls that came from members of their families wishing the Vissers and Heysteks a Happy Easter.

I could not help thinking that these men were getting ready to celebrate holy Easter, to make love and meditate on the suffering of Jesus Christ for mankind. But here I was in front of them being made to suffer the same as their Jesus Christ. That they did not have far to go to search for an example.

I thought for a long time about the contradictions unfolding in front of me at this time of the Christian calendar. That I was made to stand for hours on end by so-called Christians. That I also had a family who had no idea where I was, let alone what I was then going through, and the condition I was in.

11. *Fruit from van Niekerk*

In the hollow distance, I heard the rattle of the keys for the second time that day, and it was already early evening. Again, those approaching were stopping at every cell. Again, there was less of the usual violence normally perpetrated on the steel doors.

I found this strange behaviour disconcerting because I wanted to know the reasons for the changes. This time, I thought that perhaps it might be a priest coming to pray for us so that God should be with us over the holy period.

I heard Magoro's voice asking one Raymond Burghers, two cells away from me, if he, Raymond, was in good shape. I could not hear Raymond's response then. I also did not know who this Raymond was, but I remembered that I had been asked about him during the "Do you know so and so" sessions of Colonel Visser.

Magoro at last appeared with great pomp and ceremony at my cell door. He called:

"Pheto."

"Yes?"

Then the door was opened. He stood there with a big brown paper carrier bag.

"I've got fruits for you!"

"What!" My suspicious mind was at me again. I could never rest from being wary.

Magoro put the carrier bag down, dipped his hands into it and scooped out apples, bananas and an orange. He was supervised by the small man who had come earlier with the magistrate and Bouwer.

"Are these from my wife?"

"No! They are from my chief, our chief," he corrected himself.

110

I did not know whom he meant, particularly when he repeated "our chief", whoever that chief was. He must have realized that he had excluded the small man who was with him, or perhaps he meant to include the rest of the Black Security Policemen.

"Who's your chief?" I insisted on knowing who the man was, because I thought that this chief had put poison in the fruit.

"You don't know him," Magoro said with aplomb, looking at me. I thought he would not tell me his chief's name.

"Van Niekerk!"

"What?" Suddenly I remembered the blows again as I stood there in the cell. I remembered the first assault in Colonel Visser's office, and I heard the booming voice of van Niekerk. That had been on 12 March.

"So!" I told myself. "He assaults me. I report him to the magistrate. Next, he sends fruit to apologize, to soften me up, so that I should not pursue the matter. Is that what it is?" I decided that I would not be bought with fruit.

But it turned out that it was a totally different van Niekerk who was the chief that had sent Magoro with the fruit. After I had received it, the small man came closer to me. He did not warn me nor prepare me for what he had to say.

"Yourr kousin Michael Pheto is dead! Do you know him?"

It was a long time before I told him that I knew Michael. When I asked him how he had died, he said that he did not know, and seemed little concerned. I guessed that my wife must have requested them to let me know.

I was waiting for him to leave so that I could start my slow journey back to the blankets to rest. But I felt that he had something else to say. I waited impatiently. This time he did not fool me. I was alert.

"Yourr grroup, yourr Mihloti Thearrtrre, wants to know wherre you left the skrript of *When the Rrevolution Komes!*" He had never let his eyes wander away from my face. I did likewise. I stared back at him. The swine, who did he think I was?

"They say that they want to kontinue in yourr absence!"

"I don't know anything about a script like that," My voice was inaudible with fear.

I was both happy and unhappy that night. I thought that my wife was trying to make contact with me, or just to reassure herself that I was still alive. I was unhappy about the death of my cousin Michael. He was only 22 years old, a promising, likeable young

111

lad, and the sole support of my aged father's elder brother. But I could not feel or imagine how on earth the Mihloti Black Theatre would actually send a message like the one the policeman had tried to convey to me. There was no way unless the Mihloti group wanted to be martyrs. But the flaw was that *When the Revolution Comes* was not a script. It was a lengthy poem that the group and I used to read to our audiences. We had long committed the poem to memory and had destroyed the copy, and I knew that the poem was not among the material the search-party had removed from my house. Also, that Colonel Visser and Heystek had asked me about the performance of this poem. Anyway, I was not surprised that they wanted to know about it. They had sent their secret agents to most of our performances. I eventually told myself that *When the Revolution Comes* must be a piece of important evidence they wanted to lay their hands on. That they were trying very hard, using all the tricks of their game.

For some reason, the small man had given me the feeling that he was the prison social worker! When he was about to leave to continue supervising Magoro, I had asked him: "Are you a social worker?"

"No." He was so surprised that he did not even sell me a dummy, or try anyway.

"I'm a Security Policeman!" as if it were an honour to be one.

I did not eat the fruit. I checked all over its surface with suspicion. I checked first the banana, then the orange and the apple. I turned the fruit this way and that to see if they had used a hypodermic needle to insert some poison. I smelt the fruit and threw it against the wall in case there was a bomb inside which was intended to explode as soon as I took a bite, blowing me to pieces. But the fruit just bounced off the wall and rolled on to the floor.

Later, out of boredom, I used the orange as my football. I watched the apple and banana shrivel, and I remember that I had a strong urge to draw the fruit as a still life, wondering where the challenge was in drawing the fruit, but remembering that many European artists were well known for their still-life drawings of fruit and bottles and chairs.

Incidentally, it was the same fruit that led to my discovering of writings on the jail walls. It happened on an occasion when I was picking up the fruit after it had bounced off the wall against which I had thrown it. The writings were faint and hidden in obscure places. I started further searches for these writings like an archaeologist. I unearthed a great deal as a result. I realized that hundreds of people must have been in this cell before me, as revealed by their memories on the walls. Some had written about loved ones. Some of the writing was so lurid that I found it difficult to believe that human minds had written all that rot. There were girls' names, the word "fuck" all over the place, bizarre drawings of the female and male sex organs, sometimes mating bodies, horrid; penises in the act of orgasm, swastika signs and others I could not decipher. I also found what looked like protest poetry. There was one with the lines:

> We shall remember
> When we are free
> We shall hang you dead too.

The poem had no author's name, which was understandable. I thought him lucky to have had a pencil in there.

Consequently, there was no part of the cell I did not explore. During my explorations, I found a piece of razor blade which became a valuable and highly guarded possession of mine. I used it to shorten my finger and toe nails. Later, when I was transferred to other prisons, I smuggled the piece of razor in with me.

I do not know what eventually happened to the fruit from van Niekerk. I left it there when I was taken away elsewhere without realizing that I would not be coming back to the cell. Rotten as the fruit might have become, it must have been useful to whoever came after me.

12. Breakfast in Cairo

It was Tuesday after Easter. This had been the longest Easter weekend of my life. The Major, who had been away for the weekend, woke us up. *Tok tok tok tok,* I could hear the baton on the steel doors and bars coming a long way down the corridors. I could hear his quick footsteps, the rattle of the keys and the banging doors as these were being opened and closed.

"Everrything all rright?"

"Yes, Major."

"Everrything all rright?" at the next door, and so on, getting nearer.

"Yes, Major," another answer would make its quiet response.

113

Then he was at 320.

"Pheto?"

"Major?"

"Everrything all rright?"

"Yes, Major."

"Everrything all rright?" and "Yes, Major" had become a kind of joke with me. For lack of anything else to do it amused me to keep the Major talking, or listening, if possible, even for one brief moment.

"I hearr you komplained!"

"Yes, Major."

"Tell me anything, any komplaint you have. I am in charrge herre."

I had the impression that he wanted everyone to know that he gave the orders on the floors that were his responsibility, and that the Security Police had better know that they were in charge only on the ninth and tenth floors.

"Yes, Major. Toilet paper."

Major went on his way. His voice receded in the same manner in which it had come my way. Nobody brought me the toilet paper I had asked for. I would have to control my bowels and not use the hole in the corner.

I knew that the Heysteks and the Vissers and the Bouwers and Magoros and Patoses and Makhomisanes were back somewhere up there on those two notorious death floors, the ninth and the tenth. And I knew that I should soon be seeing them. The hyena face of Patose, the shrivelled ear of Magoro and the frightened eyes of Makhomisane.

I had hardly finished day-dreaming about what would happen to me when 320 was opened. If Major, who was not with the Security Branch, had heard that I had complained, then the men who were responsible would have heard of it much more quickly than the Major, if they were to answer for having assaulted me.

Patose and Makhomisane looked tired after the Easter weekend. Perhaps they had gone to visit their different areas of origin, Lesotho for Patose and Vendaland for Makhomisane. Or worse still, they may have spent all Easter weekend on raids, bringing more Black people for interrogation.

There was something their eyes seemed worried about. They kept on avoiding making direct contact with me, and I did the best I could to register some reaction from their faces as I needed to

114

reassure myself and be prepared mentally for anything regarding the complaint I had lodged, which had gnawed at me all weekend. I registered nothing positive. Their faces were shifty all right, but perhaps I was speculating too much.

"Pheto, they want you upstairs," Patose told me.

I tottered up from the blankets and put my grey jacket on. My favourite jacket and refuge from their blows. I was glad that no one ever thought of telling me to take it off.

The freshness outside the cell made me realize how disgustingly I smelt. Sweat, dirt, stale clothes, cell air and other peculiar prison smells plus the stench from the toilet in the corner. I was all those smells. I had a sadistic affinity with those smells, regarding them as my bodyguards, because the smells were with me wherever I went. If I needed to be given a nickname, such as I did with them, they could have called me "Smells" — I was sure they would have done it in Afrikaans.

I had not washed since 5 March, let alone had a bath or shower. I used to get water in pint-sized plastic bottles brought to me at meal times. I used the water for drinking and for washing my face and armpits. I would go over to the toilet pail, pour some water into my cupped hands, and clean myself as best I could. I would ration the water as much as possible because I did not always have it. The amount depended on the policeman who was distributing food at the time.

On arriving at the ninth floor, Heystek wasted no time. He was in a lousy mood and was fuming like a steam engine. He was unshaven, and for once did not speak in SeSotho.

"You told the magistrate we have assaulted you. We are now facing an assault charge." He looked at me and raised his nostrils. I was certain that his nose twitched because of the smell coming from me, and that he did it instinctively to ward the smell off. But I reasoned that they were responsible for my smelly body and clothes because they had not allowed me washing facilities.

"You don't know what's coming to you. We can take you to a place where no one will ever know about your whereabouts."

At that moment Lieutenant Visser, van Niekerk and the Beast burst into Heystek's office. They had all heard that I had made a report to the magistrate.

"So, Phineas," the Beast took over even before he had sat down, clasping his massive hand on my neck and holding tight. "You have rreporrted us."

I tried to twist my neck to look at him, but it was difficult as he had a tight grip. He continued. "Did I assault you? Wherre did I hit you, heh?"

I knew the answer to that one. That he had never laid his hands on me!

I whimpered that I told the magistrate that I intended no trouble for anyone...no trouble....'

"My *Kaffertjie*, you arre going to shit yourre pants today!" and dead on time on the word "pants" he smashed both his palms on my two ears, from behind me, having quickly released the clasp on my neck just in time. The shock lifted me up and put me flat on my buttocks. My hands came up too late to protect my one already buzzing ear.

This time, I was doubly certain that I could write off the music and teaching career I had steadily built up for myself. I would have to tell the students on my release, whenever that would be, that I was through with helping them with their music problems.

"*Stan op!*" (Stand up!)

I was afraid to. Lieutenant Visser lifted me up. He seemed to enjoy using me as his weights, this Lieutenant Visser. Just then, he came into line with my smell. He told me that I smelt like a porcupine. The Beast said that I should learn to wash myself. He then insisted to the others that unless I washed, he wasn't going to be involved in assaulting me further, and he was dead serious at that. They held a debate whether I should be driven somewhere for a bath! What I could not understand was why I had to be taken elsewhere to wash when I was certain that on several occasions I had heard water splashing at Jan Vorster Square, not far from my cell, when other prisoners had their baths. Makhomisane and Patose took up the chorus when they were escorting me back to the cells afterwards.

"*Hei, monna, Pheto,*" Patose said, looking pleased with himself, "you must wash, man. You smell!"

Heystek addressed himself to the others. "I told you chaps. This one we should have long killed!"

For the first time since I was detained, van Niekerk produced a government gazette that dealt with the "Terrorism Act" and read to me the clauses relating to my detention. I remained still, unmoved and unimpressed as I had asked them from the very first day to tell me what I had been brought in for and the law under which I had been detained. It seemed as though I had to report to

116

the magistrate that I had been assaulted before I could know what my "crime" was supposed to be. I could not imagine what the magistrate had said to them. It was certain that he had taken some form of action, even though they kept on saying to me that the magistrate could not stop them. That's when I felt that the inspection by the magistrate had been a waste of time. These men run South Africa. They are a law unto themselves. The Beast had just smashed my ears a moment ago. And didn't the magistrate assure me in no uncertain terms that nothing was going to happen to me again, ever?

With his fat fingers poking into my face, van Niekerk continued to read to me the reasons for my detention: "You arre held herre underr section six of the Terrrorrism...."

I did not want to listen. There was no point. Whose Terrorism Act anyway? What part did I play in the formation of whatever law affected my being in South Africa? Bullshit!

Van Niekerk read on to the end, giving a version I had never heard before, insulting me in the process, including my "arse" in his rendition.

I did not know who or what to respond to. The Beast, just behind me, was breathing down my neck. I could perceive how close he was by his own smell, which I did not like one bit. His sweat-smell was terribly overpowering, mixed with Mum and hair oil. Then there was van Niekerk, who was making heavy weather with the government gazette. I decided Lieutenant Visser, mouthless as ever, was the one to watch for some of his quick karate chops. Heystek had been busy biting his finger nails as though he had been deep in thought. Only Makhomisane had looked as frightened as I was.

Apart from the double-handed blow on my ears by the Beast, no further assaults took place that day. Thereafter, I would be brought up from the cells every morning and made to stand until four in the afternoon.

It was on one of those occasions that yet another millionth "new one" appeared. He asked Heystek who I was and where they had dug me up, as if I had been on the run.

"He is just a small shit-house," Heystek had replied, not caring to look at me.

I was made to understand that the "new entrant" was their continental expert on Pan-Africanism. He was also supposed to know everything there was to know about the Pan-Africanist

Congress of Azania, which had been banned after its anti-pass campaign of the early sixties that had resulted in the police murdering my countrymen, women and children, at Sharpeville, Langa and other parts of South Africa. The Pan-Africanist Congress had since gone underground, and most of its leaders were exiled or had been banned, arrested or banished to some remote parts of the country where the government felt that these popular leaders of our masses would be ineffective.

He went on to give me a lecture on the Pan-Africanist Congress, as distorted a talk on the subject as he could make it, one I had never heard before. If he were ready to learn, I would have given him an illustrious one, as I was very proud of the Pan-Africanist Congress and its programme.

"Sobukwe is ourr frriend," referring to Robert Mangaliso Sobukwe, the then banned and banished founder member and first president of the Pan-Africanist Congress, and the most feared and respected Black national leader of modern Black South Africa's struggle for liberation. Sobukwe had spent nine years on Robben Island prison after having led this organization and other political events, particularly the 1963 Sharpeville upheavals. Six of the years he spent on the island were as a result of a special act of parliament — the Sobukwe Clause — being enacted to keep him under lock and key. Of course, "the Prof", as Sobukwe was popularly known, could not have been their friend. If anything, he had been a nightmare to their lives. I am certain that the "expert" was doing his best to defuse whatever resistance I still had.

He went on to ask me several questions about the Pan-Africanist Congress, if I knew so and so, about the organization's constitution, trying to convince me that it was a document intent on throwing the Whites into the sea.

He was talking a lot of rubbish, but I had learned not to argue with this lot any more. The frustration of such exercises had proved humiliating countless times before. But I was resolved to personally throw this type of White man into the sea.

When he was convinced that I "knew" little or nothing about the Pan-Africanist Movement, he dismissed me contemptuously. He swivelled on the chair he had been sitting on, turned to Heystek and told him: "this trouser's shit is not a PAK-*man*, man," stressing the first "man". PAK is the Boer's version of the Pan-Africanist Congress.

The remark relieved me. Heystek and the others were then

118

convinced that I was an underground agent for the Pan-Africanist Congress, because I had myself told them I supported the movement's policy, and that I would have carried the Pan-Africanist Congress card if it were not banned. I had also insisted on that when their line of interrogation was at one time trying to press me on the activities of the African National Congress, one of the liberation movements, which is also in exile.

Finally, and suddenly, the "expert" sitting there in his khaki tunic and withered face with heavy-rimmed glasses weighing on him, turned to me, pointing a dried-up finger at me: "My frriend, listen. Yourr Pan-Afrrikan Kongrress will not help you." He continued pointing. "Yes. You will put on a show and kill a few womens and childrren and old men. But," he boasted, "you will not touch the Afrrikanerr youth. Then you will see he kan fight. The Afrrikanerr youth...."

The policeman went into a frenzy extolling the Afrikaner youth and its bravery. By then he was foaming at the mouth and I concluded that he was mad. "If we starrted herre today, at this Botswana of yourrs, we will go rright thrrough Afrrika and we will have brreakfast in Cairro!" By that time his finger was wagging so fast in front of my bewildered eyes that I could not tell whether it was a fore- or an index finger, or any one of his fingers for that matter.

I remembered that I had read somewhere in a newspaper that Idi Amin had programmed an army exercise displaying how the Ugandan forces would take Cape Town. Under my breath I told him that he would have breakfast in Cape Town, "with your backs to the sea...you motherfuckers". I wished fervently that he had heard me.

I did not know then that soon after my release, in June 1976, instead of having breakfast in Cairo, the Afrikaner youth would be having breakfast in Soweto, pinned down by Black teenagers with stones and catapults and garbage lids and petrol bombs and pickets and strikes and burning buildings and buses, and that, whereas the Pan-Africanist Congress had not yet killed any White child or woman or old man in South Africa, the Afrikaner youth had already murdered Black children who were in a peaceful protest march against an unwanted special "Bantu Education" designed for us; and that as the spirit of Soweto engulfed the whole country, the Afrikaner youth murdered men, women and children as well, with a madness fuelled by fear.

119

13. *Two nightfalls and two dawns*

It was obvious to me that the last encounter I had experienced through these men was only the beginning, and that they had hardly started on me. They still had to get the vital information from me relating to the activities in the underground political cells they had asked me about, and about which I knew nothing, had never even heard of. Somewhere along the line I had been a victim of circumstances and coincidences which were slowly unfolding.

I could not imagine how they were going to fit me into the pattern they had woven for me. All my answers to their questions had gone in different directions from what they were after, excluding questions about Clarence Hamilton.

Clarence Hamilton was part of the new and rare phenomenon of Coloured youth who were joining the Black Consciousness Movement and identifying themselves with the Black liberation struggle in more concrete terms than had previously been the case. Coloureds, who are regarded by the régime as politically more acceptable than Blacks, did not associate as a rule with Blacks socially or politically. Clarence Hamilton and his group were therefore an embarrassment to the overtures being made by the government. On the other hand, Blacks welcomed these "rebels" into their fold. The régime was going out of its way to accept the Coloureds politically because they used the same language — Afrikaans — as their mother tongue, and also, to swell its White numbers against Blacks during this era of mounting political demands by the Blacks, who now are in no doubt that physical confrontation for their liberation is an unavoidable necessity.

In 1974, Clarence Hamilton had been detained for distributing leaflets which urged Coloured youth at his school in the Coronationville and New Clare communities, near Johannesburg, not to celebrate Republic Day, which falls on 31 May. The day marks the final victory of the Boers in the formation of the present political South Africa as we know it today. Before sentence was passed, Clarence had been allowed out on bail and had been expected to return later for sentencing by the court, which had found him guilty as alleged. Clarence went into exile to the neighbouring state of Botswana.

I was accused of helping him make his escape into exile, of

having recruited him for military training, of having engaged in that type of activity since my return from London, of having left the country several times without valid travel documents, of meeting and planning with freedom fighters in Botswana and Mozambique to infiltrate into South Africa for armed insurrection, of having received military training myself and of having conducted underground cells, proof of which was the missing pages of the passport then in their possession.

But Clarence had been an associate of mine before he had engaged in the activities that had led to his detention. The association had continued during his trial and travails until his disappearance. If Clarence Hamilton had been acting for others, and if his colleagues had told the Security Police during "interrogation" that I was one of them, as Patose had hinted to me, then I was not aware that I was supposed to have belonged to their group. However, Patose's revelation was not an example I could go by. It could easily have been a ruse by the police to tempt me to talk.

I thought I had scored a victory by reporting to the visiting magistrate that I had been assaulted. For a few days thereafter they had let me be, although they continued to have me brought up from the cells to stand from morning till afternoon. I had already lost count of the number of times that had happened.

I believed that that would be the new routine they were going to follow until I talked. Although I was beginning to get used to the standing, my legs were slowly swelling, and boredom had begun to take a heavy toll on me. My feet and legs were becoming clumsy, dragging, and were losing their walking rhythm. I began to experience needle-like pain attacks, particularly around the ankles.

I looked up from the dark interior of the cell to notice the frightening white of an eye in the peep-hole of the steel door. It was about nine in the morning. The suddenness of the sight had shocked me. When its owner realized that I had spotted it, he moved over to the wire-meshed iron-barred window. It was Makhomisane.

"Hey, man. Wake up!"

I had developed a great deal of contempt for Makhomisane. He knew that he was a frightened man. On several occasions he had tried to exert his borrowed power over me, until the day I had told him that with circumstances even, I would fight him until I killed him. Although small himself, he was bigger than me. Still I told him I would fight him, I was certain I could kill him because I was so bitter that I would find the extra strength needed. For us to win our struggle for liberation, the Makhomisanes of this world would have to go. I do not know why I had not heard the rattle of the keys that day, but there he was. He opened the door of the cell.

"Get ready. Take your things. Maybe you are going home!"

Makhomisane helped me pick up the odds and ends — face cloth and soap, toothpaste and brush — that had since been allowed — thanks to the people outside, wives, relatives, lawyers and some church people. Of course, I took my jersey and eternal jacket also. I could not understand the reason for Makhomisane's anxiety. "Maybe you are going home," he kept on repeating.

Hell! My heart pumped excitedly, frightened, even at the prospect of going home! It could not be true. Perhaps I have defeated them, I thought to myself. If so, then it was damn easy!

I was to realize a few minutes later that the Black Security Police did not know anything about the day-to-day programmes at Jan Vorster Square, except to fetch detainees and to attend to other menial jobs. The whole manoeuvre turned out to be the most cruel ruse of my entire time in detention.

I was signed out at the Major's office as a transfer to the Brixton Police Station, ten minutes' drive from Jan Vorster. Brixton Police Station is the murder, robbery and theft headquarters, where the hardest Black "criminals" were broken during questioning. Every adult Black man has heard of Brixton. Black women get taken there too for vicious assaults during so-called police investigation. Brixton is already legendary for its mercilessness.

In a while, Heystek and Lieutenant Visser took me out into the street to get into their car. I saw Johannesburg, felt her pulse and looked all round, wishing I had a million eyes that could take it all in. The sky, sun, the people, cars and passing buses forever loaded with Black people. I wished I could absorb everything in that short time. Heystek and Visser led the way, Makhomisane covering me from behind. They all had their hands in their pockets until we climbed in to their little pale-coloured Ford Cortina car. I knew that it was the end of me. I would agree to everything, anything. It would be better to be sentenced for a long jail term than to go through the Brixton mill.

But the journey to Brixton was only a ploy to enable them to account for my absence from the Major's area of responsibility.

The Major would not have bothered about my non-return. As far as he was concerned, I had been signed for, and therefore was out of his jurisdiction.

At Brixton Police Station, Heystek and Visser merely "registered" me into the police station. My clothes, face cloth and other small belongings were left there. I was immediately taken back to Jan Vorster Square. I was sneaked in through the back door, via the underground garages, up in the lift to the tenth floor, this time into the Beast's office, where the standing routine was continued. I was made to face away from the door. In front of me there was a void, a window whose venetian blinds were closed.

Heystek and Visser, and many other White police who had suddenly gathered, went out and left me with Makhomisane. The Beast blasted his way into his office and started rummaging in his cabinets. "Make him stand strraight, at one spot, orr arre you sympathizing with him? Is he yourr brrotherr?"

Poor Makhomisane abbreviated what I had also heard. He passed the insults he had received on to me. "You hear him, man!"

When the Beast had gone out again, I took advantage of Makhomisane's humiliation. "Who is he?"

"Struwig. And I hate him with his small thin crooked legs and big body. He even beats his wife up. He was in court the other day for assaulting her!" Makhomisane really indulged himself.

He ceased to be the Beast. I told myself that I would need to remember his name for all eternity.

By my intuition, I reckoned that it was long past four o'clock in the afternoon and I had not been taken down to the cell as was normal procedure. At about this time, a completely new policeman arrived on the scene, just when I was beginning to think that I knew them all by then. He had given me no bother with his name. He had introduced himself as Bidou or Pitou, making fun over the fact that our names were alike.

Bidou had a permanent sneer, a scar on his bottom lip, and eyelashes like an albino. He had meticulously gone over the documents relating to me from the bundles the search-party had taken from my house. He was more interested in the passport, and had asked me questions about guns and explosives and communists. He saw my judo membership card which I had received when I was a member of the North London Judo Club. The card became of special interest to him. It led him to tell me that he too was a *karateka*, and lo! he at the same time

123

began a karate demonstration.

"Yeeeeeaaaa...ish!" as he turned and twisted and twirled his body and arms and punched the air, stopping the punches half an inch from my face, his shirt swooshing, with more yells like "Yaaaaaa...!" Bidou looked like a beast gone wild.

When I moved back and out of range of his punches, he told me that I should not worry as he had been trained to stop the punches just before impact. He asked me if I knew any *kata*. I said that I did not. He nonetheless forced me to do one, without me knowing what karate war-cry to utter. The whole incident was both funny and humiliating. Again, for the millionth time, I wished that I were tall and strong, backed also by a thorough knowledge of karate. That during the time he had given me to show my wares in the art, I would "accidentally" belt this monster in front of me so that he would be unable to recover, mutilate his ribs and throat and eyes and pull his intestines out. Having finished with him, I would turn to this shadow called Makhomisane, cut him on the bridge of the nose with one swipe and make a blind run for freedom, taking with me any moving policeman trying to stop me.

The big van Niekerk came into the room and a little conference ensued. Thereafter, there was further interrogation from Bidou which lasted for some three hours. By then, I could feel through the quietness permeating the ghostly interrogation headquarters that all the rank and file had left. That only murderers remained behind, to do their ghastly dirty work quietly in the stillness of the night.

The telephone shattered the eeriness, made terrible echoes in the corridors behind me. Bidou lifted the receiver. All I heard from him were grunts. Nothing sensible, or loud enough to bring me into the picture. I concluded that it had been intended. In a short while, Colonel Visser and Magoro arrived to relieve Bidou and Makhomisane. Van Niekerk, who had been somewhere in those offices, emerged to be relieved too.

With Colonel Visser, it had been back to square one. Back to 5 March. We were back to the same questions and the same answers. The difference was that it was then 7 April, and late into the night, and yet more new people had entered the picture who included karate demonstrations as a process of interrogation.

By the time the next telephone ring jarred the still night again, after roughly the same interval as the first, I quickly realized that the phone had been the signal for a new relief crew to interrogate and for the electric-button steel door to be opened for the arrivals as it could not be worked from the outside. I also realized that that would be the routine for the night. If one's mind overworked itself, as mine did then, the Security Police operational patterns registered very quickly. This alertness, for a sensitive, albeit tired mind, was good, in the sense that I quickly eliminated unnecessaries, thus saving myself energy for other important instincts for survival.

Bouwer, as large as life, had been the leader of the new team which included the little man I had earlier suspected was the prison social worker during my first encounter with him. All the members of this team called the little man "Smallie". The Bouwer team was completed by another named Liebenberg. I had named this team the "Picnic Brigade" because they came in with cake, coffee jars and sweets on which they gorged themselves during interrogation. This, incidentally, was the funniest team and the most bizarre too.

Each night Bouwer would enter the door at the head of the team. He would raise his right hand in the Hitler salute and shout "Sieg Heil!" to me.

The first night he did this I pretended stupidity. He repeated the act. When I still did nothing, he forced me to imitate him. I had to obey.

"*Dis reg!*" (That's right!) "Rrememberr that!"

Soon after, he would begin to question me, then emit a thin long whistle like a bird, holding his head as still as if he were dead, like a rattlesnake prior to striking.

"What's that?" Bouwer would ask me.

"It's a whistle."

Whistle. Thin, long and eerie, with his lips quivering to effect the correct dynamics, his head not moving, as though hypnotized, or in the act of hypnotizing someone.

"What's that?" he would ask again, which made me realize that my first attempt had been wrong.

"It's a bird," I would try.

Bouwer would say I was not as dumb as he had thought I was. That I was getting nearer to the correct answer, but not quite yet.

Another whistle. The same as the other times. After cracking my mind, I repeated that it was a bird, wondering at the same time if I should respond to all the humiliations I was suffering, as that had nothing to do with the matter of my "activities".

"No. It's not a bird. It's a canary!" he said with triumph.

Me: "It's a canary."

More whistling and hypnotic transformations.

Bouwer: "What is it doing?"

Me: "It is whistling."

Bouwer: "No. It's not whistling. It is singing. You will sing like a canary!"

The message went home.

Most times Bouwer was there, he made me imitate him and his canary, a legacy of Jan Vorster that I can still do to this day.

Smallie was also a strange one. He would offer me cake and coffee and sweets, saying that the sweets would help my dry mouth so that when I started to talk it would be easy.

Liebenberg had his own characteristics too. He would limp and come close to me, very close, butt me with his shoulder as if he were spoiling for a fight, look at me from my feet to my head, move his head deliberately up and down, then shake it from left to right. Suddenly, with no lead-in at all, he would say: "*Jou poephol, man, jy moet net gemoer word!*" (Your "penis", man, you should just be beaten up!)

When I was growing up, we boys knew "*poephol*" to mean penis. We had often sworn at each other by calling out "*poephol*", referring to that part of the anatomy. Indeed, even today, *poephol* simply refers to penis in the ghetto, except for those Blacks who are very sophisticated in Afrikaans. So I did not feel offended, for after all we used to play about with the word. I now know that the cripple-minded blighter meant "arsehole". This changes the picture and my reaction considerably. I am offended retrospectively and I am paying back in kind: "Well, Liebenberg, your arsehole too, man!"

As far as questions were concerned, Smallie had little to ask. He mostly nattered on about his family, his grandchildren, and then ran out to fetch hot water for their coffee. He would be continuously gobbling up the sweets. But on one occasion he too lost his temper.

"Fuck off. Now tell us. We have been nice to you, giving you ourr sweets and koffee. You make us miss ourr sleep and ourr families, and the soonerr you do this, the betterr it will be forr you."

His favourite pastime had been to remind Bouwer to ask me about "that one!"

Bouwer would oblige and enjoy himself.

"Ja, Phineas, you and yourr White woman," meaning Elina Templin. "How many times have you been to herr bedrroom, I mean when herr husband was not therre at home?" Then he would look at Smallie, whose eyes would be as small as himself, mirthful with smiles. "I mean, between men, you kan tell us. Afterr all, you got away with it. We all brreak the law at times. And that's yourr luck!"

The last team of the night comprised Heystek, Lieutenant Visser and Patose. They came in at about four in the morning and would interrogate until dawn. At this time, it had been Lieutenant Visser who was keenest.

"You still have nothing to say, Pheto? About yourr frriends and activities and passporrt?"

"I have said all there is to say," I would tell him.

Usually, Heystek and Visser left me in Patose's care then. They ended up in another room somewhere nearby. It was clear to me that they were all waiting. I did not know what it was they were waiting for, but they all certainly knew that whatever it was, it would happen. So we all played the waiting game. For two nights and three days the process did not change. All the teams had come in at their scheduled times, and had left at their finishing time. In the meantime, I had stood still. No shifting had been allowed me. Nothing. I was reminded several times to stare ahead and to remain still.

The night of the 8th was the worst. Colonel Visser would stand up, remove his gun out of its holster, examine it, size me up, then check the time and put the gun back into its holster. He had done this several times. Each time my hands dripped with sweat. Magoro had complemented him by moving away from me, away from the line of fire, as it were. I was so hot I felt like asking them if I could take my jacket off.

Then Visser went to the door behind me, with the gun in his hand, and the light went off suddenly. I panted for breath as if the darkness was drowning me. But before I could even catch the air I was so desperately gasping for, the light came on again. My hair moved. On the second occasion the scene was re-enacted, a loud shot rang out behind me next to my head.

Shit, I said to myself, *he's shot me. The sadist swine has shot me!* Just as quickly the light came on.

I waited for the pain and the blood. Only sweat poured down the inside of my palms. In the light I saw Magoro's pimple-black face near my own, his half-ear almost touching mine, with his nostrils inflated. During the darkness, he had quickly and nimbly moved towards me, but I had not heard any movement then. All I had felt were my eyes straining in the dark as if they would jut out of my head in an effort to see everything.

"What was that?" Visser asked me as soon as he returned to the desk. I told him that it was a gun.

"Oh, you know about guns then."

Visser pointed the gun at me. I almost pleaded with him not to do that as there could be an "accident", but I kept quiet. I thought about my daughter Phello, who was only nine months old when they took me away. I was longing to see her. I wished to see her before I died, if they were going to kill me, and I wondered if they would agree if I asked for permission to see Phello.

Before Visser and Magoro were relieved, Magoro took his turn too, as soon as Visser had gone out of the room. During his master's presence, Magoro would be a mere robot which said nothing, heard nothing and, one might say, a robot which saw nothing too, a perfect picture of docility.

"So, you are an educated man, Pheto."

"No. I'm not."

"Look, man. Why can't we be logical? Education, logic. It's simple. I ask you the questions, you answer me. Now, that's logicality! And we all go to sleep. Even you too. You will go home to your children."

In all his Black life, Magoro will never smell the authority whereby he will order any man's release. He had only been indulging in wishful thinking, and he must have known that.

When Heystek and Lieutenant Visser came in to relieve, I felt some respite. I knew that dawn could not be far off, and that I was still alive. I had hope in the dawn, and I would remember a favourite line in a poem that I liked to read:

"And each fighter will see the dawn."

My legs were clearly swollen. They had grown very hard to the touch, as hard as new lemons. Each time I secretly pressed and felt around with my hands, the swelling did not yield as I thought it would. The pains were coming at intervals, like birth pains, I suppose. Like needles wanting to come out of my flesh. From the feet upwards past the ankles and beyond the knees and thighs, the swollen roundness was the same size. My legs were shapeless, straight and stiff as poles, and thick. The canvas jogging shoes that I wore had stretched beyond their capacity and the shoelaces had become stiff, despite the fact that at the start they were loose. If nothing happened soon, at least the laces would break. Now and then, whether I liked it or not, I had to bend down from the waist to find some relief, as if the upper body was weighing too much on my legs, causing them to shoot the numerous pains. There was nothing my interrogators could do to stop me from bending down. As soon as I had raised my trunk to an upright position again, the armies of pain would rush back in a flash. At times I thought that the pain was in my mind, that it would soon be over.

"Pheto," that was Patose, who had woken up from one of his many naps during the long interrogation session. "Have you not yet fallen, man?"

If that was what everyone had been waiting for, then they did not have long to wait. I might as well be ready for what was to happen when that moment arrived.

It was morning again. The second dawn but the third day. I could tell it was morning by looking at the slits in the venetian blinds. I learned where to look to have some idea of what the time was. At the corners where the blinds did not fit well into the window frames and at other places like that. Then there would be the hustle and bustle in the offices and corridor behind me, of typists and clerks and other Security Police members as they greeted each other on arriving for duty. Then those who were not connected with my interrogation but who knew that I was there in the room, the Christmas party people, would come into the room, inquisitive and surprised that I was still on my feet.

It was as if we were engaged in a marathon. They, like jaguars waiting to pounce, and I, doing my best to be on guard, aware for my safety.

But I was weakening by the minute. The pain was unbearable. Last night's shooting or whatever it was Colonel Visser had fired behind me; the "logicalities" of Magoro, including when he told me that I must be a communist, clinching the statement by comparing me to Timol, an Indian who had died in the hands of the Security Police during "interrogation". Timol was supposed to have "jumped" from the same floor where I was. That, as a communist agent, Magoro said, I would rather die than divulge information, alluding to brain-washing by communists. Poor

129

Magoro. The view he was espousing must have been told him by his bosses, who instead had succeeded in brain-washing the likes of Magoro so that he hardly knew whether he still had a brain or not.

"You must be Timol's friend," Magoro had boasted, walking about during the absence of his boss.

"Why do you say that, Magoro?"

"You behave exactly like him!" he finished.

To me, what Magoro had said was a revelation. It answered many questions that had never been resolved about Timol's death. How could Magoro have known that I behaved "exactly like him" (Timol), if he had not been one of the torturers on the night of Timol's death? Magoro had not been the only one who had mentioned Timol during the last two nights of my torture. Smallie had said that I should do the same as the Indian that "ran and jumped".

I had to weaken. Everything had saddled me with anxieties that wore me down. As the day progressed, it was nearly the same as the occasion of the Christmas party. Their visits were more frequent. Different interrogators, each savouring the rich cake that was about to be eaten. Gradually, it was Lieutenant Visser who had been exerting more pressure, sometimes running into the room at the double, shooting questions even before reaching the spot where I stood. Patose became fresher too. His long ears were pricking. They all seemed to sense that the end was near. My condition also convinced me that it could not be too far off. I did not know how the whole process would resolve itself. I looked at the ill-fitting parts of the blinds to assess what the time could be. I could not last another night.

My mind was reeling, debating whether it would be better to agree to anything they might suggest, if only to save myself suffering further, or invent anything they might lap up. Again I wished to see Phello. She suddenly started haunting me, coming in and going out like a vision in front of my eyes, laughing and giggling as children do in their innocence. I also remembered Benzo. I was sweating and smelling and the jacket made my predicament worse. My mind had collages of Benzo, Phello, pain, worry, what to tell them and other confusing pictures.

Lieutenant Visser jumped in and at that moment I was whimpering, bending, going down despite his command that I should stand straight. He lifted me up, his face full of anxiety.

Patose came in closer to help Visser if he was needed. It was the moment they had been waiting for.

"What happened? Yourr passporrt. What happened to the missing pages?" Visser was hissing through his clenched teeth and bulging neck.

"I went to East Germany. I tore the pages out," I said in halting speech, remembering a journey a friend of mine took to East Germany. I wondered why that had not come into my memory earlier, instead of at this late hour when I was desperate with pain. I thought that my lie would work and I was beginning to believe my inventions.

"Then, why did you not throw the passporrt away? Why did you keep it?"

Silence. I had not been prepared for that one, simple as it sounded.

"You arre lying. What happened to this passporrt?" Visser went on, concentrating on the passport only.

"Tommy Mohajane borrowed it from me and he went to Lesotho. He went via Jan Smuts Airport," I lied again.

Tommy Mohajane is a friend of mine living in London as a political exile. He skipped the country during the Pan-Africanist Congress upheavals of the early sixties. There was no way they could reach Tommy. For a while, they checked from an album with photos of most of my countrymen then living in exile. Tommy's photo was there, and we almost looked alike. For a short while they chased the shadow I had thrown at them.

Then Visser was back. "Why did yourr frriend go to Lesotho?"

"I don't know. He did not tell me!"

"Then why did you tearr the pages out?"

"To hide the fact of the visit."

Visser was ready for the answers I offered. "You kould have left the pages therre. How would we know!"

The pains I was going through were helping Visser. I could not think straight or concentrate and prepare well. If only he would leave me alone!

"No. I sent the passport to East Germany." I was groping all over the place.

"What forr?"

"So they could do a more professional job of it there.' I did not know what else to say.

"But you kould do it yourrself!"

131

"I did then!"

"It's not possible!" he shrieked. He took the passport forcefully from the desk, where it had been left with some of the papers that they had taken from my house. They had chosen some which they considered more important than others. The passport was one of them. He showed me how it was NOT possible. The passport would have fallen apart if I had torn any page out of it. When I believed that it was indeed not possible to eliminate some pages, Visser showed me that it CAN be done!

"O God, what can I say now…"

"The trruth…you tell us…"

Eventually, I offered a solution. I bargained with them. I told him that they could advance any reason and I would accept it. I would write the statement corroborating whatever they suggested, and I would sign it under oath. But Visser would not accept it.

"You arre going to tell us…" was all he would say.

Many other questions were included. Questions on military engagements, what group I belonged to, whether it was the African National Congress or the Pan-Africanist Congress — though I had already denied the former. When and how "my people" would re-enter South Africa and from what point, whether Clarence Hamilton and his friends would be in the group, and finally, where the military training was conducted.

Patose had witnessed all this without batting an eyelid. He had shown no feeling or sympathy for me despite the fact that I was Black like him and had been under severe stress and pain. He must have seen that happen many times before and had assisted in torturing other Blacks.

Finally, the confession they all had been awaiting came suddenly, as I could not endure any more. To hell with it! They could do as they damn well pleased. Enough is enough!

Visser could not think any more either. He seemed to have givenup.

"You have told us all sorrts of lies. What is the trruth? Tell us the trruth now." He almost pleaded with me, with a kind of bark through his teeth, his neck showing thick veins, still holding the passport between his hands pressed to the lapels of my jackets. He held me so tightly that I thought he was choking me to death.

I told him that I was ready. But he wanted to be sure. He could not imagine what I would say.

"Yes. It is the truth now. No more. And the truth is that I do not know what has happened to the missing pages of my passport! I don't know any of the Coloured people except Clarence Hamilton, and I am not a Communist. That is all!"

I felt very tired after that. The silence in the room was stunning. Only my breathing and whimpering could be heard.

His disbelief was unimaginable! I must have been the devil himself. He sucked in a deep breath. "Is that the trruth?"

"It is the truth."

Patose was still as cold as ice. Visser hesitated, then went out, slowly this time. I remained standing, with my hands supporting the upper half of my body on my knees, breathing heavily, sweating, the image of Phello coming and leaving my vision all the time. It seemed like a century of waiting, but he was soon back.

"Sit down."

I did not believe that he had actually said that I could sit down. My ears were playing games with me, I thought, perhaps because it was what I most wanted to hear. If I sat down in error, I would expose myself to more of his brutality. He had better repeat what he had said. I remembered that at one time he had made me "sit" without a chair.

I took a long time trying to sit down. It seemed as though I could not do so any more. My body was dying to, but the joints in my body would not obey my desires. The ankles would not move. I must have been crazy to want to continue after two nights and three days. I felt like begging Patose to carry me to the chair on which he had been sitting most of the time. I appealed with my eyes, but Patose did not respond. He brought his chair nearer me, mostly because he wanted to leave, as it must have been nearing his knocking-off time. He rammed the chair into me, just behind me. The action had lifted me, only for me to flop into the chair, my knees still straight. Then the pains all over my body were worse than when I had been standing.

"Arre you rready to wrrite now?" Lieutenant Visser asked me even before I could get my thoughts together.

"Yes."

"That you trried to help the Kolourreds?"

"Yes."

"And that you knew about militarry trraining?"

Members of the Christmas party were back. They all chatted at the same time, just as they had done at the beginning of the long process. It seemed as though they were celebrating the fact that I had at last broken down. To them it was a triumph. Had Bouwer not told me that I would sing like a canary? That I had not been the first Black bull they had interrogated, that other bulls had kept them up for seven days or more, but that in the end they had also sung like canaries? I told Bouwer "yes" he warned me, and "yes" I was singing like a canary.

The anger of the interrogators seemed to have blown itself out. They were now talking to me as though I were a human being, as though they had been doing that since they had ordered my detention. As though none of them had ever laid a hand on me. Lieutenant Visser even asked me what time it was. I told him that I thought that it must have been going on for four in the afternoon. It turned out it was three. He even asked me if I had had any hallucinations, asking what day of the week it was. I made a few guesses but I missed.

This time, all the White policemen who had been involved had their usual conference right in front of me. The most prominent were van Niekerk, the two Vissers, Bouwer and Heystek. The conference had decided that I should be driven to the Brixton Police Station to be signed out and to retrieve the few articles of mine that had been left there. Then again, they changed and decided on collecting my belongings without me, as well as booking me out in my absence, that is my "absence presence" or vice versa, if you like. In the meantime, the others wanted me to start writing the "statement".

In a little while, they were "back with me" from Brixton Police Station. Van Niekerk typed out a letter explaining that I had been brought back from Brixton Police Station. The letter was to be presented to the Major, who would then sign it as an acknowledgement that I was back and under his jurisdiction again.

Patose and Makhomisane part carried, part supported and part walked me to the lifts to take me to the cells after my "two nights at the Brixton Police Station ten minutes' drive from Jan Vorster Square on the tenth floor of Jan Vorster Square!" There was no question that I could walk on my own without aid. Colonel Visser and van Niekerk led the entourage as we approached the lifts after having passed the remote control electric steel door from which we had emerged, and which had just as quickly been shut.

Suddenly there was a commotion from the leaders, Colonel Visser, van Niekerk and a few others. It was as if we were cattle in a small enclosure trying to make a break for it. Colonel Visser had spun round, his hands raised about his head, his face as pale as snow, his lips dry and eyes wild. Everyone shouted and tried to hide me. Patose and Makhomisane attempted to force me to the ground, behind the massive column of those in front. I fought back instinctively, wondering at what was happening, thinking that they were about to throw me into the street below, as they had done with the others. I believed then that the whole charade of the two nightfalls and two dawns had been a ploy to reduce me and take me off guard so that I should present them with no great resistance. For a brief while, I even thought that freedom fighters had arrived to rescue us. Instead, my eyes saw a rainbow at the end of the storm!

My wife had suddenly appeared from the very lift that was to take me down. Apparently she had not telephoned for permission to bring me clean clothes and some food, and there was no way in which they could have known who would emerge from the lift. She must have seen me first because I remember that she called me and screamed, that she tried to break through their column to reach me. She had no chance because there was a whole maze of them. I dared not respond, but the desperate anxiety in her voice and her efforts to reach me made me realize that she had been aware that I was in a terrible shape. I did the best I could to peep through and under their long arms and steal glimpses of her. I winked and bobbed my head up and down and hopped about, but the cramped space with so many people, some of whom were fat and huge, made it awkward. They could not push me back into the corridor from which we had emerged because the electronic mechanism of the door had been manipulated to close it, and the clod that operated it was as stupid as all of them. He did not have the innate intelligence to sense the danger in which his friends had found themselves. He had only been taught to work to certain given orders. This was one of the many times that their collective stupidity had been a blessing to me! By the time I had been pushed into the other lift, it was too late.

I did not know what had eventually happened to Deborah. In the lift, Colonel Visser asked me who the woman near the lift was. I told him that it was my wife. Patose asked me if I had seen her.

"*U 'mone?*"

"Yes!"

14. *Major Booysens*

Cell 320 on the third floor must have been allotted to a new detainee. I was now on the second floor, in cell 201, the cell where I started "writing" my prison poems. The poem "There is no sun in there", describing exactly what it says, was born in cell 201.

Many nights I had debated my next move as I lay on the pillowless grey blankets. For three days I could not walk. One morning, a uniformed member of the police force called Joe had been distributing food to the cells. He realized that the previous day's food cartons were all where he had left them, just inside, beside the iron bars.

"Are you not eating?" he asked me from where he was standing at the door. He could not come in any further. His key allowed him access only as far as the steel door. The key to the inner iron-barred steel door was kept by the Security Police on the tenth floor.

I told Joe that I could not walk. I told him what they had done to me. As he was listening, he kept on taking furtive glances down the corridor. No one was allowed to speak to political detainees. Joe knew it too.

"What can I do? You must eat because we need people like you!" Joe had advised me.

I tried for his sake to prop myself on my elbows. I could not believe that I had heard him correctly. Could Joe be one of their traps, or could it be he really wanted to help and demonstrate his solidarity with me and the other detainees?

I said that he could try and slide the carton he had just brought to me through the door. If it should spill, then that would be too bad, at least I would smell the food.

Joe pushed the fresh carton hard. I saw it come. He had aimed well and it stopped next to me as I caught it.

When he locked the steel door, he was not smiling. His face was an angry shining mask, heavy with dignity. I tried to imagine what he was thinking, but I could not. I felt a strong liking for him. His words of support made me cry for a long time before I attempted to eat. When I tried to, my mouth had no desire for the food. Joe's solidarity was all I had needed. I felt emotionally strengthened. I acknowledged that sometimes the fight for liberation had support in unexpected quarters.

"Arre you all rright?" *Tok tok tok tok.* Key rattles and steel doors

136

make hollow harsh noises that carry a long way. The corridors echoed with footsteps and cold unsympathetic voices.

"Yes, *Nkosi* Major." (Yes, king Major.)

When the Major reached cell 201, he asked if I was back. He knew that I was back. He had himself signed the letter from van Niekerk.

"You werre upstairrs, werre you?"

"Yes. I was in cell 320."

"Arre you all rright?"

"I'm fine!"

Many days passed in which nothing happened. There was no point in complaining to anyone. The magistrate had promised that nothing would be done to me but it had happened. It had been worse than the sessions of assault I had received from van Niekerk and Lieutenant Visser, Heystek and Struwig. Had the magistrate only meant that physical assaults would stop, but that torture could be condoned because the police would not lay their paws on my body?

The keys made their usual noise in my door and Smallie showed his little face. "How is yourr condition, Pheto?"

"I'm fine."

"You must not stay in 'bed' all the time. You must exerrcise some time. Move arround. Yourr legs will be orright!" he smiled.

I did not reply. I wondered why this man had only come to see how I was without taking me to the tenth floor. That was unusual, and I wondered what had happened to the magistrate. He had said he would be back every two weeks. Anyway, the police play games with us detainees. They could take us away to a place where the magistrate would never find us, such as Brixton Police Station on the tenth floor! That afternoon, the magistrate arrived. I told him that I was fine.

After the magistrate had left, Makhomisane showed his shining miserable face. I immediately compared and contrasted his weak face to the strong one of Joe, the policeman. Makhomisane told me to come with him. As I reached the door, he took his handcuffs and locked up my wrists. I complained that I had never been locked in handcuffs since I had been detained, except once when I was taken to the doctor. Makhomisane said that it was a new directive that all political detainees be handcuffed without exception as one of us had tried to escape, and that he, Makhomisane, nearly shot him dead. He said that he was sorry he had missed.

137

I checked the story later, soon after I was out. It was true. One detainee, Trevor Bloem, made a bid to run for it. Makhomisane, who was escorting him then, drew his revolver, aimed, shot at Bloem, and missed. He hit the wall leading to one of the lifts on the east side, one of the many routes to the cells. I heard Makhomisane's seniors making jokes at his poor marksmanship, asking him how many target shooting practices he had done.

Trevor Bloem, who also belonged to this group of Coloureds, had been detained on arriving at Jan Smuts Airport from a trip abroad. He had found a "reception" committee awaiting him, and when his luggage was searched some documents, according to the police, proved the need for his detention.

Trevor told me that on the day of the shooting, he had seen a chance to run for it and he took it. He didn't care, he said, where he ran to as long as he could make it. He also did not think that anyone would shoot inside those heavily populated corridors! Now he knew better. He said that he stood and raised his hands as soon as he heard the report of the gun and the accompanying ricochet of the bullet on the wall in front of him. He had been terribly lucky because they still could have shot him even if his hands were raised to the heavens! The cover-up would come later.

The directive to handcuff me was followed any time they had to escort me somewhere, and remained in force for the rest of my detention period. I would stretch out my hands in readiness as soon as someone arrived to take me somewhere. One day I did that to Colonel Visser, who seemed embarrassed by it, as if he did not know that his directive to have us bound in that manner had long since been routine. He declined to use the handcuffs on me, saying that a man like me would never try to escape. He was wrong: I have no inclination to play the house nigger in South Africa. Given the chance, I would have run for it.

"Makhomisane, where am I going?" I asked him, remembering the last time he had come to fetch me from 320. I asked him even though I knew he could not tell me. He might not even have known.

Makhomisane told me to shut up. He said that I was in the habit of asking questions and always looking all over the place. He finished by saying that I should walk with my head facing the front, straight, and quiet.

We took an unusual route. We finally stopped at an office with the words "Criminal Investigation" printed on the door. A White man of burly build and with a heavy pair of spectacles sat inside. He asked me in and showed me a seat, which I took. He then ordered Makhomisane out. I saw Makhomisane wondering what to do with himself. He looked very unhappy that he had been told to stay outside. It was as though I had been lifted to a higher echelon than himself.

After chatting about a lot of unrelated issues, Major Booysens had introduced himself, in both the official languages.

"I'm Majorr Booysens, Crriminal Investigatorr. I'm told that you have been assaulted."

Major Booysens produced the notes that the magistrate had made, already typed. He read the notes to me. They were correct. Everything had been faithfully reported, some of it verbatim.

"Yes. They did assault me."

"Do you want to make a charrge by wrriting a statement, orr I take one frrom you? And kan you identify the men who assaulted you at a parrade?"

I told Major Booysens that a parade was not necessary as I knew every one of them, but he told me that it was police investigative routine.

I agreed to make a statement but declined to go to the identification parade. I said that I wanted to have the statement on record, but dared not say anything incriminating while I was still in detention, at the mercy of the very people I would be laying a charge against. I had had enough. I further mentioned that I did not think that there was anyone who could offer me protection, so the whole exercise had no point. I think Major Booysens appreciated my fears.

On the way back to the cell, Makhomisane asked me what Major Booysens had been saying. I was tempted to tell him to shut up as he had done to me, that he always wanted to know everything, even if it did not concern him. But I decided to try and rub something in.

"I made a charge against you and we are going to court."

"Me too!" he said, hanging his long lip out.

"Yes, (swine) you too!" I lied to him. I was aware that he was new in the Security Police branch. He would easily get scared, and if that gave him some sleepless nights, well and good.

Prior to leaving Major Booysens's office, I had seen a small comic booklet. I took a quick look at the Major who was busy with his files behind his desk. I immediately swiped the little book and pushed it as fast as I could under the jacket beneath the jersey. I kept my hands very close to my body as if Makhomisane had the lock of the handcuffs on tightly. I made sure that my prized property was intact as I had pushed it home hurriedly after I had stolen it.

I read the booklet from Major Booysens's office so many times that I eventually knew every word of that particular American war sequence by heart. It had something to do with the war in Japan.

15. *Present from Colonel Visser*

On 11 May, Magoro peeped into the cell. He looked important, as he always did, as though he had something special to tell me. If one did not know him, one would have had the impression that he was the kindest Black Security Policeman who sympathized with us detainees. But Magoro was an opportunist. I remembered the day he had brought the fruit from their chief, van Niekerk. He had handed the fruit out with such a flourish, as if he himself had bought the fruit for us with his own money. However, on this occasion he quickly handcuffed me as he led me to the tenth floor. We ended up on the ninth though.

Along the way, we passed other prisoners and both Black and White policemen going about their duties, and ghetto people who had come to inquire about their arrested next-of-kin — husbands and sons or brothers or sisters. I must have appeared a hardened criminal to all these people. Within the walls of Jan Vorster Square Police Station, prisoners were not handcuffed and everybody knew that to be the order of the day. So, without these people knowing that I was a political prisoner, it was plain from the manner in which they stared at me that they thought me to be one of the dangerous criminals. My demeanour was also different. Black prisoners in South Africa always cower. I walked tall with rebelliousness. All of us political prisoners were unafraid, particularly after we had been interrogated. Before interrogation, we had the fear of the unknown that might befall us. Whether one's balls were going to be squeezed with a pair of pliers or whether one would be given electric shocks, through the same balls, and so on. However, that over, we walked with pride and were not ashamed. Our resolve, whatever the outcome, remained unshaken and strong. We knew that we had a cause. If we broke, as

140

did happen under the excruciating pain of torture, we might be ashamed. But within our inner selves, the battle continued.

Magoro directed me to one of the offices where Colonel Visser was waiting.

"Ja, Pheto. How arre you now?" after he had instructed Magoro to undo the handcuffs.

I told him that I was fine.

"Have you made up yourr mind to tell the magistrrate?" he said without elaborating what I had to tell the magistrate. I thought that I was being taken to court for formal charges and remand.

"Am I going to court? And what am I charged with?"

"We want you to tell the magistrrate that you knew the Kolourreds and that they werre planning militarry action against the state."

"No, Colonel Visser. I told you I did not know the Coloureds. There is nothing I can tell the magistrate about them. I would rather be tried on what you are charging me with, so I can answer for myself."

"Why do you want to be trried?" Colonel Visser challenged me.

I said to Visser that if they had nothing on me, then he should order my release.

My last reply stopped the proceedings. It would appear that they wanted to use me. Lieutenant Visser tried this stunt as soon as they had finished torturing me. Lieutenant Visser may have given them to believe that I was willing to be a state witness. I even remembered the day Lieutenant Visser had estimated that I might be sentenced to a minimum of five years in jail, or nine years maximum with an extra year for a letter I had written to a fellow-detainee to which I had owned up. The letter had been intercepted. Lieutenant Visser said that the letter had "complicated" me badly.

Magoro had been listening to the conversation, facing the door. I had been made to turn my back to the door as usual. I could hear movement behind me, doors opening and closing. Magoro shifted and cleared his throat, went out and returned to whisper something in Colonel Visser's ear.

"I have a prresent forr you!" Colonel Visser had suddenly announced as soon as Magoro had finished.

"A present for me? Am I going home?"

Home sweet home. That thought must stay with every detainee from the moment he is interned. The family was such a binding

141

existence, warm, inexplicable, though normally taken for granted. But as soon as one is removed from them the feeling of concern is as important as life itself. It is foreboding.

Colonel Visser stood up, followed by Magoro, who motioned me to follow them, chatting with me at the top of his voice.

"You look very well. Are you happy and resting down there?" Magoro asked me as they led me out of the one room into another. He was patting me on the shoulder as if we were old friends. I wondered what their new game was. As always, I was cautious.

As I entered the room, Deborah was in the centre, just about to sit on a chair and still trying to arrange her handbag, paper carrier bag and other parcels that she had with her. Patose, Makhomisane, Sons and now, Magoro and Colonel Visser were all there. Before they could steady themselves for whatever preliminaries, all hell broke loose. I half-flew and half-ran the short space, arms open, towards Deborah. The only thing I heard was her trying to call me, by which time we were in each other's arms. Her *doek* (headscarf) had fallen to the floor with the impact. By the time they reached us, it was too late. They had been totally taken aback. Colonel Visser told them to let us be whilst they stood there embarrassed, their hands limply hanging by their sides, some of them with their mouths open in surprise.

My wife may have been told that she was going to see me on that day. But I knew nothing of it. If she had not, then she must have been as surprised as I was.

"How are you, the children, the house, money, rent, food and debts and health?" I went on without giving her a chance to say anything.

Colonel Visser spoke at last. He was addressing himself to Deborah. At that moment Deborah and I turned to listen to him.

"You see, we kill him and brring him back!"

There was no better proof to me that Colonel Visser's dimness was beyond redemption.

We were told to sit down on opposite sides of a table. A tape-recording machine was set up and put on the table. We were directed to have our conversation so that it could be recorded. We were also warned not to speak in our mother tongue! Only English or Afrikaans was permitted. But to make sure that we did not speak in our vernacular, Colonel Visser had Patose and Magoro sitting in to listen to any of the vernaculars we might use. Visser had earlier on asked Deborah if she spoke Afrikaans. She had shaken her head to indicate that she did not. "We speak only Afrrikaans herre. We kan't speak English. Now, talk to yourr husband into the mikrrophone don't mentioning anything about the kase," he concluded.

Deborah looked surprised at what she had heard. I wanted to tell her that they did not speak English as a form of protest. That the Afrikaners were still fighting the Anglo-Boer War of 1899-1902, when the English and the Boers had fought for the occupation of our land.

Magoro and Patose occupied opposite sides of the table between us, checking both Deborah and me and themselves too, so much did the Whites not trust them. They did not dare leave only one of them with us. We were told that we had only fifteen minutes to finish all we had to say to each other. But we were warned not to speak about the circumstances of my detention.

Deborah answered all my anxious questions, but I could not reply to her awkward unguarded questions, and at times, I anticipated her, in which case I filled in the time with unimportant chatter. She was too keen to know things she was not supposed to know.

I hoped that she understood me when I had responded to her "Are you OK NOW?" with my "I'm fine NOW," because I had noticed her stress on the word.

I fathomed a way to talk about my car, which was really a substitute for me. That the car was battered, and that it needed a mechanic, but that it should be all right soon.

On the day I was released, as we talked late into the night, I realized that she had understood all my implied speech about the car and the mechanic. She told me also that on the day she had suddenly appeared out of the lift and had seen the condition I was in, she had contacted the lawyer and told him about the whole incident. The lawyer and church organizations had done their best to force the Security Police to release me urgently, but they had refused point-blank. An attempt had also been made to have an independent doctor visit me. That was also turned down.

We laughed when I told her that Magoro and Patose had not followed our impromptu manner of communication, such as when she rolled her hands into small fists, stamped both alternately into either of her cupped palms, as if emphasizing a point she was making, when what she was really doing was a means of inquiring if I had been assaulted.

143

I slept very well on 11 May in cell 201. I did not even smell the stink from the blankets and toilet when I had been brought back. The smell always assaulted my nostrils each time I was returned from their offices. It was the first thing that I would notice. Not so on this day. I was drunk and confused at having seen Deborah. At having touched her, on the same floor where she had last seen me as a ghost. I remembered the frock she had on, with green, gold and black flowers, the colours used by the South African liberation movements on their flags. I drew hope and strength from her spirit, because I knew that she meant that the flag had to fly, whatever the consequences. It was that important. She had told me that the children were well; that my eldest son, Gaboipeoe, had surprised her and the family by baking them a cake one day, to keep their spirits up; that Maseitshiro, who comes after Gaboipeoe, was helping her to marshal the two younger ones, Pule and Phello; that a friend, Barbara Waite, had helped her by paying the rent, and had promised to continue paying it until the day of my release, while neighbours and other ghetto friends had contributed food and meat. The same ghetto that seemed to hide itself on the day of my detention. It knew when to show its solidarity safely, which made us detained have hope, to know that we were not alone, only that we were at that moment incarcerated.

There is no doubt that the ghetto Blacks, given the chance, will surprise the régime when least expected to. What we now see is a mask that seems docile, revealing nothing. Many a time the ghetto has defended itself. It will do so again.

16. The transfer

The Vissers acted swiftly, quickly, with military precision, amazing stealthiness and very coldly. It was on 15 May. As usual, the keys and other prison noises could be heard deep in the interior of the building. These noises had a steely coldness and detachment, like echoes. I had my ears tuned in to where the noises were emanating from and my eyes elsewhere — the comic strip I had stolen from Major Booysens's office. All decisions taken on the ninth and tenth floors about detainees manifested their horror the moment the keys were thrust into our cells. We were like parcels or instruments waiting to be carted here or there, acted upon, beaten up, humiliated and so forth. No questions were expected from us, no preparations or information were given us and no answers were anticipated by us, why so much inhumanity had been perpetrated on our persons. To them it was normal. Our lot was to wait, expect, hope, anticipate the extent, and look into the pros and cons with weighing eyes.

I was lying on the eternals — the mat, the grey stenchy blankets, reading for the countless time the war comic-strip. I could then walk well as I was fit again. A little while ago, I had started exercising in the cell, beginning the physical training session with a jog, running about forty circles in the cramped space, first in the one direction, and then in the opposite one. Then I would do loosening up exercises: press ups, dips, flinging my arms, standing on my head and keeping my balance with my hands, leg stretches and others until I became exhausted. I had also started sharing the food given me with the prisoners who were escorted as carriers to serve us. I did this as a weight-reducing device, so that I ate half the ration supplied. At times I ate meat and fruit that my wife had by then been allowed to bring. She handed the food to the Vissers whenever it suited them to allow her to do so, usually once a week or once a fortnight. This would be when she had been asked to bring me a change of clothes. The weekly arrival of food and clothes was one of the indications by which I knew my family was still intact. Vice versa, my dirty clothes must have been my wife's monitoring device.

"*Grote! Grote!*" (Elder brother! Elder brother!)

If it had not been for the ghetto salutation, I am sure I would have been caught reading the comic strip, as it may well have been a policeman at the window. I had not heard the sound until the boyish voice called. No keys, of course, but nothing.

The salutation was that used by younger people in the townships whenever they needed the attention of someone older than themselves, or someone they had respect for. I recognized that, so I did not even try to hide the comic strip. During his approach to my cell, the young boy must have been stealthiness personified. I had to admire his caution and quietness in a place that echoed at the drop of a pin.

"Ya!" I answered scornfully. I was having the best of times reading the contraband. I did not even look up towards him when I answered. His voice continued. "*Grote, grote,* what's the matter? Are you sick?"

It was a Black boy's thin voice. I felt sad that he was concerned for me, inquiring if I was ill, yet I had not been encouraging to him.

"No. I'm not sick. I'm resting," I said as I woke up and went to the window, taking some blankets to stand on for extra height. In the meantime, the young man was hanging from the window latch, his fingers firmly pressed on the surface. I surmised that his feet must have been clamped on the wall like a limpet. I told him to get off because standing on the blankets I could see him comfortably, even though it was through wire gauze.

"How come they left you alone in the cell when there are fifty of us in one cell?" His question was a curious mixture of accusation, inquiry and sympathy.

I told him to rush to the corridor to see if there was anyone coming, because it was a long story and I wanted him to understand what I intended to tell him. But I knew inside me that it was not the length of what I intended to tell him that mattered, but rather our safety. He argued that it was safe, and anyway we would hear the keys or the footsteps of impending danger. He was a precocious little boy.

"Go, man!" I shouted at him.

He ran and was back in a second.

"There is no one coming," he assured me, and then continued where he had left off. "Why are you alone?"

"Well, you see, it's like this. They..." meaning the Whites in general, but I changed course. "We are Black Power prisoners. We want to fight the White man and end the passes." I tried to be very simple, pinpointing what I knew he must already know. "We raise the fist and we tell them we are not afraid of them. They are worried that if they mix us with you, we will teach you Black Power."

I thought that using words such as "politics" would take ages to explain. But I knew that by this time a lot of Black youngsters in the ghettos had heard of Black Power through the efforts of the Black Consciousness Movement which swept throughout South Africa from about the mid-sixties.

He had his mouth opened in attention and had the brightest little eyes in that darkness. They were keen eyes. He still had serrations on his front teeth. They looked like his milk-teeth to me.

"You understand now?"

He kept quiet for a while.

146

"But the Whites are cruel. Alone like that?" He stressed his horror.

Even this young boy understood what solitary confinement could do to one.

I asked him what he had done.

"House-broking!" he said. "House-broking and *thatha*" (theft).

"House-brea…" I wanted to correct him. But I was thrilled by the expression. I even wondered why "stock-broking" was not stock-breaking. I had never thought of it before.

"Where did you do it?" I asked him, and not "why" he had done it.

"It was a White man's place, *grote*. A Greek fish and chips," he replied.

"Oh…that's fine. But you must be careful, man. You are still young, and you know the swine will shoot you dead. We in the Black Power don't want to see Black youngsters die. We need you."

He protested. "But he was White, *grote*. We are helping you!"

I was not surprised that he was already as clear as he was about the racial divisions in South Africa, and he knew, right or wrong, on which side of the colour divide he belonged.

"But don't they lock you up?" It was my turn to ask and accuse him and begrudge him his little freedom. He told me that only the main gate leading from the corridor was locked during the day, but that their cell-doors were kept open. However, at night, the cell-doors were locked also.

This dialogue had gone in all the vernacular dialects Black people speak in South Africa, which we interchange at will, as we speak any one of them. There was also some English and ghetto Afrikaans, which is different from the Afrikaans of the Boers.

I retreated far into my mind, asking myself questions which I could answer, but which I had no immediate solutions for. He was so young, so beautiful, but already in jail, and not looking the least worried at all. Perhaps it was not his first spell there, and there was nothing to teach him either. Perhaps the only thing that was new to him was that he had never seen or talked to a political detainee before.

I told him that I was not alone. I showed him Frank Molobi's cell diagonally opposite 201, but he declined to go there. When he left, he said that he would see me the next day.

147

By this time, I had long been introduced to the night conversations or "meetings". At first, I thought the whole business was risky, but these meetings were initiated and had gone on while I was still on the third floor in cell 320. I agreed that it was absolutely necessary that we have these meetings. The second floor had Chris Weimer in cell 200, Frank Molobi in 203, Simon Monamodi in 205, Xola Nuse, Johnny Ramrock, Wiseman Hamilton, Pat McGluwa, Vincent Selanto, Eric Molobi and about six or so others whose names and cell-numbers I cannot now remember.

Du . . . du . . . du . . . du . . . du.

"Who's that?" I had responded *sotto voce* to the knock on the wall, the very first night I was brought to cell 201.

"Chris Weimer!" the response came, also *sotto voce*. "I saw you passing my window, comrade Finn, when they brought you in. You were in a bad shape," he finished his introduction.

"Ya. They tortured me. And I can't get to the window to talk to you," explaining why I could not fulfil his request to talk to him at the window.

"Expect a letter," he ended his introduction.

The jigsaw puzzle was slowly coming together in my mind. So, Chris Weimer, the man Visser and the rest of them had asked me about, was in the next cell, adjacent to mine, facing east while mine faced north.

The letter Chris had promised took two days to arrive, yet he was only a cell away from me. It detailed the group on the second floor, giving the cell-numbers as well. Sometimes, Chris wrote, it was possible to communicate with comrades on the third floor. The note had been addressed to Comrade Finn. With the letter was included a pencil stub, folded in toilet paper!

The nightly meetings took place, whenever necessary, by an elaborate system of banging on the walls, then shouts from cell to cell. The shouting went on from the time of the commencement of the meeting to the end. Frank had a cell facing the corridor, from which the police would approach. He took part as the important link between safety and approaching danger. Frank would immediately whistle "Mannenberg", a jazz piece that had been recorded by Dollar Brand, whenever someone was coming. "Mannenberg" was also used to arouse us from our mats to our windows for meetings.

The Security Police had put us in the cells at intervals between

148

us. If the cells were opposite each other, then they skipped that cell and put someone in a cell that would be diagonally opposite. This had been planned so as to minimize direct communication, or to prevent sighting each other. However, that had not circumvented anything. We screamed our lungs out softly, which was very difficult. Nonetheless, we had achieved much.

During the meetings, I gradually put together the pieces of how I was supposedly involved with this group, directly or indirectly, although I had by this time made the "statement" which had been spelt out to me by the Security Police. But I felt a mountainous relief when it dawned on me that the Security Police had made arseholes of themselves. That the activities I had really been involved in were unknown to them, and that even in their stupidity, the police must have known that they had made a bloomer. Perhaps better luck next time! The best they could do was to try and use me against this group to justify their detaining me.

At this time, our meetings were discussing strategies for what we considered to be impending trials. Most times we were involved with those who had been approached to turn state witness. I told them that the police had suggested that to me, but I had refused. We also guessed that the major targets the police wanted convicted were Eric Molobi, Chris Weimer, Wiseman Hamilton and Johnny Ramrock. I had refused to be a state witness against Chris, Wiseman and Johnny. Frank, Simon and Vincent, Thula and Xola had been earmarked for Eric.

It was also at this time that I had written a letter on toilet paper with the pencil stub from Chris Weimer and had sent it to Frank in cell 203 for further transmission of its contents through a channel of "common prisoners" such as "Grote", the boy. Or much safer still, through our shouting system.

Frank had made a copy of the letter and sent it on, but the letter had been intercepted on its way. It ended up on the tenth floor, on Lieutenant Visser's desk, and in his file on me.

Du ... du ... du ... du ... du, an announcement of one of our meetings. But this one was ominous for me.

"Yes, Chris?"

"Call Frank. He's got important news."

"Frank ..." No answer. "F...r...a...n...k!" Still there was no reply. I threw caution to the winds. "F...r...a...n...k!"

"Comrade MP," he answered. I had changed my name from

Comrade Finn to Comrade Molefe Pheto. The comrades shortened it to MP, as Frank explained to me, MP for member of parliament!

"What is it, Comrade MP?"

"Chris says you have news."

"I beg yours?"

"F...rrr...a...n...k. Chris s...a...ys you ha..ve news..."

Frank replied without warning me. "Yes, Comrade MP. The let...ter you wro...te, about us re...fu...sing to be state witnesses has been caught!"

There was silence. The message had to sink in. I had to believe what I had heard.

"What?" I screamed at the top of my voice, despite what that could have entailed for us. To speak *sotto voce* was out of the question.

"Frank! I sent the let...ter to you. To you!"

We were fighting each other now. "Did you not flu...sh it do...wn the toi...let as al...ways?"

"I did. But I wro...te ano...ther im...pli...ca...ting you!"

"Shit-house, Frank. Shit-house, man!" I was still screaming, fuming with anger, my chest threatening to explode at the repercussions I would suffer. Then, suddenly, inexplicably, I gave up. There was nothing I could do about it and there was little time to discuss anything further. I took a quick unilateral decision.

"OK, Frank. But how was the let...ter im...pli...ca...ting me caught?"

"E...ric gave it to a sma...ll pri...so...ner to pass it on whi...lst a cop was loo...king!"

"But how cou...ld E...ric do that?"

Frank's reply nearly dropped me on the floor.

"He says he tru...sted the cop! But the cop fol...lowed the little boy and con...fis...ca...ted the let...ter."

I gave up any kind of thinking. It was incomprehensible how it could happen, to me at least. It could not be true. I remembered that I had reported the Security Policy to the magistrate. A charge of assault against them might be pending, and they surely would do anything to stop me proceeding. And here it was, the opportunity they needed, easily delivered to the police by fellow "revolutionaries".

"Frank, listen. Listen with your two ears. I will own up to the let...ter. And from now on...wards, I'm no lon...ger ta...king

150

part in the mee...tings."

The message was related to the other comrades. I could hear it echoing all the way to the inner precincts of the second floor....

"Comrade MP will no longer take part in the meetings. Comrade MP will no longer take part in the meetings." And further on, "Com...rade MP will no lon...ger take pa...rt in the mee...tings. Comrade MP w...ill no lon...ger take p..." and so forth as each relay voice had taken it up.

My declaration to discontinue with the meetings was on the night of 14 May. It was a sad day for us to come to such an end. I felt that we were not careful enough, and that we would end up in a worse situation. As statements had already been made, our consciences would have to guide each one how we could save or sacrifice each other.

Lieutenant Visser had sent for me. Patose with his hyena face collected me.

"Pheto, let's go," Patose blurted out as soon as he opened the door. I gave him my wrists. On the way to the tenth floor, we passed a number of White prisoners who were lined up for court. They tried to speak to me, but Patose said that I was not to be spoken to. He put it as cynically as he could, almost hinting to them that I was a political detainee. One of them said, "He's a Communist."

I used a typical swearword which, if referred to another SeTswana speaker, would certainly provoke a fight to the finish to restore injured honour. In my anger, I had forgotten that I was addressing a White man who was scum, by the looks of it, and who would not understand anything, let alone being angered to a point where he would fight to restore his honour and that of his mother.

The White man saw red, not because he had understood, but because I was Black and had stood up to him. A fight ensued. I tried to strike him with my handcuffed hands. Patose held me back and accused me of starting the fight.

"Pheto," Lieutenant Visser said between his teeth. "You said you did not know the Kolourreds. But we have a letterr that you wrrote that they should not bekome state witnesses. Did you wrrite the letterr?"

"Yes. But I did not write to them. I wrote to Frank who is next to me."

"How did you give it to him?"

151

"I gave it to a young Black boy who was peeping into my cell, to pass it on to Frank."

"But you said you did not know them," Visser insisted.

"It's Eric Molobi I do not know. I told you that I know Frank Molobi."

I got away with it. I had avoided the Coloured issue and dwelt on the Molobi connection only. I took a chance on his daftness and it had worked. Visser contemplated for a long time. He was strangely calm. I had the feeling that they were all just about sick of me. Visser had given me that impression too.

"Well, you arre now facing a furrtherr charrge, defeating the ends of justice, and the otherr charrges." He paused, took a deep breath. "The letterr has komplikated you verry badly."

Incidentally, it had been the first time that I knew I was going to be charged. I asked Lieutenant Visser what the further charge and the others still unspecified would amount to if I was convicted. He told me. I totalled the whole sentence to come to seven years instead of the ten he had mentioned, basing the reduction on the probability of counsel argument. I had again been indulging in wishful thinking. In South Africa ten years is ten full years' imprisonment for political "crimes", and not even a minute's respite. If the sentence were life, then it would be for the rest of one's natural life.

I told the Lieutenant that I would accept anything that came my way. Then he said, "Unless you agrree to turrn state witness when we will drrop the otherr charrges!"

I realized that these men must be desperate. He had, as far as I was concerned, suggested open blackmail!

On the morning of the 15th, I was stealthily taken to the Hillbrow Police Station, about two to three miles away from Jan Vorster Square, to the north of the city centre. Perhaps the small boy came to look for me as he had promised. Perhaps he too had been taken to court. But I never saw him again, and I had wished we would met again to continue where we had left off.

17. *And night fell*

Hillbrow Police Station is relatively new, built in some of the most densely populated land in the world. The police station and cells were flatly constructed buildings — a contrast hidden by very high modern buildings and flats. I had never known of the police station's existence until 15 May, and I must have driven past it on many occasions without noticing it. Behind the police station there were courts which dealt with local petty crimes of the Hillbrow community, Blacks, Whites and Coloureds. Hillbrow is one of those areas in South Africa where, like it or not, apartheid has failed. Black and White lovers live together, open secrets also known to the police. At times, many times too, money changes hands for the police to ignore the "illicit" goings on. Further away, only a short distance from the police station, is one of the most beautiful parks in Johannesburg. I wished I could be taken there for exercise walks.

Bouwer and Makhomisane brought me to Hillbrow in the highly powered black Kommando motor car that Bouwer preferred. I sat at the back, handcuffed, next to Makhomisane. The doors had been securely locked in case I tried to jump out.

On arriving at Hillbrow, this Sodom and Gomorrah of Johannesburg, Bouwer told the White policeman on duty at the desk when he handed me in: *"Hierdie man moet alleen bly."* (This man must be isolated.) No one was to talk to me, and he emphasized that no book, pencil or paper should reach me.

Contemplating what might have caused my transfer, I felt furious at my participation in the nocturnal meetings with my colleagues, and my stupidity at having written the letter. This then must have been the result: a quiet removal from Jan Vorster Square. There could have been other reasons of course, but the letter had certainly contributed. I also felt mad at Frank. Already, I was missing 201 and the meetings from which I had resigned as well as the safety and togetherness of our numbers. I was certain that the meetings would continue. After all, we were not in the same boat, and the meetings had not been my creation. The ingenuity of the Weimers and the Molobis had felt the need for that sort of communication.

I continued to wonder at the shock the comrades would experience on discovering that I was no longer there. In fact, a few days prior to my own removal, Simon Monamodi and Vincent Selanto were missing. I remembered how Frank had nearly gone berserk knocking at the cell connecting with Simon's. He had knocked and screamed for Simon to respond without success. He had tried for a long time until I told him that Simon must have been whisked away. It had been eerie listening to him banging on the walls without getting any reply. It had been like trying to wake up a ghost. But fear suddenly struck home — the fact that a human being could disappear without any of us there having noticed it, that it could have been at night, thus heightening the tension among us as to what could happen in the night. In fact, Simon Monamodi was one of those who had turned state witness without having informed us that he had agreed. I was then the third detainee to disappear. Perhaps my fellow-detainees would think that I had been released. But I knew that they would sooner or later know the truth.

Colonel Visser had said to me that I was being taken to a place that had more sunshine than the lightless cell 201. That also, incidentally, had been one of my many complaints — that there was no sun in there. I had missed the sun, and I was certain that there was nothing wrong in asking for a walk outside, as there were courtyards at Jan Vorster through which the sun shone. I had missed the heat, particularly during a South African winter. Visser told me about the removal to the sun as if he were concerned that missing the sun was no good for my health! I knew that I had been removed because of the letter, for complaining about washing facilities and exercise until the Major had shouted at me that the police under him could not be expected to do work that should rightfully be done by the Security Police themselves. In the meantime, I looked forward to feeling the embrace of the sun, its warmth and seeing it. Stupidly, I had believed Colonel Visser.

At the Hillbrow Police Station I was under the surveillance of all sorts of members of the uniformed branch, Black and White. Every day it rained Afrikaans. the Boers spoke it with relish, the Blacks suffered it. It was afternoon, after the preliminaries of handing me over, so I did not care that I would miss the sun that day. My hope were for the following day.

On the 16th, the sun rose in a halo of glory. I felt as if I were the only man in the universe waiting for it, and through the window of the ten-by-twelve-paces cell, I saw its rays. It promised to touch the window of my confined room as it played in the ten-by-twenty ceilingless courtyard outside the cell. It did not matter that I was not allowed out of the cell. As long as the sun could kiss the window momentarily and perhaps my face and hands, through the iron bars, the only exposed parts of me.

As it rose higher, I realized that its rays slanted southwards, touching the entire south wall, signalling its move towards me. By

154

midday, it began to dance away from me, its rays receding eastwards on its journey westwards, taking a course north of the cell. At about two in the afternoon, I had given up hope. Its light was south-east, nowhere near where I was. Towards five o'clock, I saw the shadows made by my cell rising upwards on the east wall, by which time the sun was behind me, growing weaker, about to set. A lonely bird in the nearby park sang its farewell to day, to sun, to man and life and to me as it went on: *"Phez'ko mthwal", phez'ko mthwal', phez'ko mthwal'.'*

I remembered having heard this bird in Vendaland, in the northern Transvaal during my music research projects, in Mozambique and Swaziland, where I went to rest after prison, and Khosi Noge, my hostess, explaining the lyrics of the bird-tune to me. That *"phez'ko mthwal"* ' meant "up and on to your burden".

I sank on to the mat, spread out the three grey blankets, folded my black jersey to make an uncomfortable pillow and prepared myself to sleep at 5.30 in the afternoon.... And, in a little while, night fell.

18. *Maponyane, Soersant, Terrorist, Jakalas, Long days*

I could never sleep peacefully at the Hillbrow Police Station. I had to readjust to the new routines. There were far too many checks to see if the prisoners were all still in their cells. This went on at the rate of a check every four hours or so, night and day, by the different policemen as they came on or off shift. Most of the policemen at Hillbrow were of raw Afrikaner stock, fresh from some hinterland or other, and were very keen on their job. Many undertook an immediate campaign against me as soon as they were told who I was.

There was Fatso (who was fat) to whom I had complained that I could not see the point of being confined in the ten-by-twelve cell when there was the ten-by-twenty empty courtyard that was not being used at all. "At least I should be allowed just an hour ambling in the courtyard!" I said.

"Sluit hom toe!" (Lock him up!) was all he had said. *"Ek praat nie met daardie ding nie —"* (I don't talk to that thing) — indicating me with his capped head to the African policeman whose duties

155

were to open and lock the gates for him during inspection.

But I knew that my presence gave him sleepless nights. It must have been the first time that Fatso had met with Black Resistance. The Black policemen who worked under him never complained, and he tongue-lashed them continuously. It did not matter what he did to them, "playfully" or otherwise. I noticed many things they should have protested about, like the little jabs in their ribs. They took it all smiling, flinching, "their penises limp between their legs".

That, incidentally, was how two Black policemen became my companions. One, a sergeant whose name I never managed to get to know, and retrospectively that was for the best; and Maponyane, his mate. The two were inseparable and almost always worked together.

The sergeant and Maponyane were Fatso's intermediaries. I was so repugnant to him that he did not want to come into contact with me. He would stand outside my cell, directly opposite the door, to make sure that the sergeant and Maponyane did not speak to me, except to see if I were still there and to give me food. But the other reason why he did not want to come near me was to avoid beating me up just for the hell of it and to put me in my place. "To know who was 'baas'." I knew he would do it.

I did not bother to ask the Black sergeant his name. I called him "Soersant", imitating Maponyane, who had always referred to him by his rank. I knew Maponyane's name by the way Soersant addressed him. These two were mild and did not mind me being inquisitive; even they could not understand why I had not been sent to court after such a long time in detention, first at Jan Vorster, then at Hillbrow.

Soersant was squat, short and always clean and neat, outshining the entire police force there. He was very gentle with all the Black policemen who worked under him. He was gentle with me too. No non-rank White policeman worked under Soersant despite his rank, but Soersant told me that they wrote the same examinations for promotion.

Maponyane was his opposite. He was uncertain of himself, thin and tall, his uniform always ill-fitting with the gun hanging heavily on him as though he could not support it on his waist. Maponyane was also talkative, unlike Soersant, who was reserved.

"These people are mad, heh, Soersant," Maponyane said to me and Soersant during breakfast one day. "Everyone goes to court.

156

Why do they keep you here for so long?" Maponyane shook his head. "And that one," meaning Fatso, "he hates you. He says one more word from you and you'll shit. He wants to goad you. Please, my brother, whatever he does, keep quiet with your *seriti*" (dignity). Maponyane spoke in SePedi, which I also speak. He went on, "And you know what he did the other day?"

"No. What did he do?"

"The day you told him you want to walk in the courtyard. He assaulted a Black *moruti*!"

"What for? Why did he assault the priest?"

"Oh, he's mad. Because he was angry all day because you told him. You told him and I felt good too. Man, I fear you!" he laughed.

Soersant just looked on, allowing us more stolen time.

"Ya. But what did he assault *moruti* for?"

"*Oh, wa papa*, because *moruti* did not keep his place in the queue in the charge office. For queueing, mind you!"

Maponyane added that Fatso suffered from "Black Hate", that he had already assaulted many prisoners without provocation; he had been slightly reprimanded, but continued nonetheless.

"A Boer is a Boer, man," Soersant said with resignation.

Soersant and Maponyane left to finish their inspection and feeding rounds, joined by Fatso outside. I heard Fatso's voice cursing other prisoners further away.

As week after week passed, if the two were on duty, I felt good and safe. We developed a warm friendship to a point where Soersant would not lock me up in the ten-by-twelve, but only pretended to, even at night. But before signing off-duty, he would come, apologize, and lock.

"Please understand, *wa papa*."

"Don't worry, Soersant, and again, my brother, I thank you."

Every day was the same. Boredom. May, June, July, August; no change. September, October. Shit. Long days of thinking. But I felt such peace in me. Perhaps the chance to reflect became a balm.

In the meantime, I had devised several pastimes to avoid insanity. Strangely enough, one of the devices was to pretend I was actually mad. I behaved and acted as I thought mad people did, imitating those I had seen in Soweto and elsewhere in South Africa. I imitated White hobos in the city of Johannesburg, or the Black soldiers who had returned from the Second World War stark raving; there were many of them who were rewarded with bicycles and boots and blankets and khaki shirts and heavy trousers for their efforts for the "freedom" of the world! I know because my *Rrangoane* (small father or uncle), who eventually disappeared in the ghettos, was one. I walked about the cell, or the courtyard, if I was in it, imagining myself carrying the usual trinkets that mad people collect. Garbage, papers, tins and other paraphernalia, with their oversized clothes. Standing, talking alone or to everyone, cursing and laughing.

Yet I was worried no end that I should go mad. To check whether I was not already mad instead of acting, I would "go back" to normality by asking myself questions like "Am I mad?" and replying with "No, I'm not mad!"

My favourite pastime was relating to insects that fell into the courtyard through the small wire rectangles in the open ceiling. There were all sorts of these insects, and in all colours. Most arrived there to die. Very few were strong enough to fly away, despite my efforts to lift them up and throw them into the air to fillip them to freedom. Ladybirds were the most common. Black and yellow spotted ones, black and ochre ones. I would watch them, follow them, talk to them in all languages, even an invented insect-man-language. But I excluded Afrikaans. I would ask them questions, why we were all there, or why they had volunteered to imprison themselves when freedom was such a valuable asset, telling them that I had no choice. I would stand in their way to see if they would make a diversion. They always did, with annoyance, I thought. They would stop suddenly, slowly, obviously reluctant, and then take another direction. Sometimes they would stand there in defiance until I moved away, yielding to them the right of passage which I felt was theirs. I remember saying to myself that if Blacks in South Africa would refuse to budge over their rights like those insects, the régime would soon fall.

The winter of 1975 was the coldest that I could remember in South Africa. At one time temperatures reached five degrees below zero. On that day, when Maponyane and Soersant brought in the food, I remember feeling sorry for Maponyane who was draped in a headscarf, his nostrils dripping watery mucus which he could not feel because of the cold.

"*Man, wa papa, u thata, monna.*" (You are tough, man.) "It's cold! The Vaal River is frozen, ice, man! Eh ... Soersant, what did the White one say?' Maponyane was searching for the correct word, shivering in his uniform, his jaws clamped down but his teeth rattling.

"Five below zero," Soersant replied importantly, but still humble.

"Aha! ... There they are, *wa papa*, in that English of Soersant and the White one. Five pilow siro!"

Maponyane was so simple, but so amusing and human. Many times I caricatured him after they had left, sometimes whilst they were still there. He would only laugh at my imitation of him.

It was on such cold days that ladybirds were my saviours. Despite the cold, the chance to walk and stretch is the most rewarding if one is confined. The warmth of huddling in the blankets could not compensate. On coming out into the courtyard, I would immediately realize that there were only one or two ladybirds and other insects instead of the usual large numbers. In searching for them on such cold days, I would find them in obscure crevices and corners and filthy places like that. I would quickly rush into the cells and put everything on that would provide warmth. I would put on double layers of trousers, jerseys and my favourite jacket that had cushioned all those blows and boots from van Niekerk, Visser and Struwig. Or, I would shed the clothes accordingly.

Many of the insects died only a few days after their arrival. When they did, I would conduct a solemn funeral for them and put them away in the corner of the courtyard with a lot of rubble, eventually to be removed during the sweeping rounds by convicted prisoners.

"Go in peace, my ladybird brother, whether you be man or woman," then I would intone: "Amen."

I became very good at determining whether one of them was dead even if they were all stationary. The dead ones looked like a beetle car that had no wheels. The live ones were still that much bouncier. The conclusion was always difficult, but it usually turned out to be correct on testing. With the passage of time I became knowledgeable. I could tell at a distance whether there was to be a funeral or not.

I also became their protector. When the police arrived for their daily checks, they rushed into the cell as if they would not find me there, to the point where I believed that a policeman's thrill was finding that a prisoner had escaped, being the first one to sound the alarm, and then capping that by recapturing the prisoner.

The poor insects would get in the way of their jackboots. I

would grimace with anticipation, wincing for them and hoping that the boots would miss them. Many times after the boots had left I would see fatty spots of death and the crushed black and yellow or ochre wings outstretched, flat, dead, splattered. Afterwards, I would still bury the remains, collecting their pieces, cursing the devil that was responsible. One day, without thinking, I stopped a sixteen-year-old policeman as he was heading for one with his boots on his hurried way to my cell, followed by his Black assistant in similar jackboot manner.

"*Meneer . . . meneer . . .*" (Mister, mister.) I came out with hands outstretched, pointing at the ladybird. He stopped dead, surprised, the Black policeman accompanying him eyes wide open.

It was risky for me to do that. The little runt could have panicked, drawn his revolver and shot me dead as he did not know what I was up to. I thought later about the foolhardiness of the act and resolved never to risk that again. The Black policeman seriously suggested to the 16-year-old that he thought I was mad. I wondered whether his diagnosis was perhaps correct, that I had, in fact, gone berserk.

"*Baas*, this man is mad!"

The White boy-policeman simply said: "He's a terrrorrist!"

Word must have gone round. Later in the day, two senior august White policemen came to inspect me.

The first one said, "Arre you all rright?"

"Yes."

"Arre you surre you'rre all rright?"

"Yes!"

"What do you want?"

"I want to go home!"

The other said that I was all right and they left. I'm sure that it was the closest I came to being sent to a mental home.

After June, the coldest month, it became somewhat warmer, though generally it had been a long cold winter. The opposite of an Indian summer in the West. My programme of doctor, friend and burial minister to ladybirds and other insects continued. My longest poem, and the last one in prison, "*Hikuba* (because) those that wield power *ba teke nuna* (have taken the man)", was written here:

Her head and face
Cupped in sinewy hands
She let the tears flow
Down her elbows
Splashing amoebic stain blotches
On her *muenda* ...
  Hikuba those that wield power
  Ba teke nuna.

I then sing on for another eight long stanzas.

After June, bees and locusts were now dropping in as well as
ladybirds. Bees were the most sad. None of them ever left after
arriving. In a day or two, their legs would begin to fold up, so that
they rolled over and could not support themselves in the same way
that I could not after the two nights and three days of torture,
when I was reduced to having to crawl on my hands and knees. I
would, several times, over long periods, try to prop them up to no
avail. They took a long time to die too. Sometimes two to three
days of an agonizing wait for death. A day is a long time in a South
African prison, and it seemed as though they knew they were going
to die because, try as I might, they made no effort on their part.
Normally, by this time, I had long failed in trying to repair their
broken wings and legs. As soon as I certified them dead, I (and
who was I anyway?) would take them to the rubble in the corner to
perform the death ceremony, remembering the many funerals I
had attended in Soweto.

My most unwelcome pests were mice. On several occasions I
was woken up by their noise, rummaging and trying to chew my
canvas shoes away. Then the damn things would hide in the grey
blankets and mats. It was difficult finding them, as they were the
same colour as the blankets and mats, their small size adding to the
problem. I was thankful that the cell-lights were switched on and
off from outside, and in most cases they were left on out of spite by
the likes of Fatso. That made it easy for me to find the mice.

Despite the fact that mice could not harm me, I still had a fright
when one of them would suddenly shoot out in panic, scamper for
safety, only to meet a naked giant preventing its escape and
wanting to kill it. I killed three of them by aiming at them with one
of my canvas shoes. I would then use the shoe to sweep the remains
into the courtyard, leaving the dead thing in direct line of the
police so that they either saw them or stepped on the soft slithery

discomfort. One night, a White policeman was so frightened after seeing one that he jumped up high — so high I hoped he would never land on the ground again.

He asked me who had put it there. He was embarrassed because both the Black policeman he was with and I had seen him frightened by a mouse.

"Why did you put it there?"

"I did not."

"Who did?"

"I don't know."

I wanted to say that he did. I said it in my heart though. I knew that he would never understand if I said that he had put the mouse there.

I felt sadistically happy at what had happened to him. The next morning, the Black policeman who was with him the night before stole the keys and came to my cell, telling me how the White had talked about the incident all night long, telling the other White police that I was a cheeky bastard. But the Black policeman told me that he had come so we could have a good laugh at the White one, about how he had been scared by a mere mouse. I had a good laugh with the policeman, of Xhosa origin, who had imitated the whole incident and had enjoyed it more than I did.

I realized that there was no love lost between the Black policemen and their White counterparts in South Africa. "Man, since you came here, we are ridiculing them. You mustn't leave this place soon, *mfo* (brother)."

I learnt many things in prison, though. Positive and impossible ones. There is one thing I am sure can never be achieved by a human being, which is to try to walk or run in slow motion. I practised that for days on end. Long hours of labour. But I could never do it. Or, even worse, to run, still in slow motion, and then stop dead in mid-motion, off the ground, if only for a brief moment, and then continue. My mind told me that it could be done. That I had to do it. With all the time I had, my body failed to respond. The thing was, I knew exactly how to attempt it, and what I wanted. I also trained my left leg to kick a ball with the same effectiveness as the right leg. I had a tennis ball with me which I used for practice in pursuance of ambidexterity. I also learned to be alone for endless time without missing anything.

On two sides of my cell, on the north and south, Black people were always brought in and out of the cells. The police always brought them in at night from nearby Hillbrow. These people were supposed not to have had passes and night passes on their persons when they were stopped or raided. These offences are punishable by jail sentences. Other offenders included those "trespassing" in White residential areas, as well as "Magoshas", as Maponyane told me when I asked.

Hillbrow is a painful sore on the face of White South Africa. It is mostly populated by White immigrants who come from countries without a legal colour bar. No sooner were these settled than they were caught in bed with Black women, a "crime" earning the culprits anything from six months to two years in jail. However, those sentenced were always the Black partners in the "crime". Whites usually escaped lightly as the trials of the parties were separated, despite the fact that they were found in the same bed. In Hillbrow, a number of beautiful Black girls live openly with White men. The police knew this, at least the Hillbrow ones do, an open secret that even I, in prison, was made aware of. The Hillbrow neighbourhood knew this too, and so did a lot of White flat superintendents. At times, a convenient blind eye took over. At times, it was difficult for the police to make arrests as the "culprits" had perfected their security measures. In the meantime Hillbrow lives and pulsates on, next to its new police station, and next to the old prison, the Fort. Hillbrow lives on its bed of many crimes, while petty crimes like passes and trespass and permits and night specials and prostitutes do not escape. The committers end up in the two cells next to me, and other cells there too.

As soon as the steel doors and iron bars of these two cells next to me were locked, the recent arrivals would start singing. It did not matter whether the prisoners knew each other or not. They all knew the ghetto songs, the prison songs that I first heard at Jan Vorster, then here at Hillbrow. Many of these inmates were paying their fifth or sixth visit to jail. Anyone would start a song and the rest would pick it up. I would also join in and in a short time the whole police station would be singing, in sympathy with each other, and as encouragement to each other. These would be sonorous sad songs, whose lyrics would be political messages dealing with the lives of Blacks under the yoke of the White man in South Africa; or the songs would be talking about labour relations, about wives and sweethearts who did not know where their loved ones were. The rhythms were strong, which threw me into all sorts of contortions. A lot of times I clapped my hands and danced until

163

the song was ended. I also noted that there were good composers in the prisons. I knew most of the prison songs of the time in Johannesburg.

The south side cell was reserved for women and girls; the north one for men and boys such as Grote. The prisoners were piled in fifty or sixty to a cell, just as Grote had told me. The next morning they would all be gone. The same night, others would be brought in to replace the ones who had left in the morning. And so the cycle went on.

I always heard the raiding trucks arrive every night, woken up mostly by the howling police as they shouted, screamed and cursed the arrested Blacks when they off-loaded them into the cells. The misery of these prisoners relieved my boredom, even though I did not see them, and I very much wanted to, but I knew that no policeman would take a chance and show me. Soersant and Maponyane would also not dare. At weekends I would have the best of times as they would be kept from Friday until Monday morning, by which time their numbers would have been raised to more than sixty in each cell. It is sad to admit now that their misery was my relief.

They were brought in late, but late at night, and woken up cruelly early in the morning and driven off to court to await the magistrates who only arrived at nine or ten. They had nothing to eat or drink before they left. But they were strong. I would hear their receding songs as the trucks took them to the courts at Fordsburg on the outskirts of Johannesburg, or to the Johannesburg courts where sixty convictions were passed per hour, about one person found guilty per minute by the White magistrates and their White prosecutors and Black interpreters. Some of the Hillbrow prisoners were tried in the court behind my cell.

During my time, two Black women had remained there much longer than anyone else. One day, I decided to communicate by using the nightly meeting system we had used at Jan Vorster Square. Out of similar bordom, they responded.

"Who is it?" one of them asked me. Actually, I had thought that they were political detainees.

"Molefe."

"What do you want?" another asked.

"To make company!"

"Why did you not go to court?"

164

"I'm a political prisoner."

"And so?"

Oh, shit! There we go again! Do I have to go into another teach-in, such as the one for Grote, who was brilliant anyway? Where have these women been all this time? Have they been sleeping through a revolution, as the initiated said in Soweto of those uninvolved? And the unavoidable question would follow. "Why are you alone? You must be a policeman."

Sometimes, we who are involved get accusations from all angles. The police and the state accuse us of being communists, bent on disturbing the peace; yet on the other side, doubting Blacks accuse us of working with the police. This situation is painfully amusing at times.

One weekend, the "maddest" group of young girls was brought in. They had all been taken in one swoop at one spot. I think those who had brought them in gave them to Maponyane to lock up, because I heard his voice: "Come on, you bloody Magoshas. Go in ...."

Maponyane and Soersant had never become angry. The long time that I was there I had never heard them raise their voices against Black prisoners. They were a unique combination that was beyond compare to the other police, both Black and White. I wondered whether the two had a conspiracy to treat Black people well. If so, then their contribution was remarkable up until this day of the mad girls. They must have angered Maponyane.

But they were good company for me that weekend. They sang and shouted at the tops of their voices all weekend long. They sang sexy ribald songs which made me randy and resulted in wet-dreams that weekend. It was through them that I realized there was a new trend in Soweto's party scene, which I found still in existence when I came out of prison. The girls would be singing, pretending to be trumpets and trombones and drums. At the height of their versions of those instruments and songs, one or all would scream "Hola hola ..." in ecstasy.

I knew that I had never heard "Hola hola" in Soweto or anywhere else. It must have been a vogue that saw its birth after my detention. I cracked my head trying to work out the significance of "Hola hola" without success. But so many things happen in Soweto, which never seem to run out of inventions. No sooner would one vogue disappear, than another would replace it, almost overnight. Soweto forever changing like an amoeba, it is difficult to keep pace with developments. Just like its own language invented and understood by Soweto, particularly the young, for its own survival. Old people, whose tongues have less flexibility, attempt to keep up with these developments with amusement.

These young girls were really wild. I felt that they were not bothered about being in jail, just as Grote had not been. Incidentally, that was how I lost the tennis ball. On the Saturday morning after their arrival, I was practising kicking with my left foot again. The girls must have heard the ball bouncing off the walls. Suddenly, a voice range out from their cell.

"*Buti* (Big brother), do you have a ball with you?"

I stopped and replied that I had one.

"Please lend it to us!"

I argued with myself whether I should do it or not. I came to the decision that with so many of them, the ball would be of more value to them than it was to me, alone. It would be so nice for them to share it, the more so, I reckoned, because they were mere children caught in a web created by the White man. I knew that they must be women physically, from their songs and language, but in all other aspects they should have been at home studying under their parents' supervision.

"OK," I shouted back. "But return it Monday before you go to court."

One replied that they would give it back to me when we all left for court, as both men and women were taken there at the same time, except that sometimes they were put in different trucks. I told her that I would not be leaving for court, but refused to tell her the reasons. My past experience was that it took too much time explaining, and I was tired of the other questions that normally followed which I could not fully answer, being at the same time annoyed that some Black people in South Africa were unaware of what was happening. All the same, the girls agreed to return the tennis ball on the Monday morning.

For a long time I tried to throw the ball through the little squares in the roof of the courtyard towards their cell. Eventually, the ball found one of the holes and it bounced into their courtyard. I heard a scream of delight when they saw it bounce into their cell. I imagined their pleasure and felt happy for them. And when they thanked me, nothing ever touched me so emotionally and to the same extent during my entire prison life.

When it was their turn to return the ball on the Monday morning, one of them hurled it so hard that it by-passed my cell and went on to the one on the north side of mine, the one for the men, who had shortly left to be loaded on to the trucks to go to court.

All the same, I was grateful that they had remembered to return my ball.

I had tired of begging for anything but something to read. I realized then that I could swap food just to be able to get some reading matter. I thought of the many battles I had already fought. I had won some and lost many. The last victory had been permission to use the courtyard, although it was not available when Fatso was on duty. I remembered pressing one of the visiting magistrates that I could not see the point of such White meanness when I was all by myself in the cell and there was a whole unused courtyard which I could not exercise in, that I thought Whites were a civilized people, and if that was their measure of civilization then it was not worth learning anything from. I do not know what the magistrate had gone on to do, but I remember that the day following his visit the cell was opened and I almost dived into the courtyard.

I was not allowed to do anything, even to clean the cell in which I was kept. Convicted inmates did that every morning. The police would open the courtyard and then the cell for them. I would then be locked up with them whilst they did the cleaning. When they had finished the cell, they would go into the courtyard and I would remain in the cell. One day I literally fought for the broom with one of the prisoners so that I could use my muscles. But the prisoners also did not want me to do anything. Word had gone round that I was a "Black Power" prisoner. They felt they owed me some respect! That also was one of my grateful moments in prison. Grateful to know that so many Blacks were full of support for the freedom struggle, or that they identified with it. Particularly with those in prison. By the time I was released, I was aware of the high level of political awareness among Black prisoners that I did not know existed before. A lot of them knew much more about politics than I imagined.

The police and the warders were wont to open the cell, leaving the prisoners to clean while they went elsewhere to have a chat or something. I realized this immediately and saw the potential in solving my hunger for reading matter.

The very first day in May that the prisoners came to clean my cell, I noticed that they brought a cardboard box full of garbage, sweepings, dirt, old and even new newspapers, journals and magazines.

Newspapers! I would have to read them. By hook or by crook.

"*Hoeist, grote?*" (How is it, elder brother?)

This had been a number of days later. I responded in the same way, without using "grote" as that was meant for me.

"*Jy's nog hier!*" (You are still here!) The young fellow was surprised at still finding me there when he thought I would have been in court a long time ago. "These dogs are cruel, man!" He finished his angry question in lingua franca.

I took advantage of the sentiment expressed.

"Gents, my mother's children," I begged. "Those newspapers, man, please!"

I did not have to beg. I could have simply asked for them. In fact, demanded them.

"*Jesses, ga hulle, man grote!*" (Jesus, take them, man brother.)

I lunged into the garbage box. Grabbing. Anything. Incomplete ones, everything. Some wet and smelling, advertisements and commercials. I sped into the cell and hid them in the only place available — under the mat and a camouflage of blankets.

The three of them felt embarrassed and surprised at the manner in which I greedily sought the papers out, including the nasty smells that came out of the box, soiling my hands and clothes.

"My mother's child, don't worry. We'll bring you papers, new ones every day, as long as we are brought to clean your cell. We'll even take theirs as we start there, and they don't even read the papers, these things," meaning the police. "We will also tell our *blas* (brothers or inmates) to look after you."

I told them that they should be careful as I was not supposed to read newspapers or books, or even to talk to them as we were then doing. They promised me that they would be careful. The fact that we were all becoming a part of the conspiracy made them more daring.

From that day onwards, I was never in want of supplies. At times I had a fresh *Rand Daily Mail*, the Johannesburg English morning newspaper, or *The Star*, the evening one, though the latter arrived the morning after. I sometimes had *The World*, the one with Black news sold mostly in the ghettos. At times I had a lot

168

of the Afrikaans newspapers too; as it turned out, one of the brothers could not read, so to him any newspaper was good. I remember spending some moments of anxious stolen time trying to get him to differentiate between the first letters of the *Rand Daily Mail* or *The Star* or *The World*. With *The World* it was easy, as he could look at the photographs of Black people. With the *Mail* and *Star* I had problems. It was worse as we had constantly to watch out for the police and the warders. Then I tried to get him to differentiate using the colours of their insignias or emblems. Here, too, the brother turned out to be colour-blind! I thought of ever so many devices as he was one of those most often brought to clean my cell, much more than the others. The others could do better jobs than just plain cleaning. Sometimes they would be "drafted" to the better jobs, as this regular brother told me when I asked him about their whereabouts on the days they did not show up. But eventually, I realized that he was good at recognizing designs, such as squares and circles. We looked out for special permanent features in the different newspapers.

From that day onwards, I was never out of newspapers irrespective of who was brought to clean the cell. On certain days it had not been easy, such as when their supervisor was the 16-year-old White policeman. He would lock himself inside the courtyard too and continue to remind them that they should not speak to me. That problem the brothers also solved. One of them would put the paper or papers underneath his prison jersey. As soon as they were led into the cell and courtyard, two of them would immediately come into the cell whilst the third with the hidden papers would pretend to clean the wash-basin in the corner next to the insect "graveyard". The 16-year-old would rush into the cell to stop us conversing. In the meantime, the newspapers would be tucked between the basin and the wall. All this was done through eye-communication only. Hardly a word was spoken on days like that. But the tension would weigh heavily on me because I was worried for them. The lot of the so-called common "criminal" at the hands of these brutes was not worth the risk. Theirs is an indescribable suffering.

I never read the papers during the day. But come the night, I would read everything in print. At times, I rationed myself, particularly over weekends, as sometimes the cells were not cleaned then. I read the same paper over and over again, many times, until the print wore off leaving my hands with a slippery, musty feel, black like fine soot.

The papers left the same way they had come in. The plan to flush them through the toilet, after cutting them into thin strips, was abandoned early in the experiment. The first day I tried, the toilet flooded the cell, bringing all the torn shreds back like a lot of filth spewed out by the sea. I used one of the blankets to cover the mess until the next day when new material arrived. We all had a laugh when I told them about the toilet incident.

Although the newspaper supply-line was risky, I knew everything that was happening in the outside world, particularly news concerning political trials and detainees. For instance, when the internationally known Afrikaner poet Breytenbach was sensationally arrested at Jan Smuts Airport, presumably after having done some work for the liberation movement, the African National Congress. When Eric Molobi, with whom we had nightly meetings at Jan Vorster Square, went on trial; and that Simon Monamodi, Xola Nuse and Thula appeared, disappointingly, as state witnesses, despite the tensions and the decisions of the howling meetings at night. All these, and other data, were not news to me by the time I came out.

But some of the information came via the police themselves! After Breytenbach had been arrested, the 16-year-old policeman came running to my cell. He was so happy, the little brain-washed runt, he felt he had to tell me of their victory.

"We kaught one of yourr terrrorrist frriends. Brreytenbach!" he blurted boastfully.

I wanted to tell him that he was late with the news. If he was to be my informant, he had better beat others to the punch. However, I could not resist telling him that my political freedom in South Africa was not dependent on White friends. That it depended on me and on Black people. He ordered me to shut up. When the magistrate next came to visit, I reminded him that I was not to speak nor be spoken to, but that the young policeman was a nuisance to my peace. The truth of the matter is that my culture does not allow, and would not countenance, a young person of his age talking to me in the manner he did. White or Black. I knew that we were heading for a confrontation, and that the sooner I devised some means to stop him, the better it would be for me. I never saw the young twit again.

Most of these men had an animalistic hate for "cheeky" Blacks. One of them always called me "Jakalas", the Afrikaans Black-interpreted version for jackal. In Afrikaans it is *Jakal*. But this policeman preferred Jakalas, the Black pronunciation! One day I decided to ask him why he referred to me as Jakalas. He enjoyed himself with guttural laughter, terribly sadistic. He said that the way I came out of the dark cell to collect my food reminded him of a jackal. I looked at him for a long time and I decided that he was a sick man. That even psychologists would throw him on the garbage heap.

Then there was the one who became buddy-buddy with me after we had had a confrontation. He had come with Maponyane on the food round one day. Out of the blue he picked on me. I was no longer surprised by anything from these men.

"We trrying to do so much forr you, but you arre a terrrorrist. The *skools* the goverrnment is building forr yourr peoples ..." He went on to cite so many other goodies and incidents of how his government had tried to uplift the Black man in South Africa, comparing that to other countries of the "Third World". During the drivel coming from this insensitive fool, Maponyane became uncomfortable, shifting, obviously worried for me, by then knowing my unpredictable responses. I remembered that Maponyane had warned me that Fatso intended to belt me if I dared to utter one more word. But Maponyane and I were caught unawares by the sudden free lecture. I dropped my guard for the hundredth time because I was so full of hate at the unequal odds. I decided that I was going to let him have it and take the consequences.

"When a man is fighting for his country which was stolen from him he is not a terrorist. He is a freedom fighter!"

Maponyane froze. He quickly cleared the pots and bottles in which they brought the tea and moved out of the line of fire between me and the White man. But Maponyane heard it all. I was told about it later by the good old Soersant as soon as we met.

"Maponyane tells me that you taught another swine a lesson!"

I told Soersant in SePedi that the White policeman was "playing on my head", and that I had done nothing to provoke him to do that.

Most of them did not trust me. I still do not understand why none of them ever searched under the mats and the blankets in the cell. One night, very late or very early in the morning, two of them came for inspection.

"Arre you surre you haven't got newspaperrs therre underr

yourr 'mattrrress'?"

"There is nothing here," I said, pretending to stand up so he could search and please himself.

"No, man, sleep. I was only asking." He had given up.

The bloody fool! The mat was a cover for a whole arsenal of newspapers!

19. The charges

20 November. It was midday. No one came to the cell at that time. It was long past lunchtime, which was normally at eleven in the morning. If anyone was going to come, the rattle of the keys would warn me to take the correct action. I had got the *Rand Daily Mail* to read, sitting at the door of my cell, facing the steel door of the courtyard. Several times before, I had taken some chances, daring the police by reading the newspaper whilst sitting at the door of the inner cell, and on a lot of occasions barely escaping their sudden appearance. It would be no new experience if the key suddenly rattled then, with me and the paper making a quick disappearing act to the inside of the cell. Over the long period that I had been there, I had taken many chances by engaging in activities I should not have or which were forbidden, like the reading of the paper, worse still, in the courtyard; or attempting to make conversation with the inmates in the other cells, and sending messages outside. Some of these activities had been successful.

The keys suddenly attempted to find the keyhole with the usual accompanying violence inherent in everything they did. I shot up like a champagne cork popping, disappeared into the cell, dived for the mat and pushed the paper underneath it, lying relaxed as if nothing had happened, head facing up, legs folded one on top of the other. I heard the voices of Patose, Magoro and Makhomisane.

"O my God. The Security Police. What's up now?"

However, the visit was not unusual. The Vissers and the Bouwers had come here before, trying to get me to turn state witness. Come to think of it, may be that was another reason for the transfer — divide and rule. Divide us and break our resistance. They had attempted that many times during the period at the Hillbrow Police Station, the Vissers still promising to drop the other charges if I agreed, and that they had crack prosecutors from Pretoria who would rehearse me for the role. I had steadfastly

172

refused, believing, as we Africans do, that "*Se sa feleng se ea tlhola*" — it is a long lane that has no end.

Magoro, as their captain, was in charge. "Pheto. Take your things. Don't hurry. Just make sure you have everything."

Something told me that this was it. Home! I was going home at last, and with triumph. I would arrive and hug and kiss my children and my wife. Home to the ghetto at last which I would immediately embrace as I had missed it so much. The chatter of the ghetto children, drunks and derelicts, the decent and the upright, knife wielders of the unlit nights, the danger and the safety of the ghetto. Taxi-drivers and their endless hooting motor cars, the lot. The ghetto. Love. Children. Home.

I finished. Two bundles of clothing were under my armpits. I awkwardly extended my hands for the handcuffs to be locked around my wrists.

Makhomisane asked Magoro, "Shall I tie him up, Captain?"

Magoro showed his authority with a flourish. "No. There are three of us. He can't try anything," he said.

But as we left, Magoro held my old jacket by the sleeve, which was more humiliating with the two bundles of clothing. I felt like a thief with the exhibits of his exploits. A stupid one at that. Caught, as it were, in the act, and with the evidence.

"Magoro, I look like a thief with these bundles and you holding my jacket. Use the handcuffs, man!"

I had long realized the embarrassment they suffered whenever they were with us detainees because they knew what we stood for. In this case, they knew that my complaint was a gibe at them because I knew and they knew that I was not a thief. I was held for involvement in political activities connected with efforts for a free Azania, the name we now use for our country in South Africa. In any case, that's what they and their masters were alleging were my crimes. And they, Black like me, had chosen to tuck their tails behind their backs.

"OK, Pheto. But don't try anything funny."

Makhomisane was not happy. He put his hand in his pocket, I assumed the one with the perpetual gun. I felt very uneasy because Makhomisane was a nervous wreck. One unintended wrong move by me and that would be it. He would shoot.

Patose, who was quiet all the time, with his hyena eyes darting left and right, led the way. I was in the middle, between Makhomisane and Patose, with Magoro in the rear. We formed a little triangle in motion. But I remembered similar triangles before in these prisons. They usually had me walking in the middle, with one always behind.

They drove me to Jan Vorster Square, then we were in the lift, up to the eternal ninth or tenth floor.

On arrival, I found three young Coloured men who, I soon learnt, were Chris Weimer, Wiseman Hamilton and Johnny Ramrock. They were in another room apparently waiting to have their fingerprints taken and were due to appear in court. Patose left our group to go and assist with fingerprinting. I overheard all this as I was waiting in the other room. I did not think that I was going to court as I had been made to understand that if that were the case I would be informed, and that my wife would also be told so that she could arrange for my defence. So, "I'm going home!" I thought. That seemed a logical conclusion to arrive at. Not the "logicality" of our stub-eared friend! When Patose had finished fingerprinting the three, I was called.

"Give me your hands," he commanded me.

"God! Shit, man! It's court then," I said to myself. But what about my "legal" right to defence? What was I going to do as no one knew I would be appearing in court?

Patose finished taking my fingerprints.

There was a flurry. Movement, hurried and anxious. Magoro was running in and out. He said to one of the Whites who were supervising, "*Sy's hier, sy's hier!*" (She's here!) Magoro was frantic as though he had committed a grave mistake.

I was then leaving the fingerprinting room to join the others, Chris, Wiseman and Johnny. Patose was not aware of the drama unfolding as he led me to join the others. He just took me out unguardedly.

As I looked up, I thought I was dreaming. Many thoughts raced through my mind, crowding upon me. God goodness mercy. My wife!

"Molefe!" she called.

This time, they prevented us before we reached each other.

"What is it?" she screamed.

"I don't know. Find out!" I screamed back at her.

I heard her talking to a new White policeman who was then, I suppose, in charge at Jan Vorster. She was talking at the top of her voice. I did not know what the White policeman had said to her, but what she was shouting about had something to do with the court.

"You promised to send a policeman to tell me when my husband would be going to court. How can he go to court without lawyers?" Deborah was fighting mad.

The White policeman was trying to say that there had been a mistake.

"No. It's purposely done. I'm going with him now, it is purposely done," she insisted. She was hammering the policeman with endless words and I was worried for her lest the beast clout her wide mouth, or throw her down into the cells.

"You don't want me to know!"

The policeman finally said that she could run up to the law courts where she could meet me. I called out loud that she should refuse. There was no way in which she could reach the courts before us as we would be driven there, and the courts were four to five blocks from Jan Vorster Police Station. She would also not know which courtroom as there are many courts there.

We won. My wife and I and the three, Chris, Wiseman and Johnny. The three young men joined in the battle that Deborah be driven to court with us. I immediately took a liking to these men, whatever they might have been forced to say in "interrogation" about me. They were brave. I would also stand up for them.

Johnny and I, and Makhomisane and Deborah, were bundled into the back seat of the Hillman, with two White policemen in the front. Chris and Wiseman were taken in another car.

It would appear that one of them had made a mess again. Deborah had been given permission to bring food and fresh clothes without knowing that I was scheduled to appear in court that same day. The routine would have been that Deborah left the clothes and food with them and then, after a search of the articles, these would have been brought to me at the Hillbrow Police Station. Often, these articles did not reach me on the same day they were brought in.

Deborah and I found it difficult later to convince friends that she had on two occasions caught the police with their pants down. First, when they had just finished torturing me; secondly, on the day they were smuggling me into court. If she had not been there herself as witness; and in the second instance, with Chris, Wiseman and Johnny seeing the whole episode for themselves and having quickly grasped the treachery, no one would believe my tales.

175

I heard the formal charges for the first time in the magistrate's court. Every move had the mood of a secret trial. There were only six people in court to see all four of us. I would have had no one had Deborah not surprised them.

The charges against me, as read by the policeman Deborah had hammered earlier on, one Captain Kroonwright, were: that I had recruited terrorists for military training; that I had ferried them several times across the borders without travel documents; that I had defeated the ends of justice by helping a convicted political, one Clarence Hamilton, to escape to Botswana; and that I belonged to banned subversive organizations — the African National Congress and the Pan-Africanist Congress — and because of my travels overseas, I was dangerous, experienced and therefore, he Kroonwright, was against bail being granted me as I would abscond into exile.

The mystery of my long stay in prison was over, after about 270 days of uncertainty. Of course I had anticipated, from their point of view, what I was supposed to have done. All that remained, now that they had at last brought me to court, was to prove the allegations, if it was necessary at all. White justice in South Africa is a farce. They might as well tell us what our sentences are, and I never cease to wonder why we Blacks allow them the semblance of justice by going through these trials. I had been there for so long that I could tell almost anything that was going on in there. But despite my wildest claim that I could anticipate and know what was going on in there, the South African Security Police are still capable of amazingly bizarre allegations. In their desperate manoeuvres to procure a sentence or conviction, the magistrate was told that I belonged to *both* the African National Congress *and* the Pan-Africanist Congress! The ideological differences between these two liberation movements are so wide apart that there is no way, at the present moment, in which simultaneous membership is possible. The South African Security Police should have known that. The magistrate should also have known it. But the collusion between the bench and the police and the prosecution is so blatant that astonishing blunders such as these are allowed to go on court records without remark. However, we Blacks understand the corruption of those who are in power in South Africa today. It does not matter how or on what evidence we get convicted. The essential issue is that the "trouble-making communists" should be removed from society, locked up, to allow the most "democratic,

176

all-knowing" society in the world get on with the job of racial oppression! However, the other very essential issue is that we Blacks know that we are not guilty, none of us, of any "crime" whatsoever.

A Johannesburg attorney, Raymond Tucker, who had been briefed by their families to defend Chris Weimer, Wiseman Hamilton and Johnny Ramrock, was in court. But as it happened, he was the same attorney my wife had engaged to defend me when and if I were to be brought into court! Neither Deborah nor Raymond Tucker knew that I was due to appear that day, or any other day for that matter. As soon as my case was called, Raymond Tucker stood up, to the surprise of the Security Police, to announce that he was representing me as well. He requested that I be granted bail, assuring the magistrate that I had had my chances of travelling abroad but had always returned to South Africa, and that I had a family, which factor would be a deterrent for me to abscond.

The magistrate preferred the concocted story and evidence of Kroonwright. He refused the request for bail for me. He remanded me to the Fort, a notorious prison, only a block away from the Hillbrow Police Station where I had been since May, which I had left only a few hours ago.

My three fellow detainees were granted bail. We were all driven to the Fort. They, to await bail payment on their behalf; me, to await trial, which was set for 10 December.

On the way to the Fort, one of the White policemen driving us there asked me how I knew the day of my court appearance, and how I sent a message to Tucker and my wife.

I was already known by them as a "Mister, I don't know"; they usually passed such remarks about me as a kind of humiliation process. Well, I told him just that.

"I don't know."

"Man, you arre the worrst krrook we everr kaught!"

The gods will remember me because I also remember them.

20. The Fort

The Fort was my third prison in nine months. It had been shuttle after shuttle, adjustment and readjustment. But all the same, a

177

change, if one can refer to that as change, like a holiday. The only difference was that this "holiday" had been a nightmarish one.

In the townships, Blacks know the Fort as Number Four. But the majority of them were not aware that it was a corruption of, or was intended to stand for, the Fort. The similarity between Fort and Four to them was thin, and it was of no consequence whether the name was adulterated or not. At the same time, the notoriety of Number Four arose from the fact that there is a section four at the Fort which, I was informed, was reserved for some of the most hardened convicts. The Fort was divided into numbered sections. It is also a high security prison, hence the fearsome aura it had attained.

From the outside, the Fort is a gruesome, massive, well-constructed squat structure which has been dug out of the ground more like a bomb shelter. It is built of aggressive stone all round. Recently, some red bricks have been added. The top that passers-by can espy is all barbed wire with the eternal sentinel, guns at the ready.

It is at this same Fort that prisoners kill each other for the simplest ignoble excuse such as proving oneself to be tough prison material. It is here that the toughest, most notorious ghetto gangsters are held, and where several gang murders have occurred; here that some prisoners became "mistresses" of the feared long-timers and others who have survived through their brute strength. Sometimes, if not always, men become mistresses of others for protection. It is this jail that houses more than one thousand prisoners who are crammed into cells like beasts, where human quality is at its lowest, and every instinct, from policeman to warder to prisoner, is mere animal reaction full of hate. Black prisoners are dehumanized here for all kinds of so-called crimes by laws made by White people against Black people, where "high-risk" prisoners are constantly chained even during exercise periods. It is in this jail that warders and policemen assault prisoners *every day*; where at times, during the assaults, the unfortunate incarcerated die and nothing is done about it, because "it had been in the course of duty and the administration of justice".

Our arrival at the Fort was an immediate nightmare. After having been entered in the prison records in the office near the entrance, we were given green cards detailing our names, date of arrival at the prison and our crimes. In my entry, the officials wrote: "*Terroriste Wet*" (Terrorist Law)!

The section to which we were committed was like an asylum. Prisoners in their hard coarse canvas uniforms were running in all directions like hundreds of ants, carrying huge pots, brooms, laundry, some things that looked like office papers. Some of the prisoners had nothing in their hands, but were running all the same. Black and White warders stood by at selected strategic places with their caps pulled hoodlum-fashion, menacingly over their eyes, their truncheons swinging in their hands. An endless din permeated the entire atmosphere like a busy factory. The trotting prisoners continued an endless chorus of "*my baasie*" (my boss) — "*my kroon*" (my majesty) — "*my kooning*" (my king) each time they had to pass a White warder or policeman during their eternal trot. Instructions were howled out in Afrikaans and the responses were also in Afrikaans. To me, it seemed that even life was in Afrikaans.

The four of us looked like uninitiated mining recruits from some rural backwoods recently arrived in a big city The warders who were escorting us ordered us to undress so that they could search us. But they seemed more interested in our bodies than in our pockets, and the search was done in the courtyard right in front of all the prisoners who were running. Some of the prisoners just stared at us during the search.

I personally had not expected that that form of human degradation still existed at the Fort. I remembered that many years ago, one of the most crack journalists that South Africa ever gave birth to, one Henry Nxumalo, had exposed the whole sordid business of searching Black prisoners at this prison. His exposé had blazed on front page spreads, revealing that prisoners were made to bend over naked, and there were photographs to prove the authenticity of the story which had shamed South Africa to its lowest level. Some of the prisoners were caught by the photographer in a jump and clap posture, their legs high in the air. South Africa was later to read that the practice had been abolished by the authorities. The reality was that the laws had been further tightened so that no more information could leak to the outside world about the treatment of prisoners in South African jails. I also remembered that Henry Nxumalo had been mercilessly murdered, and rumour had it that he had been on another hot story. But there we were, still being stripped and searched humiliatingly.

179

With one voice we protested, reassured by our togetherness, and for the first time out of solitary confinement. I had been particularly unfortunate. I had early on been singled out, and was put through a thorough search of my body, only to end up in a second search. The first search had not been different. The White man who had searched me then seemed more interested in my penis than in any contraband.

With our protest, the warders went wild. I was certain that they felt that they were being presented with an excuse for a beating orgy. *"Julle gaan kak hierso!"* (You are going to shit here!) "You think it's outside!"

They moved towards us menacingly. We were outnumbered. We gave ground and undressed.

The warders searched our bundles of clothes, shook them in the air and threw them into their different bundles on the cement floor. They spun us right round as if we were little tops. That done, we were instructed to pick up our clothes while the White warders were told by the Black ones that they had found nothing on us.

It was only when the Black warders were told where to lock us in that they realized that we were "special" prisoners, not that that would have made any difference. I fondly remembered the good old Soersant and Maponyane, just down the road, at the Hillbrow Police Station.

We were thrown into a cell dug out of the ground, which was surrounded by other cells above and on either side. It was also the cell nearest to the exercise yard. As we found our way down the stairs with our searching feet, into the darkness to which our eyes had not yet become accustomed, we were surprisingly greeted with shouts of "Power ..." and *"Amandla!"*, with fists thrust into the dungeon's low ceiling. Then we were hugged and slapped on our backs by those inside. We returned the salutes, even though we were not yet certain who those saluting us were.

There were seven other detainees in the cell who had also been remanded to the Fort from wherever they had been kept. There were Joe Molokeng, Kgoti Moletsane, Patrick Mayisela, Bruno and Vincent Selanto, former Jan Vorster alumni of the nightly meetings; Sandile, who had resisted and fought the Security Police before he was finally subdued and taken, and Beki, who had been brought all the way from Natal, one of the provinces of South Africa, near the coast, some five or six hundred miles away. We were eleven all told.

It was a wild scene and a raucous welcome. It turned out that though we did not all know each other, we had read about one another as each had been detained, thanks to Black journalists who made it their job to inform the Black community. What remained was fitting the names to the persons. We took a liking to each other like a big family.

We expressed surprise that they were not in solitary confinement, and that we were allowed to join them. I imagined that solitary detention would continue, remand or no remand, but South Africa has neither rhyme nor reason for the manner in which it governs Black life.

The seven immediately familiarized us with the prison routines. The bell for sleeping rang at 5.30 p.m. The one for waking up was at 5 a.m. There were other times they told us about, like for cleaning the cell, folding the blankets and emptying the night-soil and urine tin that stank like hell from the corner of the cell where it was kept. I could not understand why we had to sleep so early and wake up so early too.

The night we arrived, the cell reverberated with freedom songs from our eleven throats in the dungeon, towards the other sectors of the prison. It was most heartening when cell after cell joined us until I was certain that more than one thousand voices were singing protest songs. Then other non-political songs would answer our songs; songs about the ghetto and sweethearts and our country. We also joined in the other songs.

The four of us were swallowed up into committees that the seven had formed for the running of day-to-day existence in the cell. We contributed a breath of fresh ideas like having concerts, poetry recitals, symposia on political topics involving world systems such as capitalism, socialism and various other "isms". The seven told us about the complaints they had against the prison, which we immediately inherited.

Each person was delegated a responsibility and some duties to perform. However, we were collective overseers on each duty. I ended up being the first spokesman concerning complaints, besides other general ones I was assigned to do. We also planned strategy to counter the brutalities that might result, as we knew that White South Africa always responds with violence to Black demands.

The complaints included food — the worst I have ever seen in my life meant for human consumption. Breakfast was gruel of yellowish half-boiled mealie-meal "soft" porridge ladled on to flat tin plates. No spoons were supplied, so we had to scoop up the sticky stuff with our fingers. Brown watery sugarless "coffee", which was brought in a large saucepan, was to be sipped from the same breakfast plates. Lunch was half-cooked corn bits that had been stripped off the cob ages ago. Supper was the same as breakfast.

Wednesdays and Sundays were "special" days. Supper was a mixture of old rotten boiled fish whose stink would reach us, permeating from the prison kitchens, long before the fish itself arrived; and when it did so, it was hardly recognizable as fish, with hundreds of thin bones that made it difficult to eat, quite apart from the disgusting smell of it. The alternative, not on the same day though, was pig-skins boiled with old shrivelled carrots and dirty pale green beans. All this garbage was then ladled on to the foul mealie-meal porridge. On the day it was pig-skins, the fat had long curdled by the time it reached us, with the pieces of skin sticking out of the mess like shark fins.

We also decided to include in our complaints exercise time, which was supposed to have been thirty minutes but was normally cut down to fifteen or so, depending on the warders and the mood they were in. We resented being pushed around and howled at.

One incident which showed our determination was the day Kgoti decided that for his exercise he was going to sprawl on the floor and sun himself instead of walking up and down like a mad man or like a bear in a cage. One White warder ordered him to stand up and walk, as though exercise was some punishment he had to undergo. Kgoti refused. We all backed him up and came to his assistance against the advancing Boer. The mood became so ugly that it was a matter of seconds before we exchanged blows with the handful of warders who had rushed to their colleague's assistance. Suddenly they retreated, but soon came back with a small army of reinforcements, Black and White, truncheons at the ready. We still did not budge. Kgoti remained in his chosen position until time was up. We had won the day. The incident also made an indelible impact on the other prisoners who had watched from their cell windows. When we returned to our cells, we were saluted with clenched fists from all the windows.

Every day, immediately after morning inspection, we were allowed to bath in the smelly toilet complex on the south side of the courtyard, empty our bowels of every "indigestible" we had eaten the night before (we had a strict rule that no one should use the tin in the corner during the night because it smelt unbearably), take the nose-assaulting night-soil tin out and empty it in the toilet complex, then rinse it to give it some semblance of freshness, and refill another container with clean water for drinking. All these requirements had to be completed in the time span of our exercise period. No wonder that every prisoner was always on the trot. We fell into the habit too because we gained a little more time. However, we hated the rush and we intended to have it stopped, at least for ourselves. We could not do it for all the prisoners. We had been kept absolutely isolated from them.

To add insult to injury, that unbelievably shameless, most degnerate species of human degradation, the White warders, would actually stand at the entrances of the toilets to watch us squatting over the floor toilet-pails trying to shit the slimes out of our bodies! I could not believe that type of indignity, it was beyond me to comprehend their nonchalance at their own debasement.

Then there was waking up time. The bell would ring at 5.30 a.m. We would jump out of our blankets, fold them the special prison way we were shown and prop them up against the wall, then clean the cell and give it a shine. But before we could finish, the warders would be there for inspection. Not only that. We were supposed to stand at attention during roll call and counting. If all the above requirements were not met, punishment would follow in the form of withdrawal of meals, depending on the gravity of the offence!

Our argument to disobey the prison rules were that we were not yet convicted! Although we knew we could not win any concessions, or all the battles, such as the one for the improvement of the food, we decided to throw every bit of our energy into our attempts. We resolved that at the next inspection we were going to break all the rules that we were expected to obey.

Clang clang clang clang, the thin but piercing sound of the bell went. We heard it loud and clear. I espied the prisoner ringing it fleeing with lightning speed past the window as though his bottom had caught fire. His back was towards me as he disappeared further into the gigantic jail. He certainly had not been on fire, unless somewhere hidden inside his hard canvas prison pants. Soon the keys crashed into the steel door in search of the keyhole. The Black warder came cascading and crashing into the cell, heralding his White superiors. When he saw us, the fright in his eyes told us that he had seen an apparition of a naked white devil with the longest penis on earth! His eyes had popped that large. He had to act quickly to save his own skin.

"Hei nina! Sukumani!" (Hey you! Stand up!) shaking himself violently in the process, an act calculated to frighten us.

Not a man moved from the lazy positions we had assumed. There was only solid silence. Before he could repeat his order, his seniors had already poured themselves into the cell too. There were three of them. Two fat ones and a very thin one, so thin that the light made shadows on his cheeks. He was the lowest in rank of this trio and the onus was on him to make sure that everything was in shipshape condition, that is, "happy" prisoners, clean cells, no riots, the lot. His commanders would be praised from higher up, and he in turn would be given his pats-on-the-back by his immediate seniors for doing a good job.

"Op! Op!" (Up! Up!) He indicated with his sinewy hand, his cheeks pumping and filling as though he had no teeth. He nearly lost his voice and eyes. He could not believe what he was seeing. I was certain that in his entire life as a warder he had never seen the type of open defiance we were exhibiting. Perhaps a prison break, yes, where the Black escapees would have to run for their lives. But the unexpected, relaxed, defiant challenge had been too much!

"Arre you on strrike?" one of the fat seniors asked, directing the question to no one in particular, moving his roving eyes past each one of us. Still, no one moved. Then he said, "Who is the leaderrs of this thing?"

"We have complaints," I spoke without warning, but according to the plan we had formulated that I should be the first one to speak, followed by a panel of other speakers in the order we had arranged.

"I kan only speak to one of you. I'll send forr you."

They left before we could all say our pieces. The Black, who had been frozen all the time, woke up from his shock. He ran up the stairs to open the doors for his masters. They were off.

There was silence in our cell. As soon as we heard them enter the next complex, we all jumped up and yelled with one hoarse wild victory cry, our fists in the air. "Power, power," as we hugged each other.

We knew that it was only the beginning. That they would be back with a vengeance. We did not gloat over our quick victory.

We planned as we thought best for the next move, that whatever happened we would do things together.

By the time two of them returned, the same thin White one and his Black robot, we were ready. They told us that their Colonel wanted me to go to his office to register our complaints.

"You! Kome. The Kolonel wants you in the office."

I refused. The two advanced towards me with the aim of forcefully dragging me out. They must have been given orders to bring my dead body, if need be. But Mayisela, Sandile and the rest stopped them in their tracks. They bolted out and came back with reinforcements, as usual; this time, the fat Colonel led them. The Colonel said, "When the Kenel kalls you, you do not rrefuse herre." Then he ordered his entourage, "Brring him with you!"

We lost that one. In his office, I told him that I was not prepared to say anything in the absence of my friends, because I did not want to misrepresent them.

The Colonel wrote something down on some official prison paper. He told me what he had written.

"I've jus wrritten herre that you say you werre in my office, and you say you have no complaints, togetherr with yourre frriends."

The matter was closed. He had given us the hearing we had demanded, and we did not use it.

I told my colleagues what had transpired. However, we never stood to attention again when they came for roll call and inspection. We had won an unqualified victory.

The first time I heard the human flood of voices I thought the prisoners were rioting outside in the exercise yard. It was like a sluice-gate had suddenly been opened, except that this one gushed out Black voices.

"Hey, what's going on?" I asked, surprised and frightened.

"Oh, it's visiting day. The relatives have come to see their folk, and they're talking to each other." Molokeng said unconcernedly. He then offered to lift me on his shoulders so that I could see through the window, which was not far from where the noise was coming from.

There exists a four-foot no man's land created with long wire gauze fencing, which separates the convicted from their family and friends. The visitors all spoke at the same time, lined up on their side of the wire fence, while the prisoners, also lined up on their side, responded at the same time too. Worse still was that both sides could barely recognize the people they were talking to, because of the gauze netting, so that in the confusion, hurry and anxiety it was quite easy to speak to someone else instead of a relative, someone totally unknown to the visitor, or vice versa. The whole thing was like a war of words, which the contenders threw into the no man's land, only for the words to clash midway between their intended targets and fall to the ground, vanquished, because in most cases all the parties ended in not communicating.

I had decided to concentrate on the few nearest to me, to hear the sort of messages they were exchanging. Further away from me was just gibberish that made no sense at all. One continuous hum. Here is an example of the pair nearest me:

"Do you hear me?" the voice from outside pleaded. "RI5. Greet Satch!"

"I can't hear you!" the one inside had requested for loudness.

"I said greet Satch. The old man will be coming from the ...."

"What?"

"The farms ... on Sund..."

"I don't hear!"

"Open your ears!"

"There's noise here ... yes ... what did you say about Satch?"

"The old man ..."

I gave up listening to them. I was convinced that they could not hear each other. I felt grief for them. They hardly saw each other. It was so easy to speak to a stranger, hence the message that had just been relayed did not seem to hang together for either side.

"Molokeng," I asked when I had come off his shoulders, "is it the same with us, when our people visit?"

"No. Even if our people come together, we are called separately, one after the other. But we still shout like them, though, and we can barely make their forms out."

"Well, at least it's better."

"Ya, but the warders are watching and listening. So be careful!"

"Even here?"

"Even here."

I reflected for a long time afterwards. The Black man's lot is worth nought here, in this country. This was very hurtful to relatives who had been missing their kith and kin, who had finally perhaps traced them to the Fort, or any other jail for that matter. It was time to speak and advise. Where is this? Where is that? Borrow money from so and so. So and so owes me so much. Go and collect it. Write to the brother in Natal. Tell him to sell the cow. And all that was supposed to take place in thirty minutes. It was never that long. Three minutes, four, with luck, ten, then everyone was hauled off. Next lot of visitors. Next lot of prisoners. Talk to your families!

The sequence would have started like this. Name call. Show your prison ticket. The one with the details of your conviction, and of course, identification. Now, kneel and wait. Kneel, Kaffir bastard, kneel! Now it's time. Rush, like a blue and white wave. Talk quickly to your relative. Say everything. Shout at the top of your voice otherwise nothing will be heard. There are so many of you. Can't you see, Black swine, understand? We have no time for you. Three minutes and it's all over. Tap tap tap, hard and rough on the metal piping by the warders signifying that the time is up. Last shouts. Like a boxer who throws in the last punch after the bell has gone. The stolen punch. Then both prisoner and visitor realize, so much forgotten, so little said. Next time, when they come to visit, remember to pour it all out. Quickly. Don't forget the last one. The one that comes after the bell.

In the meantime, as I was a prisoner awaiting trial my attorney and advocate, Raymond Tucker and George Bizos, had both come to see me a couple of times to take my version of the statement as well as to prepare for my defence, which they told me was still scheduled for 10 December. Tucker and Bizos told me that they had at last been supplied with the statement I was supposed to have made "voluntarily" and had signed under oath. Of course, the two statements varied greatly. However, even at that stage, they told me that they had not yet received the charge sheet from the state.

It was December. I was certain that I would not be out or tried until after the festive season. I had resigned myself to that fate. I was not in the least anxious as Christmas had long died in me. It had long ceased to mean anything at all. Evoked no emotion whatsoever. And, in fact, I had come to loathe it over the years. But that did not mean I was not a Christian in the western sense. I consider all Black South Africans to be more Christian than any other people I know of, given the existing conditions and the injustices they have suffered from the White "Christians" who came to settle in our motherland, who later used the Bible and the gun to steal our land. Yet my great-great-great ancestors

187

continued to turn the other cheek. I also have been turning that
cheek, and the man has been slapping it all the time and now has no
more space to slap. How much more Christian can I be?

I wondered what it would be like at the Fort at Christmas
though. Would the food be better? Would the prison officials send
some dominie, priest, to pray and give us tidings of peace and
goodwill to all men from Christ?

"Molokeng. What do you think Christmas is like here?" I said,
singling him out from the others.

"Heh, heh, heh," he laughed. "Bro Molefe, what makes you
think of that?"

"Because we will still be here then."

Almost the whole group shouted, dividing itself into four
against three; the other four, Vincent Selanto, Chris Weimer,
Wiseman Hamilton and Johnny Ramrock having had their bail
paid and been released.

"We won't."

"We will!"

"We won't!"

"We will, man!"

Beki, the quiet one from Natal, remembered. "Bro Molefe, your
trial date is for the 10th!"

I chided him that the magistrate would probably be on holiday,
near the sea, somewhere near Beki's home.

The keys forced their way into the keyhole. We were all ears.

"Phineas, kom. Yourr lawyerrs is herre!"

I was Phineas here. There was no nonsense about some Black
name and Black Consciousness.

The announcement was made by another pathetically thin
warder, a White one, wearing thick-rimmed spectacles which did
n ot fit his face. He looked very sad. He escorted me about a
hundred yards to reception, where I found Tucker waiting. On the
way, he suddenly popped the question: "Do you prray God?"

I was incredulously surprised. Just like that, after having
walked some fifty yards silently contemplating each other.

"No."

"Why not?"

"I have my gods. The ones I worship, and they are different
from your god," I told him.

"No, my frriend. You must trrust God and prray to Him. He

188

will listen to yourr prrayerrs."

We walked on a while in silence. I was thinking what to tell him next. But he was first again.

"The day of salvation is nearrerr than we all think!" He bent a little in my direction to make his point. He was becoming fervent, like a possessed person. I became bothered. There must be a lot of these misled derelict poor sorts here.

"And," he continued, looking at me, admonishing me with his thin finger, "beware of Kommunists!"

Well. That was it. The *coup de grâce*. The function of his conversation, which had choked him until it spilled out. The final curtain was so sudden that I burst out laughing. I laughed because I knew from the time he had started to talk that there was a catch somewhere. It had certainly taken him a long time to come to the point.

My last answer to him was that the reason I was in trouble was that I had forsaken my gods a long time ago and had prayed his god. That my gods were therefore punishing me for having neglected my own religion.

"Hello, Molefe," Tucker beamed at me. Seeing him there was like a new birth. The hope of my release.

"How are you, Raymond?"

"Very well."

I remember that this particular visit was on the 8th. He told me that he had at last received the charge sheet, only a few days before, but that the sheet did not include all the charges that had been mentioned on my first appearance in court. He said that only one charge remained, that of "defeating the ends of justice by assisting Clarence Hamilton".

"Is that all?" I asked with my eyes as wide open as the city of Johannesburg. "What's happened to the rest?"

"I don't think they will be brought up. They probably have nothing on you," he said cautiously.

I did not want to bother him further with unnecessary data. We went to work on the details of a chance of my acquittal. On the question of state witnesses, I told him that I thought we were home and dry. We discussed a few more details and then he left.

"Have hope. We will try our best."

I dreaded the discussion about god and communists on my way back to the cell. I would not know how to handle it and the simple imbecile who must have been told, together with the rest of them there, that we were communists, was doing what he had been ordered to do to save our poor souls from communists. He reminded me of the African warder who one night told us that the songs we were singing were no good because the lyrics were inciting us to shoot the White people.

"Now, go to sleep peacefully and don't think!" he had finished his warning.

The journey back to the cell was uneventful. He kept as quiet as a stone. He had suddenly changed moods, had remembered that he was still White and therefore superior in the order of things in South Africa, and that he had to remind me lest I forgot. He barked orders at the Black assistant who had been sent to help him to bring me back to the cells. He insisted that I and the Black warder should walk side by side in front of him. I felt the Black warder's reluctance to walk beside me, because, except for his uniform, he and I would both look like prisoners. Finally, we ended up in single file, I in front, the Black warder in the middle and the man of prayer bringing up the rear.

"*Draai hierso* (Turn here)," he shouted at me as I made a turning for the dungeon. He indicated a different direction altogether to that leading to the cell. By this time, a fat, mean-looking White warder had joined my escorts. He had a baton in his hand.

"I am in the basement cell," I protested.

Fatty replied sternly, "Do as you'rre told. Upstairrs!"

"*Ko godimo, monna, ko godimo!*" (Upstairs, man, upstairs!) The Black assistant barked too. "Don't you hear what the White says?" prodding me with his own baton. "*Ko godimo,* or we'll let you shit here just now!"

It took me a long time to register what was happening. I could not believe it. This was the dread of my prison life. It seemed as if things were becoming worse.

I was thrown into a large cell with fourteen little cages inside. The cages were actually smaller cells with wire gauze at the top through which air came in. Each of the fourteen little cells was six by four. My outstretched hands touched the cage walls leaving no room for further stretch, if the need arose. It was dingy and dark. There was not a ray of sunshine that could penetrate. A small brown plastic bucket was on the floor, emitting the stalest shit and urine stench, worse than the smell we had endured in the dungeon.

190

The bits of waste matter that had been left inside the bucket had dried up and had turned a greenish yellow colour. That process seemed to have worsened the smell. There was also a four-foot steel pole with a hook at the bottom. The pole had been cemented into the floor. The device was used for high risk prisoners, such as the ones who came into the exercise yard with chains around their ankles. The hook on the steel pole was to lock the prisoners to it. The inevitable steel door was there, a large one at the entrance. The silence in there was audible.

After the main door had been secured, I heard receding laughter from the man of prayer, Fatty and the Black one. The look of disbelief on my face must have prompted their sadistic mirth.

It stunned me to realize that it must have been their comeback after our "victory". No Black man was going to lounge about during inspection in prison. They must have been smarting through all the days of our short-lived victory. Theirs had certainly been the last laugh.

I heard a voice from one of the cages. "Who's that?"

"Who are you?" I responded in the dark.

"Eh! Bro Molefe. It's me, Molokeng."

"The others? Where are they?"

Beki replied, "We are all here!"

Although we were in different cages, it was easy to talk.

"What's happened?" I was animated. "What did you do whilst I was with Tucker?" I asked no one in particular.

"Nothing that we can remember. Only Struwig came, looked at us and left."

"Struwig!" My hands started to sweat. I remembered how he had kicked my ribs. Perhaps the Security Police were going to come and kill us at night there, I thought. No one would know. We were isolated from the other prison population. I saw the whole manoeuvre as preparation for mass murder. One after another, all seven of us would be taken out, butchered, or perhaps killed right there in the cages.

Again at night we sang. *"Senzeni na ... senzeni na ... senzeni na...."* This song had become a protest song sung to a well-known hymn tune in Black churches.

Alone in the narrow cell, I silently praised these men. Their spirit was strong. They had not broken. If these young men could with fortitude bear that type of animal brutality from our enemy, then, then like hell there was hope. For the third time in my prison

191

life I wept silently. I could feel the path of the tears on my cheeks. First there had been a warm burst, then quickly a cold trickle followed, and the puddles formed little lakes around my ears.

The second time I wept in the cells had been at Hillbrow. I had been taken to Jan Vorster Square to receive fresh clothes and food that Deborah had brought. On coming out of the lift, I had seen a teenage Black girl sitting, waiting in front of the lifts. I had passed her without bothering to take a second look.

"Pheto," Patose had blurted out as he drove me back to Hillbrow afterwards.

"Yes?"

"Did you see the little girl who was sitting next to the lift door?"

"Yes, I did."

"Who was she?" I wondered why he had persisted.

"I don't know her. Never seen her before," I said.

"What's your daughter's name?" Patose was unrelenting.

"Maseitshiro."

"Hmmm," he gloated and laughed. "That was your daughter!"

A slow heat of hate rose in me, from my feet through my body to my face, when I realized the toll their interrogation had taken on me, to a point where I disowned my own daughter. I knew that I would like to strangle Patose slowly, to relieve him of his miserable life ... his heartlessness, his police-bred attitude to life. To end the miserable life he was leading, and I saw the whole act as one of mercy. I had never met so demented a soul in my life.

I wept late into the night that day. As we Africans say, "I wept like a woman."

On the 9th, earlier than the usual 5.30 a.m. waking-up time, the main door of our new cell kept on opening and closing at intervals. Then the smaller cages in turn were opened and similarly closed. I remembered my earlier fear that we might be liquidated in the small cages.

When the closing and opening of the steel door and cages stopped, I had already surmised what had been happening. We were being taken out singly, I knew not where. My turn might still come. But there had been no logic to the way they had done it. We had been interspersed at cage intervals per person. I was somewhere in the middle. How come they had skipped me?

Long after they had gone, I realized that I was going to spend the night alone in the huge cell. Or, perhaps, it was me they were going to kill, but in order to do that, they had preferred to remove my friends first? I did not sing. The whole night I waited without sleeping, crouched until the next day ... sitting, huddled, taut, watching. I had convinced myself that I wanted to see what was going to happen to me, instead of being taken in my sleep.

The key, as usual. The steel door. Fresh air. Not too fresh though.

"Go and wash," Fatty called out to me as soon as I was on my feet in the cramped cage.

"It's about five in the morning and the bell has not rung yet. We wash at seven," I had protested because I did not trust him.

"*Hey, jong, jou gat, man!*" (Hey, you, your arse, man!)

I went out.

"Herre arre yourr things."

Fatty's Black assistant, who had been waiting outside, gave me my little bundle of odds and ends which they had not given to me when they threw me into the cage.

God, I'm going to court! I knew that I was due to go to court on the 10th, but with the extra solitary confinement in the small cage, I had lost all hope. I wondered what had happened to my friends, but I dared not ask Fatty or anyone else. The best I could do was to get to that court and tell people and friends who might be there that the six men had disappeared.

Indeed I was going to court.

Bouwer and another Security Policeman were there at 7.30 a.m. when finally I emerged at reception where an African doing clerical work in the prison recorded that I had been taken to court. I asked him in the ghetto lingua franca how come he was working in the prison office and yet he was a convict.

"*Hulle rwa ons, die mogoes,*" (They're robbing us, these fools,) he told me. He said that most of the Whites there could not read and write properly or understand the filing system, so some prisoners with education worked there but were not paid their due rewards. Still, he said it was better than being taken to a potato farm or to some other menial job. He said that he had been in prison for eight years.

We exchanged some brotherly pleasantries before I left. He wished me luck, after having heard what my "smog" was.

"*Mooi loop, grote.*" (Good luck, senior one.)

I thanked him.

"Pheto. How is it, man?" was how Bouwer greeted me. He did not give me a chance to respond as I was led into his favourite black Kommando car. Makhomisane had already put the handcuffs on me. "You'rre going to courrt today."

"I hope so." I was cynical. You soon become a cynic if you live under cynics for as long as I did.

"Yes you arre!" Bouwer emphasized, "And you will plead guilty so you can be with yourre wife tonight."

"Mr Bouwer, how can I plead guilty and be let free?"

I was doing my best to restrain my anger at the insult Bouwer was casting at me. It was an insult and an affront to my being. Did he think that I was as simple as that, after all their manoeuvres? First to compel me to make and sign a statement on things I knew nothing about. Then trying through all these months to turn me into a state witness, and when I had been adamant, manufacturing five or six charges which their magistrate had believed and then refused me bail? When Tucker had nothing to argue my case on to get me bail, as he had not known that I was due in court the day I appeared, despite the fact that he was my legal representative? And then, to hide their shame to justify their detention of me, producing a non-factual charge for which, mock trial or not, I had already served nine months in their prisons without having been sentenced by some court? How could this imbecile convince me that if I pleaded guilty I would be home that night with my wife and children? What made him care so much then, after he and his colleagues had let me — rather, let so many of us — rot in their jails, who would be worrying about my wife and children, him or me? The bastard! To say that I was hurt was being generous to this Bouwer.

"I'll plead in mitigation forr you with the magistrrate. You arre a good man and you werre misled!"

Yes. Your *gat*, man, I was misled. Misled, my goddamn foot I was!

This detention has taught me a lot that was more painful than jail itself. I remembered the letter that the Security Police had found at Eric's house during a search there, written to Eric by Clarence Hamilton, my "friend". The letter had mentioned that I was suspect, that comrades should be careful of me; Colonel Visser had had such sadistic joy in reading it to me, showing or exposing my foolishness at the sort of friends I had. At the time I decided not to believe him, thinking that it was a trick to turn me into a state witness — the usual divide and rule tactic. But during the nightly meetings at Jan Vorster I had checked whether Clarence had written such a letter to Eric, and I further verified the matter with Chris Weimer, Wiseman and Clarence's brother, as well as Johnny Ramrock, who all admitted that such a letter had been written by Clarence. They told me this under very conducive circumstances, at the Fort, when it was not necessary to holler as we were not in solitary. Prison, political prison, is a university. I learnt things I will never forget.

"What will you say," Colonel Visser had then gloated, reading the letter from Clarence to Eric, and this during my second night of horror and non-stop interrogation. "What will you say if I tell you we have a letterr frrom Clarrence Hamilton to Errik Molobi, saying that you arre untrrustworrthy!"

I told Bouwer that my lawyer would be there to advise me what to do.

"Therre's nothing he kan do forr you. Nothing!"

The Kommando stopped at the law courts. I was whisked out to some waiting-room, which was a semi-cell, with the normal prison bars, and left there with the perpetual Makhomisane. When I was led into the court there was no one there. Not even Tucker. Nor my wife nor friends nor relatives. No one. I wondered what on earth was happening. I learned later that everyone had been searching for the courtroom in which I was to be tried. They had been given the "wrong" courtroom number.

Vincent Selanto, who had attended to listen to my trial, knew their tactics well. He had by then been to court himself, after his bail release, to answer charges of "perjury" because he had refused to be a state witness on falsified statements. Vincent had decided to search through the other courts when I was not found in the one the police said I would be appearing in. He eventually saw me, sitting there alone, through a chink in the door of one of the courtrooms. He had quickly alerted everyone. We later found out that I had not been listed on cases to be tried that day!

Tucker came over to give me some encouragement. Bizos also came and asked me how I felt. He seemed to study me closely before deciding on his strategy. He then went on pacing up and down, as there were some inexplicable delays. Bizos strode up and down and to and fro. He radiated confidence and could not wait to take on the opposition. Geoffrey, Tucker's legal assistant, busied himself with legal documentary preparations relevant to our case.

We were ready. They were not.

"How do you plead?" the magistrate, one de Villiers, asked me.

I looked at Bouwer and his colleague, Ben Letlaka, who was there in court as the Security Policeman who had arrested me nearly ten months ago. I looked at the prosecutor, and then at the magistrate. They were all White, except for Ben Letlaka.

"Not guilty!"

21. The trial

For Anni Dryden, Jessica Strang, Christopher Strang, Mary Benson, Stella Rene-Tailyour, Robert Loder, Caroline Thompson, friends in England who paid the legal costs.

"Not guilty!"

By this time the court had filled up, thanks to Vincent Selanto. I looked across the stairs separating the court from the public gallery, searching for Deborah. She was there carrying Phello, my youngest daughter. Beside her sat Pule, my 10-year-old son, and Maseitshiro, the teenager I had not recongized the day she had come with Deborah to Jan Vorster Square. Deborah had brought the children so that I could see them in case judgment went against me. It might be a long time before I would be able to see them again. My friends from MDALI were there, artists, poets, actors and singers. After raising the clenched fist salute to them, I stretched my arms across the separating stairs for my daughter Phello. I kissed and hugged her, oblivious of all else, the first time I had touched another human being without hindrance in nearly ten months, and when that human form is one's girl-child, the sensation is indescribable. Phello must have been surprised at the thin bearded man fussing over her. I was glad she did not cry. Neither did she know where she was.

George Bizos, confident against the odds, as in many political trials which I had seen him defend, came to reassure me again.

"How do you feel now?" he asked me.

"Good," I said.

"We'll see. But we'll do our best."

I thought that he meant Tucker, Geoffrey and himself, including me in the package.

"Silence in court!" some official announced at the top of his voice before the magistrate re-entered the courtroom from one of the many adjournments we had already become bogged down with. The fight for my release had been contested for well over an hour by then. The police or state had managed to raise one state witness, despite their earlier threats to me that they had several, including a fictitious woman from Botswana. The mysterious woman was only too obvious by her absence.

Then the "state witness", Ramsey Ramushu, swore to tell the truth. He told the court the truth in the best way he could. But the truth vindicated me. And it was the truth, nothing else but the truth. He was a brave man, Ramsey, who refused to attest to suggestions made to him for my conviction. I still do not know how he managed it all. Perhaps the technicality lay in the fact that he was not cautioned as an accomplice, because, if he had been, he would have been charged with perjury. Ramsey, being the man he is, must have spotted the flaw and decided to "go to town" in his own way! I told myself that Azania needed men such as Ramsey today.

In place of other state witnesses, Bouwer jumped up from where he had been seated next to the prosecutor, purple lines of anxiety criss-crossing his face. He entered the witness box with numerous piles of newspaper cuttings relating to the Clarence Hamilton trial and his eventual flight to Botswana. Bouwer meant to show that I had spirited Clarence Hamilton to freedom fully knowing from news coverage that he had been found guilty and was due for sentence at a later date.

Ben Letlaka, who had been literally pushed into the witness box, proved to be a damp squib.

"Is the accused the man you had detained on the morning of the 5th of March?" the prosecutor asked him.

"Yes," he replied.

"What did he say when you detained him?"

There was silence from Ben Letlaka. Doubt. He fidgeted, searching for a lie. He could not find one, and did not want to delay the answer too long lest it would show.

"Nothing," he said finally. Bouwer became more red. Ben Letlaka was throwing the case.

"Did he come quietly, not frightened?" The prosecutor was doing her best to suggest to Ben the tactics of foul play. But Ben, like all of them, was stupid. He replied that I came quietly. To my mind, the admission was a slip in my favour, even though I could

197

still not see the point of Ben's testimony other than that they had no state witnesses.

Boom. "Court adjourn!" the same official advised us. "Tea break."

For goodness sake! Not another adjournment and tea break. Why the hell couldn't we finish the business?

The magistrate left the courtroom. I went back to the waiting-room-cum-cell. But I was allowed to have the tea that my family and friends had brought.

When the time came for cross-examination of the state witness, George Bizos chose not to cross-examine. He stood up with his rotund likable face and announced: "Your worship, the defence will not cross-examine the state witness!"

A flurry. Pandemonium. "Court adjourn!"

Ramsey Ramushu, the "state witness", left. He was free. This we all knew. His mission had been accomplished. It was our first victory, that is to my mind, because I personally saw him as co-accused. The fight that remained was then for the main accused.

On resumption, Bizos stood up again. "Your worship, the defence will not call the accused into the dock!"

There was further confusion from the prosecutor, from Bouwer and the magistrate, including the gallery. Bizos had warned me during break that he would not call me into the box. He denied them the one chance they might have had to get me in a spot. Anything could have happened. Bizos had taken no chances.

"Court adjourn!"

Even a greenhorn like me, inexperienced in legal procedures, could tell that the state was being made to look stupid. Clearly, Raymond, Geoffrey and George were playing a game that had the court in circles. They made everything move fast, gave no quarter, were on the attack all the time. The state was on trial, and not the other way round. Also, whatever political statement I thought of espousing from the copious notes I had been compiling was not going to be given a chance of being heard. Now and then Geoffrey, their legal partner, had referred them to some point of law from the big books he had on the table. I admired their teamwork.

The prosecutor was forced to summarize, much earlier than she had anticipated. She demanded a conviction, basing her argument on Bouwer's attempt, with the numerous press cuttings he had used. She hardly said a thing about the "state witness", but she was just as feeble as Bouwer. She had convinced no one, the more so because she had not been permitted the opportunity to have me in the dock. Her case was in ruins. She quoted several past convictions from some references she had made to support her plea for a conviction.

It was then George Bizos's turn to summarize and ask for an acquittal. He agreed that I might or might not have assisted Clarence Hamilton to flee, but that nowhere had the court been made aware that the accused actually saw Clarence Hamilton across the border into Botswana, or that the accused crossed the border into Botswana to meet the same Clarence Hamilton; that Clarence Hamilton had had ample time from the time he had been found guilty to the time of his escape to have made it on his own, which was probable; or that Clarence Hamilton might have been taken to the border by the accused, but then later returned to Johannesburg and decided on his own to leave. The issue that the accused had belonged to a now banned political organization had no relevance to the case (the latter fact had been mentioned in evidence). The said organization, the African National Congress, was at the time referred to a legally practising political organization in the country. Also, the fact that the accused had political opinions was of no relevance. It was not illegal to have political thoughts in South Africa, he asserted. George Bizos, having said much more than I can recall, asked for an acquittal.

"Court adjourn!"

The magistrate had looked up instances from similar cases. He started reading past instances of convictions that had been of a similar nature. I thought then that he was going to find me guilty as it was clear that he was laying the ground for that. The defence, I thought for once, were flabbergasted. It could not be! There were sad expressions in the gallery. The court became restless. But with the argument that the defence had mounted, de Villiers would have been stark insane to pass a "found guilty" sentence.

Next, after rummaging with his papers, books, the recorder and sipping water countless times, I heard the magistrate say, "I want no demonstration in my court. You may go!" He had given up. He knew he had a hopeless case. No matter how much he may have desired to send me to prison.

It was the suddenness that stunned. De Villiers had led the court in one direction, and then had changed course in midstream. I had already prepared myself for the worst. But David Pheto, my cousin, had anticipated the magistrate well when he had said that he wanted no demonstration in his court. David was the first one to stand up from the public gallery, cross the separating stairs and embrace me.

"I'm proud," he said, "for what you have done for our name. For once in the history of our struggle in this country, our name will stand proud."

I was touched by what he said because I knew what he implied. Many Phetos have been or had made their mark as policemen in South Africa. Many of them had ascended to very senior positions in the force. An uncle of ours, who died not very long ago, had become a sergeant with powers to officiate over oaths. On the day of his funeral, a high-ranking White police officer from Kliptown, where uncle had been stationed, was sent to represent the police. Not only that, he draped the coffin with the South African national flag, "Die Vierkleur", the first time, to my knowledge, that a Black policeman has had that "honour". Then there was David's own father who had been a policeman, a fact that David often talked about which I thought had made him very sad. And now, David's own brother was a policeman.

One of my cousins, Johnny Pheto, became a respected policeman in the Johannesburg precinct for a number of years. He has since resigned. In Pretoria, north of Johannesburg, one of the Phetos had a high-ranking position as a detective. In Mafeking, not far from the Botswana border, there was another high-ranking Pheto policeman. Back in my own ghetto of Meadowlands, not far from my house, another cousin, Labious Pheto, was a cop. There were a few other Phetos that were policemen whose names I cannot now recall. It was in that light that David needed vindication, and it was in that light that I had understood his remark.

Despite the magistrate's warning, there was pandemonium in his court. What did he expect when they had made such a mess of their presentation? Black fists pointed towards me. My smiling crying friends were like peach blossoms in Soweto.

I remember that Miss Morake and Miss Molope, with whom I had taught at the African Music and Drama Association, had brought a large packet of food for me. They told me later that it had not been intended for my lunch in court, but to take to prison with me. They had not meant it in a sadistic manner. They knew that acquittals in political trials in South Africa were few and far between.

I went over to shake hands with Raymond, Geoffrey and George. Theirs had been a strategy that I shall long remember.

I looked around for the members of the Security Police, the prosecutor and the magistrate. They were nowhere in sight. Their pride and power had been tucked between their legs. We owned the court.

When I first reached Deborah, I asked her if she knew where Molokeng, Beki, Sandile and the rest of them were. I told her that all I knew was that they had been quietly taken away from their cages.

"The police took them to Leeuwkop Prison," she said.

At least they were alive. My imagination had gone out of control thinking about the fate that might have befallen them. But Deborah went on, "You too. We could not find you the last few days. The police said you were at Leeuwkop too. We checked Leeuwkop. They said they did not have you there. Molokeng told his wife to tell me that you were left behind, alone. He told his wife where you were, and how it was there," at the same time trying to describe the cages from what she had heard. "I panicked, but Tucker found you at last," she finished.

Leeuwkop Prison is one of the maximum security ones in South Africa, on the road to Pretoria. It nestles among secluded bushes, a beautiful natural area, spoilt by the presence of this prison. It is near to nowhere, with no direct public transport. Families of the detained had to organize car-pools in order to go there so that they could afford the journey.

Finally, I walked out into the streets, for the first time in 281 days, alone, without handcuffs menacing my wrists, without two or three sad-faced, sadistic Security Policemen or thin and fat warders escorting and monitoring my every step. I was alone, to meet family, friends and the setting sun.

I recalled to a Black journalist outside the court buildings that I had just finished the longest "holiday" of my life.

"Any celebrations?" he asked.

I shook my head. "There won't be any."

22. *Presents from prisons*

There is no sun in here

There is no sun in here
Only the rain outside, incessant.
There is no shade in here,
A mist, grey, blue-black
Through meshed wire-windows ...
There is no nothing in here
Except my breathing
Which I and the two unblinking
Policemen on the ceiling
Of cell 201 can hear.

April 1975

Mother Mbila-Mutondo

Mother Mbila-Mutondo
Tell me through your
Many children
Whose backs I beat
When night falls in Phiphidi
Who am I where I walk from.

Mother Mbila-Mutondo
I ask you because
I see you find you pass you
In valleys and falling mountain lands
Always
Waiting and wondering with the cracks
Of experience in your bark
Whither next earth child
Who am I where I walk from.

Mother Mbila-Mutondo
The many counts I leave you
I have built muscles of steel
Shining proud and glistening silver

202

On my legs and neck looking for
Who am I where I walk from.

Mother Mbila-Mutondo
I see pregnant futures in
Glorious Mozambique sunshine dawns
I know my presence with
Shadowless midday furnaces
But treacherous sunset dances
My questions away
When I ask
Who am I where I walk from.

Web of spider, juice of honey
Twig of Marula
Pulped together in sound and wisdom
Become the children of one mind
In the songs of Muthomi
And the hands of Muthugulu
Sing the last song from Vendaland
And tell me
When I ask
Who am I where I walk from.

May 1975

Hikuba those that wield power _Ba teke nuna_

Her head and face
Cupped in sinewy hands
She let the tears flow
Down her elbows
Splashing amoebic stain blotches
On her *muenda* . . .
    Hikuba those that wield power
    Ba teke nuna.

To the month
Down her thighs
The blood jaggedly
Courses and plies a dogged
Route like a stupid river

I once saw meander
In Vendaland
Through the mealie-lands green
When she has been
To the moon
 Hikuba those that wield power
 Ba teke nuna.

The eyelids of heaven
Were shut at half-close
When sleepless rains
In March chose
Her dying days as April rose
African rains out of season
Are an omen.

Bad news is coming
Good news is coming
All news is coming
Wait and see mother
Let it not be the Siamese twins of Mundau
Or that Kgosi Pilane walks
The midnight hour
To throne his throne with an heir
Wait and hear mother
 Hikuba those that wield power
 Ba teke nuna.

It is said that
Guileless men in Kommando motor cars
With black guns glistening in the dark
Have taken Black pearls
To political prisons ...
It is said that
The Molobis have lost
Their best Black pearl
It is said that
The Phetos have lost
The one who refuses to wear
The White man's women's clothes for men
It is said
In the distant vicinity

Other Black pearls have gone
Leaving
Overripe ready virgins
And political widows
To the canines
The two two-legged hideous
Hyena and wicked wolf
The carcass-licking and blood sucking
Scavengers who prowl
With tail-hidden scowls
When the men have gone ...
Indeed one hyena
Was seen to guffaw
A pale wink
For the red sun to set
But was found dead
In the morning
With its pathetic pink penis
Pointing to the skies
Still caked in blood ...
    Hikuba those that wield power
    Ba teke nuna.

I want to go now
Riding on the invincible wind
Be it the East wind or the South
To speed on to the land
Where the sweet mango grows
To shoot through green and white wild horses
Like the arrow-fishes of a Black God
Harkening to His command
To be where I and my little ones,
Yes, the innocent ones
Who wave jovially
At Chaka's beaming face
To be away from where
Men's hearts are steel
And their ears cannot hear
Black truths
To be where I can see
The thaw peel

And know that one day
Black-hand-linked-to-Black-hand
Like Frelimo in freedom
Will walk the Table mountain land ...
    Hikuba those that wield power
    Ba teke nuna.

But when the shrill note
Of jubilation
Ululates
The return of the
Been-tos prison prison-graduates
I invited the moon
To come out for the dance
I dared the sun to out-dance
Me and my mate the moon
I ran to tell the mountain
To tell the rain
To tell the lightning
To tell the snake
To spit in their eyes ...
The sacred sweat
Of the dance of the moon
And the sun
Is for when WE circumcise ...
    Hikuba those that wield power
    Ba tsheke nuna.

Phello is not the
Last one
Even before
The cleansing blood
Of the red, black and white cockerel
Had effected a reunion
With earth
Wombs and breasts swelled
Black man-childs hollered
And beat their breasts
And their names were ...
    Hikuba those that wield power
    Ba tsheke nuna.

May 1975

A small glossary of vernacular names in the order of their appearance in the poems.

Mbila-Mutondo	Traditional African musical instrument of Vendaland
Phiphidi	name of a region or place
Morula	a type of wild fruit tree
Muthomi	name of a traditional musician of great fame
Muthugulu	name of famous musical-instrument maker
muenda	Venda women's cloth wrap
Hikuba	because
Ba teke nuna	have detained or arrested the man
Mundau	name of well-known Mozambican sculptor
Kgosi	king (chief)
Pilane	name of well-known Ba-Kgatla tribal king
Molobi	activist
Pheto	self
tsheke	released
Phello	name of girl-child.

23. Who am I?

The worst horror about the abominable helplessness of my life was when I was at high school. I belonged to a local boxing gymnasium. For extra fitness, five of us used to wake up as early as 4 a.m. for a jog on the tarred main road to Pretoria, which was not far from Alexandra Township. We would then run back to our homes, wash and go our different directions. Some to school, and those who were already employed, to their places of work.

One particular morning, I was unable to join my friends for the run. By the time I left for school, they had not returned. I wondered what had happened, as on previous occasions, when one had failed to turn up for the run, we would normally meet before we went our different ways.

That night, our trainer told us as we arrived that there would be no training. He had received a report during the day that one of our gymnasium mates had been killed on the road during the morning jog by a hit-and-run car driven by a White man, with three others inside. He then let one of my friends continue the narration of how it had happened.

"Well, we were running as usual. It was dark and around the

207

area of the trees, where we normally end the run for the return journey." He was speaking slowly and deliberately and we were all ears.

"This car, which had passed us, was reversing towards us. There were four White boys inside. They knew what we were doing because we were in our shorts or boxing trunks. As I was saying, it reversed towards us, went by us, then whirled round and came directly at us. We took no precautions because we thought they were lost and wanted us to direct them, or they were police seeking passes. Suddenly, the lights were brightened up and the car picked up speed. Kekana shouted to us to jump clear and look out and run. But Freddy was too late. It hit him. It hit him so hard. It hit him. I saw him because he was a little in front of me in our running formation. And also, he saved me. I saw him fly sideways, wake up, and then drop limply, by which time that car was way past and its front and back lights went off ... switched off." His eyes were watery. "It did not stop. Then its lights came on and it was gone."

Someone in our listening group wanted to know: "What did they say ... you mean jus like that?"

"Jus like that. But when the car hit Freddy, I heard one of them shout at the top of his voice ... 'Ka...ffirs...'!"

The quietness that ensued gave me to believe that the message of racist South Africa had sunk home. That the White people suffered from "Black hate".

Our trainer warned us not to jog in the morning again, especially along the roads where White people drove. Rather, he said, we should use the area around the gym, which encompassed two streets and two "avenues", several times before we began the actual training.

Nothing was heard of the car driven by the White boys. No arrests were made despite the fact that a report was made at the nearest police station. The car with the White boys had never existed, had not killed Freddy.

A week later, the entire membership of our gymnasium went to bury Freddy at the Alexandra cemetery. We had on our boxing kit as we sang him farewell.

That incident remained vividly with me for a long time, so much so that for weeks afterwards I was consumed with hatred for White people, and that hatred eroded my energy. There we were, letting off steam from our apartheid-frustrated lives by pursuing healthy habits. There we were trying to forget the White man's inhumanity. One would have thought that they, the Whites, would appreciate that, and leave us alone, my young uncomprehending mind told me. But I did not understand the dynamics of racialism and had underrated the peculiarities of its illnesses.

I was on the London tube, on my way to my flat. The tube was nearly empty as it always was late at night. I had come from the judo club in north London, and was going south to Balham, where my flat was.

There were only three of us in the coach. Two White men and myself. Suddenly, one of them, the one sitting opposite to me, spoke to the other. He told him that we come from the West Indies and Africa to crowd them out of house and home. That Enoch Powell was right. We should be sent back. Then he asked me where I came from. I told him to leave me alone. He would not. He harassed me, poking his fingers into my face, asking me the same question repeatedly. A fight ensued. We fought for what seemed an age. The tube went past two stations, while we struck, kicked, held and punched each other in our thick overcoats.

I was unfortunate, as usual. It turned out that the man was huge and strong. But I fought on. Luckily, I wound my hands around his jugular vein, using the lapels of his own jacket. I held on as his eyes began to roll, weakened he was, by the vice I had on him. The other passenger, who had been quiet all the time, intervened:

"Leave him alone, will you!"

The tube stopped at one other station. This time four big well-built Caribbean men hopped in. As soon as they saw what was going on, they did not stop to ask questions. They "bought" the fight on my side and belted and kicked the man about. I told them that the other had joined in too. They "lent the men to themselves". The five of us lashed those two. At the next station, one of the Caribbean brothers said we should get out and run. We jumped out and ran in different directions into the London night.

I arrived home bleeding from nail scratches on my face and neck.

"What happened? Finn, what happened? Tell me!" Deborah was hysterical.

I told her that I had been mixed up in a race fight.

I thought of Freddy, about eleven years ago, back in the slums

209

of Alexandra Township. And there I was, in the height of "civilization" in London! It looked like there was no escape. White people just won't leave the Black man alone. In Alexandra Township or London.

My father had never been to school. He could neither read nor write. Now and then, he had a job, working for White people in Johannesburg and the nearby suburbs. But he never seemed to hold on to a single one of those jobs long enough. Six months in a job would be too long. I could never understand why he found it difficult to stay in any one job. Now I know.

I heard him many times complain to his friends over a calabash of beer. That the Whites called him a boy constantly, and he said that it was more humiliating when he was called a boy by White women and young girls. Because of that, and that alone, he would pack his few belongings, tools and other paraphernalia he used for work, and leave. He would load these on to his beloved bicycle and ride off without collecting whatever was due to him in terms of pay. He said that he had never even told his employers that he was leaving.

He worked hard, and together with my mother's support they saved enough to put a deposit on a small plot of land. We called those plots "stands". At that time, I was about 11 years old, and he was still paying off the plot. This was Alexandra Township where, my mother told me, I was born.

My grandfather, on the other hand, was a chunk of a man weighing some 400 pounds. He had had some education. He would plague me with the English "Nelson Grammar" which he still read and never let out of his sight. It had become dog-eared with handling. Then he would also wreck my mind with percentage calculations each time he saw me in his vicinity, with his perpetual exercise book and pencil. If I saw him first, I would avoid him. But if he spotted me first, then that would be it. We were constantly on the look-out for each other. I think my grandfather had some money in the bank, because he was always working out his interest over one, three, or five years.

"How many perrcent inturrest tree quarrters on hundred pounds ober seben yearrs?" he would ask me.

At that time, I must have been in standard four at school, so he reckoned I could do the calculations. But I could not. All the same, with his exercise book and pencil we would plough through his banking prospects. I remember that we had always quarrelled because our answers seldom tallied.

Grandfather had a number of Black names such as Pule, Molefe, Pheto, Morake and Serunyane. But he had been simply "labelled" John Pheto by White officialdom and arrogance. He was lame. His left leg had been amputated just above the knee and he used crutches to hobble about. He told me he was born in Botswana (Bechuanaland Protectorate then), in a village called Mochudi, in the Kgatleng district. He had moved from Botswana because he had heard that money could be made by renting oxen to stranded Boers further south, for ploughing.

He was well-remembered for an incident in the East Rand, near developing Johannesburg then, involving a White farmer. The farmer had come to see Grandfather about hiring some cattle. The farmer had spoken to him perched on his horse. It is said that my grandfather approached the rider with his cattle-whip and asked him which gate he had used to enter his property, though there was no gate in sight to delineate his property. The White man indicated where he rode in. My grandfather had lashed both man and horse with his cattle-whip, dropping him on his pants, simultaneously telling him that he had no right to jump over his "fence", no right to enter his property without using the "gate", and no right to talk down to him from his horse!

When I questioned the fact that there was no gate and how was the White man expected to get in, I was told that it was part of the culture of Africa. I found out that there was a time in certain parts of the country, when visiting people had to "carry" a symbolic gate, whereupon they would choose a spot wherever they were visiting, put the gate down, open it, enter, close it and then proceed to where their host might be. The White man had none. But on reflection, I think that my grandfather could not accept the idea of the White man talking down to him from his horse. It was the height of arrogance for the White man to have done that. Also, it was a question of age. The White man had not respected my grandfather's age.

The Kesi, my father, had wanted to learn to read and write. I became his teacher when I was in standard five or six. As soon as I took a book to read, he would be there. We went over sums and the order of the alphabet. But he was not interested in the detail. He only wanted to learn to read in SeTswana, to write his name, and no more. I had to convince him that the alphabet we used in SeTswana was the same as that used for English.

"How come?"

When my father was able to read and struggle to write his new name, Johannes Pheto, and count to some extent, he stopped wanting to learn. He was so proud that he could write his name though it took him some sixty seconds to barely scribble "Johannes Pheto".

One day, I was sent to his brother's house to collect a "parcel". My mother was angry. "When are you going to get yours?" This had been a secret the two families had kept for some time, until the day I was sent to collect the "parcel". I was back quickly with it. My greater father (he is not my uncle in my culture) had given it to me without revealing what it was, except to say that it should be returned soon, as he himself intended to travel to Johannesburg in a day or two.

The parcel turned out to be the pass, the document every Black has to carry on his or her person, to be shown on demand by any policeman, government official or, for that matter, any White man. The document that determines where Blacks may travel, engage in business, live and marry.

My father and his brother were spitting images of each other, and for years these two simple uneducated men had realized that and had taken advantage of the adage that, to Whites, every Black looks the same. They had fooled the system through all the problems caused by the pass.

I asked my father why he did not have one. He told me that a while ago, in Alexandra Township, there had been a move to defy the pass laws, to burn the passes and never carry them again. Their leader had been a strong old man called Makue, who had organized the campaign. But on the agreed day, members of the "conspiracy" did not show up. He and Makue walked a mile and a half to the then Native Commissioner, where Makue threw the pass on the Commissioner's desk and told him that he would never carry a pass again. Old man Makue had died without one. At his funeral, which I attended, several speakers remembered the incident and had eulogized it.

The Native Commissioner had refused to accept my father's pass, because my father "was not a leader". The Commissioner told him that he had been misled. On the way home, my father threw his pass away. He never carried one until he died. I do not know how my family buried my father without the pass as I was in England then. I hope they did not bury his brother!

When my father heard of the African National Congress, he took up membership. I believe, in his mind, anything that spoke of throwing off the White yoke of oppression was fine. He must have had enough.

My maternal grandfather, whose other name, Gaborone, I bear, was my other influence. Incidentally, he too had had his proper names replaced with John. He was then known as John Mojatau. The Whites called every Black man John. The habit was still in existence when I was growing up. I have been called John many times too!

Grandfather Mojatau also had a stand in Alexandra Township when I grew to know him well. He had no need to work for White people. He was fairly well educated. He had also rebelled as the effect of a man from Nyasaland, now Malawi, called Clemens Kadalie. This man, he told me, had the White man "peeing his pants!" Clemens Kadalie had organized a massive movement which involved all kinds of Blacks in the Cape areas, called the Industrial Commercial Union. Through it, many demands were made from the ruling White establishment, particularly in the area of employment. Strike action had been used to bring the Whites to their senses. When eventually Clemens and his movement lost momentum and, according to my grandfather, "when new movements with White people stole their members", Grandfather moved from Kimberley to Johannesburg and ended up in Alexandra Township. He had already amassed some money with which he had bought his plot, had built rooms on it to rent out and had never looked back. He had one of the cleanest properties I have ever seen and a great house for his family.

My mind had stored these influences in some hidden nook.

My mother, MmaSamuele, as she is known, had worked for some Erasmus family and other White families about six miles from Alexandra Township. She worked as a washerwoman, cleaner, children's nurse and general "do-everything" for twenty-three years. When I reached high school, I could not endure her early journeys to these White families any more. There was the big family, six children then, and she was ailing too. But worse still for me, was watching her pray very early each day, at about four in the

213

morning, for protection from God, *"Ramasedi, mosireletsi oa khutlong tse nne tsa lehatshe"* (Owner or giver of light, and protector of the four corners of the world). I must have been aware of those cruel prayer sessions for at least eighteen years. But she must have prayed for all the twenty-three years and more. The pathetic figure in the dark praying by candlelight was too much for me. That, incidentally, was the beginning of the end of my formal academic education. I took a job and helped out.

At high school, the principal, G. Nakene, one morning made what I considered a startling announcement.

"On Tuesday, all the male newcomers over the age of sixteen and those who were not sixteen last year, should go to the pass-office and get their passes!"

I remembered my father, and my greater father, old man Makue and his burn-the-passes-campaign, my grandfather who had whipped the White Boer off his horse, my maternal grandfather of the industrial union of Clemens Kadalie and their long struggles.

It was not until I carried a pass that my real nightmares as a Black youth in South Africa began. Try as I would, I could never get the document right or fixed as the law required. If it did not have the monthly signature of the employer, then the annual tax, the general poll tax payable by all Black males irrespective of earnings, was not included in its many folders. When the tax was right, then it had no permit for me to be in Johannesburg. And when the permit to be in Johannesburg had been fixed for as long as I worked for employer so and so, it indicated that if I stopped working for employer so and so, I should betake myself out of Johannesburg within seventy-two hours to where I had originated from, or else, prison. When the pass had all the requirements I thought it needed, then it had no house permit which was "easily" available at the township's superintendent's office. At the superintendent's office, a birth certificate was required, which I did not have ... still do not have. A baptismal certificate from an independent Black church was not recognized, and I happen to have been baptized in such a church.

I would end up punch-drunk from all these requirements, and for all these years, up to now, as I write this book, the pass I am carrying is full of "legal-requirement-holes".

After prison, the White moguls of Johannesburg would not offer me a job, and I tried many. The African Music and Drama

Association did not seem keen to take me back. The few talks I had with its management gave me the impression that they wanted to find out whether imprisonment had softened my stand *vis-à-vis* the White man in South Africa and the issue of the Black artists versus the establishment. Besides, I knew that I had given them enough trouble when I had worked for them. The management was White with a few token Blacks. Liberal as they were, I felt that my type of Black was not suitable, not that it had been suitable before. For the Blacks on the committee, I had the least respect. There were times when I hated myself for my involvement in the whole charade and farce.

Eventually, I asked a White friend to "register" me and sign the damn pass document every month. But with this arrangement, there had to be the monthly levy that all employers of Black labour had to pay at the labour exchange offices. I could not give her the money as I was still unemployed then. Anyway, there was no way in which my "employer" friend could pay the levy even if she had wanted to as we did not actually go through the paces of "registering" me. It was one those arrangements to beat the system.

I thank my two grandfathers who talked to me without knowing that they were educating me in a manner none of our schools and so-called universities could. I thank my uneducated father who told me much and taught me resilience. That way, I was able to continue the struggles they begun.

My grandmothers? They were two old sweet women I adored, but we boys belonged to the company of men. The girls to the company of the grandmothers.

Looking back, I am baffled that it was the decision to study music, round about 1959, that eventually brought me into direct confrontation with the enemy. Four years in a London music institute foraging into Bach and Beethoven, trumpets and trombones, concerts and compositions, dissecting the mathematical orderliness of the European mind at work in his art, and thoroughly wallowing in some of their creations. Then in December 1970 I was back home, to teach, and with a clear mind to commit partial, if not total suicide of my European experience towards a rebaptism of myself in my culture. With the suicide, I took with me a number of my charges and other artists in the

215

community to wage political war through the arts. The exercise has left me with no regrets, and I look at it as only the beginning.

Conclusion

I met Mojalefa Ralekgetho, a Black South African living in New York who had heard that I was coming to the United States and had come to look me up. He is married to Sokorro, a warm Black sister. I told them that besides the visit to the States, I intended to finish a book whose manuscript was, through contacts, *en route* to me from South Africa. Mojalefa and Sokorro accepted me as part of the family, and asked for nothing in return. There were food and familyhood, on top of which Mojalefa typed out most of the manuscript. Without that first overture, this book would not have been completed ... at least not then, not here in America. My thanks to Mojalefa and Sokorro are unlimited.

Portia Franklin's apartment, 406 La Mont Street NW, Washington, DC, situated in a woodland area and very quiet at night, was my second home. It was in this apartment that the last fullstop was marked. She too offered the same facilities as the Ralekgethos, including typing too. I also find it difficult to thank Portia Franklin enough. When I add that the African gods have been more than kind to me, I refer to events of this nature.

At long last, I hope, I have finished the narrative of a nightmare that had lasted for 281 days in South African prisons, 271 of them in solitary confinement, a chapter of my life I want to forget as soon as possible because there is still so much ahead of me, so much to achieve, that to be harping back on those days would be an unproductive waste of time.

Somewhere within my inner right ear, some nerve had been damaged, brutally bruised, as the Johannesburg ear specialist, Mr Joe Seeger, told me after he had examined the ear. Joe Seeger examined me without charging any fee. He advised me to return so that he could keep a check on the bleep-bleep sounds the ear had somehow recorded during the time I had spent at the Hillbrow Police Station, where some machines behind my cell kept on bleeping all day and night, and decided to store for all eternity. Whenever I am in a place that is very quiet, such as Portia's apartment, the ear begins to ring with the bleep sounds. Very early in the morning, very late at night, such as now as I am writing. The

216

bleeps remind me of the first brutal assault, of the blow that landed on the ear. Joe Seeger is another of those people I am grateful to.

There is also Dr Nthato Motlana, of Soweto, to whom I went for a thorough medical and physical check-up soon after prison. Dr Motlana also took no fee for either the examination or the medicines he supplied. I thank Dr Motlana for words of political solidarity as well.

At the moment (during the writing of the book), there is political turmoil in my country that has been sparked off by the death in detention of Brother Biko who, evidence has indicated, was brutally murdered by state agents during the "so-called interrogation". It is difficult to comment, watching, as it were, for the first time, from far away. The truth will still out despite all that has been said and written about Steve Biko's death. I hold a different view. I doubt that he died in the cell. I believe that the police murdered Steve Biko, with premeditation and with an order to do so (from higher authorities), on the road between the prison at which he was held and Pretoria; many excuses given do not hold water! I am prepared to be proved wrong for my assumptions after a thorough investigation in which we Blacks have been involved.

I am due home soon. [I was then, 1977, until friends and family warned me not to return as the Security Police were searching for me.] Through the media, I have read that most of my friends have been detained and redetained. Black organizations have been banned, all seventeen of them, three of which I had belonged to — the Union of Black Journalists, the Black People's Convention and Medupe, the Black Writers' Organization which had been newly formed just prior to my departure, and of which I was elected first chairperson. But all these incidents were no surprise to me. The South African White racist régime had been known before for worse atrocities than what was then happening. That type of reaction from the régime had been a part of Black life in South Africa. I was rather taken aback when the world reacted in the manner it had done. Was this world honestly opening its eyes to what had been happening to Black people in South Africa after all these years? I did not believe it. The western world had been a partner in these atrocities!

Finally, I have no doubt that the South African Security Police will want to know what communist funds had sponsored me during the four months of completing this work. I would like to state that there were none. That for a livelihood I had commuted from Washington or New York, to various parts of the United States to read my poems (which were well received, thank you!). That I watched the honorariums that accrued from the readings. That as soon as the funds were down to fifty dollars, I would be off on the road. When these had reached about 200 dollars, I would be back scribbling and typing away. In this respect, I would like to thank Ray Gould of Rockland City for finding me places to read. I thank also a number of Black American artists I met in the United States, like writers Quincy Troup, Jane Cortez and Alice Walker, sculptor Mel Edwards and many others who supported me. County Cullen Library in Harlem was my launching pad, and it too, and the staff there, I want to thank.

I have no doubts that the Security Police in South Africa will want to know who really wrote the memoirs. Frankly, I would like to record that they did. Their fists did. Their animalistic hatred of me and my friends of what we were attempting to achieve for our people, did. Their isolating me, shuttling me from prison to prison and holding me in solitary confinement, wrote the memoirs. Their brutalization of me and all the other detainees did. I am only a recorder of their deeds, and I am certain that many more books will be written, as long as racism remains rampant in our country, and as long as children can be shot at like wild game by White people. But again, because I know that they are so thick-skinned and incapable of understanding how they came to write this book, I carry the burden of saying that I have written it.

I thank all my friends with whom I spent some time in jail. Eric Molobi, the first one to fall to two concurrent five-year prison sentences which he served on Robben Island; Frank Molobi, the Weimers, Wiseman Hamilton, Ramrock, who have all since fled the country. Vincent Selanto, who refused to turn state witness. The Molokeng group of the dungeon at the Fort. I shall also remember, for some time to come, in these prisons, our singing, songs of our struggle. I would also like to thank, most humbly, the so-called common prisoners in South Africa, many of whom took great risks to help me.

Molefe Pheto,
Washington, DC, 1977